# Verizon Untethered

## AN INSIDER'S STORY
## OF INNOVATION AND DISRUPTION

AS TOLD

BY **IVAN SEIDENBERG** AND OTHERS

FOREWORD AND INSIGHTS BY **RAM CHARAN**

WRITTEN BY **SCOTT McMURRAY**

A POST HILL PRESS BOOK
ISBN: 978-1-64293-266-9
ISBN (e-book): 978-1-68261-760-1
Library of Congress Control Number: 2017960745

Verizon Untethered: An Insider's Story of Innovation and Disruption

Post Hill Press
New York • Nashville
posthillpress.com

Published in the United States of America

Produced by The History Factory
Washington, DC • Chicago, IL • Chantilly, VA
www.historyfactory.com

# TABLE OF CONTENTS

# Preface

When I retired in 2011 as chairman and CEO of Verizon Communications, it was with a great sense of appreciation and indebtedness to the company and all of the people I worked with and met along the way. My 46-year career in telecommunications, starting in the Bell System and including 25 years spent as a senior executive of Verizon and its Baby Bell predecessors, was an extraordinary journey. Many of my friends, my wife and my colleagues urged me to consider writing a book or memoir of my career.

Initially, I could never find the right balance to capture the big picture, the view of my career and that of our leadership team as others might have seen it, as well as pay proper respect to the company itself. Besides, I knew I could never have remembered enough to do justice to all of the people involved over the years. Meanwhile, I read every CEO biography I could find but never found the right approach for me. My colleagues continued to encourage me to think about it.

When I was CEO of Verizon, I served on the boards of other organizations and continue to do so in retirement. I learned during one such board meeting that the company had started a project to record and tell its history. The agency it retained to help it capture its heritage and put it to work was The History Factory.

I immediately contacted The History Factory to find out more about the company and its work. It was a terrific match, and after a few conversations, we were developing a plan for telling the Verizon story. The idea was for The History Factory to conduct oral history interviews with 40 to 50 senior executives, including Verizon directors, to capture their experiences through the years. With that information, we would build a baseline framework that would tell Verizon's history through a professional storyteller without my thumb on the scales. My role would be limited to monitoring and providing direction for accuracy and for those parts of our history on which I had a unique perspective.

Independent of this process, I have been fortunate to have had a 30-year relationship with global business consultant and icon Ram Charan. He has been a mentor, teacher, critic and friend. We also discussed the idea of a book or perhaps something less ambitious, such as a few articles touching on particular areas of strategy, governance, succession and the culture of organizations. Ram and I met or spoke for almost three years about twice a month to see if there was anything of value to be learned from my experience at Verizon and before. Then we got lucky. I told Ram about The History Factory and its approach, and the idea of collaborating with a professional storyteller. Ram concluded that that combination and the original research from specific interviews with 40 to 50 executives and board members would be a novel approach to conveying the Verizon story to a broader audience.

After a few more months of thought and some conversations with key people, I concluded that we were creating something that would pass my internal test: create a history of the journey, capture the views of many different people, provide a platform for my commentary and perspective when needed, honor the people who built the company, and offer some lessons that might be of use to others. We were getting there.

One last preparatory step was to contact my successor at Verizon and close friend Lowell McAdam and sound him out on the project. He was terrific. Having been a very key part of my journey, he was quick to encourage me to consider the approach and indicated he would enthusiastically support the effort and even participate in the interview process. So, here we are. Now we have a finished product from preeminent professionals helping us tell this remarkable journey of so many people who had a hand in building Verizon. I am delighted and proud to serve as the village guide and archivist in helping to make this all work. And finally, after all of the interviews, we settled on a title that reflected dozens of conversations in strategy meetings and board presentations in which we were trying to untether Verizon from its past but naturally build on the foundation of that very history. "Untethered" remarkably captures in one word our life's work to remake Verizon and place it in the middle of this new world with so much excitement and potential for our customers, employees and shareowners.

Ivan G. Seidenberg

I could not have succeeded in my career without the unceasing support of my wife and children. Phyllis and I wanted one more opportunity to thank the Verizon family. During my career, there were literally thousands of employees who offered encouragement and support. Their hard work and commitment to our business will always be a great source of pride and appreciation. We will donate the proceeds from the publication of this book to the VtoV Employee Relief Fund for the use of Verizon employees and their families in need.

# Foreword

Fifty years ago, as a very young Harvard Business School profes-
sor, I started consulting with the senior leadership team of New
York Telephone. I also worked closely with the senior leadership
of parent American Telephone & Telegraph, AT&T, and conducted
advanced management programs for rising Bell System leaders beginning in the late 1970s. This highly regulated utility was not a seedbed
of corporate revolution. Or so I thought at first.

Then I got to know the team led ultimately by Ivan Seidenberg and
his successor, Lowell McAdam, who transformed, and continue to
transform Verizon Communications and the global communications
industry. Time and again the unconventional route to success taken
by the Verizon leaders left me nodding my head in appreciation and
sometimes in wonder. I have referenced the Verizon team in several
articles on leadership and corporate succession over the years. Even
so, I always thought their story should be better known.

Verizon's industry dominance was not foreordained. *Verizon Untethered*
offers a unique and timely view inside the transformation of an iconic
industry and the rise of underrated also-ran turned dominant player
Verizon Communications. The Verizon leadership team honed some
simple, useful and replicable concepts that can be used by leaders nav-
igating their way through the new era of discontinuity, competition and
relentless globalization.

- The CEO and leadership team operating in today's messy, complex and fast-changing external environment will be tempted to immediately turn their leadership focus inward. This can be a fatal mistake. It is imperative for them to first focus on how the industry as a whole needs to be reconfigured and repositioned. Only then is the company likely to prosper.

- Real-time, simultaneous strategizing and decision-making, not textbook, sequential planning, is required to achieve goals during periods of accelerating change. From the most challenging competitive position among the so-called Baby Bells, Verizon engineered its rise to industry leader.

- And they reframed their relations with regulators and legislators to overcome restrictive oversight in order to meet customer needs. Former parent AT&T agreed to the breakup of the Bell System, mistakenly thinking that a new set of regulatory rules would free it to prosper in a competitive marketplace. By not understanding that the industry needed to press for market-based regulation sensitive to changing customer needs, the phone company was exchanging one set of regulatory chains for another. Verizon, realizing that it had to either change or die, was at the vanguard of breaking free of the regulatory mindset dating back to when railroads were the industry of the future and reshaped industry regulation around the customer. In so doing it successfully navigated the transition from utility to budding technology company.

The Verizon leadership team also recognized before many business leaders and entrepreneurs that, in an increasingly interconnected and rapidly evolving world, companies don't thrive by just answering to their shareholders. They also have to act to serve customers, employees and regulators acting, ostensibly at least, in the public interest.

*Verizon Untethered* is based on more than 50 in-depth interviews with Verizon leaders conducted by the leading heritage management agency The History Factory. Assertions raised in interviews are cross-checked with company and third-party resources for accuracy.

Because of my work with other companies and industries around the world over decades, I have been able to compare events at Verizon to those taking place at leading companies in communications and other fields. In that sense this is a longitudinal, 30-year research project based on my personal observations of Verizon and its leadership team, especially frank dialogue with leaders behind closed doors.

The Verizon leadership team stands apart from most leadership teams today in their willingness repeatedly to put the enterprise before the individual. At first blush, this might look like a hopelessly old-fashioned notion in the age of the selfie. Yet, I would argue this is a trait that future leaders and boards of directors across industries would do well to understand and embrace.

Seidenberg not once but twice in the service of company shareholders and employees subordinated himself and put off taking sole leadership of the company to advance the enterprise's odds of success. And many others in this story exhibited the same trait to help build this industry-leading enterprise. They understood that the risk of not acting and thereby destroying value during a period of accelerating technological change and industry consolidation—a situation faced by leadership teams around the world today—was much greater than the risk of stepping in as No. 2 or co-CEO. In my 50 years of experience, it is a rare leadership team that will subordinate itself for the benefit of the industry, customers and the company. That principle, that the company comes first, the individual second, is what will define successful leadership teams of the future.

Multiple leadership principles, some new, some timeless, emerge from this narrative and will be of great use to the next generation of leaders across industries and around the world. By taking a look at a company that successfully executed exponential transformation, we can take the strategies of Verizon leaders and apply them to our own experiences. Throughout the book, I add my own commentary and analysis. I have written five books on how to plan leadership succession, manage boards and prepare for disruptive change. My expertise informs my own understanding of the Verizon story and what today's businesses can extract from these lessons.

At the end of each chapter, we include a brief list of key takeaways for leaders of the future. The Verizon leadership team took its company from the bottom ranks of its industry to the top by using skills that readers need to understand to identify high-potential people in their own organizations and put them on a path to success. And the team used their imagination. These takeaways will help readers apply Verizon's leadership lessons to their own lives.

When we encounter key turning points in the Verizon narrative, we hit the pause button and include brief essays reflecting on and emphasizing the leadership themes that have been developed during the particular era being discussed.

- The first essay examines the chessboard strategy still used by Verizon to create an exhaustive list of strategic options.

- The second explores the relationship and dynamics between executives and a board of directors.

- The third delves into the actions involved in creating and driving the search for the truly innovative leaders of tomorrow, and in managing the succession process at multiple levels in the organization.

These essays serve as connective tissue to help animate the Verizon story as it applies to broader leadership issues. I use my own expertise as a consultant to draw parallels between the trials and tribulations endured by the Verizon leadership team and today's rapidly changing leadership landscape.

The Verizon transformation continues. Chairman and CEO Lowell McAdam and his team are moving Verizon to the center of a new, fast-changing competitive chessboard once again to meet future challenges. Competitive and regulatory hurdles are not going away. Meanwhile, next-generation technologies promise another quantum leap in the scale and scope of products and services offered to customers. The disruption facing Verizon today is as great as any time in the history of the modern communications industry. As Verizon reinvents itself in this way, I look forward to the next chapter in one of the most compelling corporate and industry success stories of our era.

Ram Charan

# 01

# CHANGING
# MINDSETS

1982-1984

"We're going to blow up the phone company in order to save it."That's what Larry Babbio took away from AT&T Chairman and CEO Charles "Charlie" Brown's address to a group of phone company leaders shortly after 8 a.m. on Tuesday, January 5, 1982. Babbio, one of AT&T's operating company technology czars, was among those who had assembled in secret and on short notice at AT&T's sprawling corporate campus in Basking Ridge, New Jersey, for a military-style briefing from Brown. With scant introduction, Brown told the group that after more than a century in operation, the Bell System was proposing to divest itself of the very foundation of its nationwide telephone network—its 22 local operating companies.

Brown's proposal was a shock, but it wasn't a complete disconnect for those who had been closely following current events. It was triggered by a months-long antitrust court case brought by the Justice Department that decidedly was not going well for AT&T (see sidebar "The Last Mile"). The proposed divestiture was more of a strategic retreat for the phone company. Brown's plan would allow AT&T to keep its highly profitable Long Lines long-distance business as well as its Western Electric manufacturing facilities and one of America's research crown jewels, Bell Laboratories. That in itself was a victory compared to the Justice Department's initial demands in *U.S. v. AT&T* dating back to 1974, when it asserted that AT&T not only should have to divest Western Electric but that the manufacturing arm should be broken up. The

Justice Department filing suggested that Bell Labs might meet a similar fate if the government had its way.

In return for agreeing to divest itself of the local companies, AT&T was confident it would be able to finally get out from under a separate consent decree with the U.S. government dating back to 1956. That decree had kept AT&T out of the computer business even though its own Bell Labs in 1947 had invented the solid-state transistor, the basic building block of the modern computer and electronics industries. Brown had often shared his vision of the worlds of telecommunications and computers converging. Now it was going to happen, and he was determined that AT&T would lead the charge.

## "THERE WILL ALWAYS BE A TELEPHONE COMPANY"

The Basking Ridge corporate amphitheater was full of middle-aged, white men, nearly all of whom—like Babbio—had spent their adult lives working for the phone company. Until that morning, it was hard to think of a job that was more reliable. As Babbio's Italian immigrant grandmother back in Jersey City had told him after he had been offered a job by the phone company right out of Stevens Institute school of engineering in 1966: "Take it. There will always be a telephone company."

At the same time, most of the men in the room were engineers who personified AT&T's commitment to public service. At the heart of Brown's presentation was an engineering problem. After the group's initial stunned reaction and some grumbling, the challenge of assembling self-sustaining Regional Bell Operating Companies (RBOCs) from scratch became the focus. There was little yearning for the good old days voiced by the audience, said veteran AT&T public relations officer

Ed Block, who was also at the meeting. That in itself was a tribute to the Bell System's can-do attitude, he thought.

The uncertainty Babbio felt that day in early January 1982 was shared by other members of the next generation of phone company leaders. Ivan Seidenberg was in the audience for a similar presentation Brown led at AT&T's 195 Broadway headquarters in Lower Manhattan following the Basking Ridge meeting. Sitting with dozens of other phone company officers on folding chairs hastily arrayed in the building lobby, Seidenberg felt as if his world had been turned upside down. He acknowledged that Brown's decision was courageous in the face of the government's unrelenting crusade to break up AT&T. In an ideal environment, there might have been room for debate as to whether the breakup was the right legal and regulatory response to developing market forces. But the Justice Department clearly wasn't interested in ideals, he realized. "My first thought was, 'The government won!'"

At the same time, there was a sense of excitement and challenge for those willing and able to embrace a future that suddenly didn't look nearly as predictable as the past. As the countdown to divestiture got underway, the slow but steady phone company career escalator they had been riding had the potential to turn into an express elevator. "How cool is this going to be?" Seidenberg recalled thinking by the time the presentation was over.

As the divestiture process progressed, the 22 local operating companies would be grouped into seven RBOCs, dubbed Baby Bells: NYNEX, comprising New England and New York State; Bell Atlantic, covering the mid-Atlantic region from New Jersey and Pennsylvania down to Virginia and the Chesapeake Bay; BellSouth, covering the Southeast; Ameritech in the Midwestern Great Lakes states; Southwestern Bell, stretching from Texas to Missouri; US WEST in the Mountain States, the Pacific Northwest and the northern Great Plains states; and Pacific Telesis in California and Nevada.

# THE LAST MILE

AT&T's battle with the Justice Department for nearly a year in U.S. District Court was the latest iteration of an antitrust case, *U.S. v. AT&T*, first brought by the government in 1974. And AT&T had been fighting in the halls of Congress and other public and private arenas for years before that, precisely to keep the nation's largest monopoly intact. Second-to-none reliable phone service, world-beating scientific innovations and nearly 1 million jobs spread across virtually every congressional district in the country gave AT&T a lot of firepower. Why surrender now? wondered its legions of supporters.

Brown, AT&T's former chief financial officer and an avid futurist, believed that to succeed in the years ahead, the phone company had to respond to and anticipate customer needs. It had to abandon its approach of assuming that AT&T always knew best. "Mother Bell simply doesn't live here anymore," Brown told a group of company executives shortly after assuming the top job at AT&T in 1979.

His willingness to take a fresh approach applied to legal issues as well. As the Justice Department court case against AT&T progressed, presiding Judge Harold Greene's interim rulings clearly favored the Justice Department. By the latter part of 1981, Brown was seriously thinking the unthinkable: What would happen if he broke up the company before the government itself had a chance to dismember one of the world's greatest corporate enterprises? Adding to the pressure on Brown was the fact that in 1980, a jury deciding a private antitrust suit against AT&T had awarded upstart long-distance calling provider Microwave Communications Inc. (MCI) an unprecedented $1.8 billion in damages.

Meeting in secret in late 1981, a phone company team proposed dismantling more than a century's worth of work. Its plan would end up giving more than three-quarters of AT&T's assets—from millions of telephone poles, innumerable copper wires and tens of thousands of service vehicles to the most sophisticated call-switching equipment—to newly created Regional Bell Operating Companies (RBOCs) composed of the 22 existing local Bell Operating Companies.

These were the companies that controlled what was referred to as the "last mile," the twisted pair of copper wires that connected almost every U.S. home to the phone network. This was the communications chokehold that the Justice Department wanted out of AT&T's grip in order to spur industry competition.

These AT&T offspring would not be operating in a vacuum. Also offering phone service in various regions of the United States were nearly 1,500 independent phone companies. The largest of the independents, GTE Corp., not only provided local service in markets across the country, it was also a nationwide long-distance phone service provider. That combination of long-distance and local service would give it a competitive leg up on the Baby Bells, which were prohibited from offering long-distance calling in their formative years as part of the divestiture proposal, as in some ways would GTE's sheer size. Once the Bell System had been carved up into seven RBOCs, GTE's $9 billion in revenues from "telephone operations" would trail NYNEX's and BellSouth's $9.5 billion in revenues each but would easily outpace Ameritech with $8.4 billion and Bell Atlantic with $8 billion and the rest of the Baby Bells during their first year as independent phone companies.

# "CULTURE, NORMS AND VALUES"

Many industry experts and Wall Street analysts argued that not all of the RBOCs were created equal. Favorable demographic growth projections gave the edge to the Baby Bells in the South and the West. Slower population growth projections in the Northeast and the mid-Atlantic and a legacy of activist, state-level regulation, coupled with a heritage of complex relations with organized labor in these areas, left these Baby Bells carrying an extra burden going forward. Factor in the complexity of operating a regulated monopoly in New York City, and the consensus was that NYNEX, in particular, faced more than its share of challenges.

It was a reputation that would dog NYNEX for years. In fact, the company would be seen as a bellwether among the Baby Bells. If telecommunications deregulation can make it here, New York securities analyst Daniel

Reingold reasoned, it can make it anywhere. "NYNEX faces perhaps the most significant competitive threats of any regional Bell company," the Merrill Lynch securities analyst told *The New York Times*. "What happens to NYNEX will say a great deal about the future of competition in telecommunications."

One of the great ironies of the breakup of AT&T is that the perceived industry underdog, NYNEX, would combine with Bell Atlantic, its better positioned neighbor, and over time become the industry top dog. Leading this transformation would be a generation of rising telecommunication industry executives. They were challenged to act quickly in light of competitive pressures and shareowner expectations. They were able to outgrow the regulated Bell System culture and not be weighed down by its deadening bureaucracy.

They embraced the concept of industry transformation that AT&T CEO Brown and many of the first generation of RBOC leaders would recognize was the key to thriving in the new telecommunications marketplace. The difference was that team Verizon would make that concept a reality. This is their story and the story of the industry-leading corporation, Verizon Communications, they helped create. As one of those creators, Ivan Seidenberg, would later observe, "Leadership has less to do with any single individual . . . than it does with the culture, norms and values of the institution itself."

## "FINANCIAL UNDOING" OR "BRILLIANT MASTERSTROKE"?

Babbio, an engineer who embraced complex technical challenges, had transferred a few years earlier to AT&T from New Jersey Bell Telephone Company, one of the 22 operating companies. He was leading a number of cutting-edge technology projects, including running the

# UNIVERSAL SERVICE

America was forever transformed by the industrial revolution that swept the nation in the decades following the Civil War. The growth of the railroad, steel, electricity-generating and oil industries propelled the country to the vanguard of the developed world. Household names among the scions of the new era included Cornelius Vanderbilt, Andrew Carnegie, Thomas Edison and John D. Rockefeller. A parallel revolution in human communications occurring at the same time was the handiwork of another giant of American industry, Scottish-born Alexander Graham Bell.

Bell's first telephone patent granted for the invention of the new technology in 1876, and the formation of Bell Telephone Company in Massachusetts the following year laid the foundation for the phone system that spread across the country, state by state. To facilitate the creation of the nation's first long-distance telephone network, in 1885 the company created a subsidiary of Bell Telephone called American Telephone & Telegraph Co. (AT&T). In 1899, the child became the parent as New York-based AT&T, to get Bell Telephone out from under restrictive Massachusetts corporate laws that hindered its ability to raise capital to fund future growth, bought all the assets of Bell Telephone and the national phone network it had created.

By the early years of the 20th century, AT&T was on a path toward creating a national telecommunications monopoly. It effectively pressured hundreds of independent phone companies to sell out to AT&T by denying them the right to connect calls to the Bell System. And it bought a controlling interest in Western Union Telegraph Co., the giant of American telegraphy.

Facing an all but certain antitrust suit by the Justice Department, AT&T chose to compromise rather than risk being dismembered or even nationalized (as, in fact, it would be briefly during World War I). In what was known as the Kingsbury Commitment, named after an AT&T vice president who signed the letter, the phone company agreed to sell its Western Union stake in 1913 and agreed to interconnectivity with independent phone companies. It also said it wouldn't buy any more independent phone companies without the approval of the recently created Interstate Commerce Commission (ICC).

Phone use soared as interconnectivity made the telephone a much more practical and efficient communications device. The agreement started AT&T and the remaining independents, including the predecessor of GTE, and the U.S. government, down the path of providing universal phone service to the American public. It was a policy envisioned as early as 1908 by the hugely influential president of AT&T, Theodore N. Vail: "One Policy, One System, Universal Service." There would be plenty of bumps along the way as this government-regulated monopoly evolved, and multiple legal actions would follow, but the telecommunications system developed and continually enhanced by AT&T would quickly become the envy of the modern world.

latest in high-capacity fiber optics cables between Chicago and New York that were capable of carrying millions of calls a day. Another of his projects were two small pilot efforts underway in Chicago and Washington, D.C. These were rollouts of the latest generation of in-car Advanced Mobile Phone Service (AMPS). Both technologies, it hardly bore noting at the time, had been developed at Bell Labs. And both would figure prominently in Babbio's future and that of the as-yet-unborn telecommunications giant Verizon Communications.

So Babbio naturally leaned forward when someone in the amphitheater asked Brown who was getting the mobile cellular business, AT&T or the RBOCs? Brown didn't appear to Babbio to have given the idea much thought. That was not a big surprise, since cellular was a minuscule, money-losing business at the time. In fact, the consulting firm McKinsey & Co. had advised AT&T in 1980 that the nationwide customer base for its heavy cellular phones, costing thousands of dollars each and with very limited service areas, would top out at about 900,000 by the year 2000. (That would turn out to be more than 100 million shy of actual usage.)

Brown turned to one of the lawyers on stage with him for an answer to the cellular question. The lawyer didn't seem to have studied the issue either, Babbio observed. But the attorney's opinion was unequivocal. "It's a local service; it goes with the telephone companies," is what Babbio recalled the lawyer saying.

In retrospect, Babbio would realize that the lawyer's matter-of-fact response was a turning point in the history of telecommunications and in the career of the future Verizon vice chairman and the rest of the Verizon leadership team, as well as its hundreds of thousands of employees. "I'm not sure he had thought about that answer before, in fact, he gave it," Babbio said. "But that's the way it came out, which led a long time after that, I think, in many ways, to the strategic undoing of AT&T."

The idea that divestiture was the beginning of the end for AT&T was hardly the consensus in 1982. It was widely assumed that the parent AT&T represented the fast-growing telecommunications company of the future. The $115 billion in assets AT&T would slough off on the RBOCs by year-end 1983 represented the slow-growth past. Richard Wiley, former head of the FCC, which regulated the phone company, spoke for many communications industry cognoscenti when he made the widely quoted comment at the time that "AT&T's agreement was a brilliant masterstroke. . . . They gave away the future railroads of the industry, kept the moneymakers they already had and won the right to go after everything else on the high-revenue side."

# FAST AND SLOW TRACKS

Babbio, who served as senior staff to the divestiture committee assigning technology assets among the RBOCs, bounced between Bell Communications Research; Bellcore, a research unit jointly funded by the Baby Bells; and Bell Atlantic for a few years before settling in at Bell Atlantic. There he rose through the management ranks in parallel with another of Bell Atlantic's future leaders, Jim Cullen. New Jersey Telephone alum Cullen also had a freshly minted master's degree in management science from the Massachusetts Institute of Technology. He led strategic planning for Bell Atlantic starting in 1983, even before the Baby Bell had technically been born. Later, he served as president of the New Jersey Telephone subsidiary of Bell Atlantic and rose through the senior management ranks from there. Across the Hudson River, Fred Salerno served on the nationwide LATA (local access and transport area) divestiture committee that sorted out the details of which assets belonged to whom among the 161 LATAs that formed the local pieces of the seven regional operating companies puzzle. He had risen through the operations leadership at New York Telephone, the traditional route to the top of one of the operating companies, and now NYNEX. All three of these managers were fast-tracked for leadership through the Bell System's demanding on-the-job management training program for recruits straight out of college. Known as the Initial Management Development Program (IMDP), it was designed to produce middle managers within three to five years. It was up or out after the first year, and as many as 80 percent of those recruited washed out of the program. Those who survived and thrived would be in line to replace the World War II generation of leaders who were expected to begin retiring en masse in the 1970s. Babbio, Cullen and Salerno, while each from different backgrounds and each excelling in his particular arena, had advanced through the system and were following a relatively traditional path to career success at the phone company, even if it was now broken up into Baby Bells.

And then there was Ivan Seidenberg. He wasn't eligible to participate in IMDP. He dropped out of a four-year college program after a year and later enrolled in night school in New York City, taking eight years to get his undergraduate degree in math while working full time. A night school master's degree followed.

## "NO, YOU DON'T"

For much of the two years following the divestiture announcement, scores of Bell System managers worked in six nationwide committees as they sorted through all the detailed steps required to create the RBOCs. The primary issues with which the committees were grappling included the details of separating the long-distance business that would stay with AT&T from the local exchanges of the newly comprised regional carriers. In addition, the committees had to determine what one part of the system would now have to pay the other for its services and sort through technology, asset-swapping and rate-related matters tied to divestiture.

# POLE FARM

The divestiture process did have its lighter moments. At one point Babbio was tasked with escorting AT&T CEO Brown to a semirural site in northern New Jersey, where the phone company maintained what was known as the Pole Farm. Here, wooden telephone poles and other parts of the exterior "plant" were exposed to the elements to determine how well they stood up under varying conditions and with various creosote and other coatings.

Brown was still smarting from a decision a few days earlier by Judge Greene, who was presiding over the divestiture, to award use of the iconic Bell logo to the seven operating companies, not AT&T. Babbio did his best imitation of an enthusiastic travel guide as he described what Brown was seeing on the farm, even if most of it was pasture. In one direction were outbuildings in which two horses were standing. Their tails swished in the direction of the phone company executives.

At issue was whether AT&T should push to keep the Pole Farm, as the engineers at Bell Labs were arguing, or let it go to the Regional Bell Operating Company that would become Bell Atlantic, which operated in the region. Brown, scowling in the direction of the animals, said, "Horses' asses. They're all over the place these days." The two men walked back to their car, and Brown decided to let the RBOCs have the Pole Farm.

AT&T CEO Brown had no way of knowing at the time, but he met the future chairman and CEO of Verizon early in the divestiture transition process. Seidenberg had been tapped to be the senior staff for one of the most important divestiture committees. His was tasked with proposing a new tariff structure for originating and completing long-distance calls among the RBOCs and AT&T as well as long-distance providers MCI and Sprint, which would require FCC approval.

Seidenberg and nearly 80 AT&T managers sat apprehensively in a conference room in New York one morning awaiting Brown's arrival.

As was his style, Brown arrived less than a minute before the start of the 8 a.m. meeting and nodded at Seidenberg, who was standing in the front of the room, to proceed with his presentation. Brown gave the first chart a quick look and said, "I know that." Chart No. 2: "I've got that." Brown said he knew the information on the third chart as well. But this time Seidenberg responded, "No, you don't." Those were not words that Brown was accustomed to hearing.

Brown paused, and no one else in the room dared speak. He asked for more information, seeming to accept Seidenberg's interpretation that this was an extremely complex issue with important and costly implications for AT&T and the RBOCs. Seidenberg's argument was that there was no way the FCC was going to accept that the phone company tariff proposal was a fair one based on its dim view of AT&T's past monopoly pricing. That meant the FCC would suspend it, he said, based on his experience working with the regulators.

Seidenberg argued, contrary to phone company custom, that they needed to develop a Plan B as some form of compromise that would enable them to keep functioning even as they continued to pursue Plan A. Brown didn't agree or disagree. He told the group to keep working on solving the problem. The rest of the room didn't share Brown's tendency to withhold judgment. Many of those present ripped into Seidenberg during the question-and-answer session. They were angered by his willingness to even consider something like a Plan B, which was so contrary to the terms of the consent decree that the government just signed and contrary to the way AT&T expected to do business.

# "LET'S LISTEN TO THE YOUNG MAN"

The group charged with proposing a solution to the access tariff issue reconvened a few weeks after the initial meeting at which Seidenberg had floated the need for a Plan B. They met in the office of Walter Kelly, a native Bostonian who was the AT&T vice president in charge of regulatory issues. Kelly, whose starched white shirts and magisterial mien gave him the appearance of an old-school phone executive straight out of central casting, shook his head and smiled as Seidenberg walked into the office.

Eyeing Seidenberg's long dark hair well over his ears and beard—an homage, in Seidenberg's mind, anyway, to baseball pitcher Rollie Fingers and the Oakland Athletics baseball team that turned facial hair into a fashion statement in the 1970s—Kelly said, "What is it with you young people?" He noted that neither he nor his wife could convince their sons to shave either. Sighing, Kelly locked eyes with those in the room, whom he knew were opposed to Seidenberg's solution based on the first meeting, and said, "Let's listen to the young man." By the end of the meeting, they agreed to pursue a Plan A and Plan B strategy, preparing them for the FCC's eventual decision to scuttle Plan A.

The meeting made a lasting impression on Seidenberg, who would share the story with his fellow leaders over the years. "I don't care what people look like when they come and see me. I pay attention to what they have to say," he said.

# "SOMEONE YOU SHOULD KEEP YOUR EYE ON"

After the meeting, Seidenberg received numerous messages wishing him the best of luck as he considered the next step in his career. The callers clearly thought that going toe to toe with CEO Brown and his legal team was likely to be a career-ender as far as AT&T was concerned. As it turned out, the FCC suspended the tariff in Plan A, just as Seidenberg had predicted. A compromise was fashioned in which tariffs were pooled in a quasi-escrow account and apportioned later among the RBOCs.

Others may have bid him adieu, but Seidenberg's principled, informed stand caught the attention of the man who was going to be the first chairman and CEO of NYNEX, Delbert C. "Bud" Staley, who at the time was president of New York Telephone. Staley told Seidenberg that he was aware that Seidenberg would get offers from other RBOCs but that he should be sure to come and see Staley in a few months before making a decision.

Seidenberg also caught the attention of Ram Charan, a young Harvard Business School instructor working as a consultant advising Staley. Charan happened to sit in on a presentation Seidenberg was making one day in NYNEX's White Plains, New York, headquarters. He was impressed by the no-nonsense leader's ability to clearly see opposing points of view and think creatively in response to new information as he fashioned solutions. "This is someone you should keep your eye on," Charan told Staley.

## BRONX STREET SMARTS

Being able to read people, friend and foe alike, was part of the survival skill set Seidenberg honed growing up in the Bronx during the 1950s and early 1960s. His world consisted of the streets and the six-story tenement apartment buildings where family members and friends resided.

While the neighborhood was filled with diverse races and ethnicities, home had more of a Central and Eastern European flavor. The extended family on both of his parents' sides hailed from Russia, Romania,

Hungary or Poland, and there was plenty of hearty, international cooking to go around. President Franklin D. Roosevelt was the family hero, and hard work and community involvement were the family bywords. The occasional vacation was a day trip to a lake near Brewster, New York. Seidenberg's father was up at 4:30 every morning and off to run his one-man air-conditioning and heating contracting business. And his mother was there making her husband breakfast and preparing his box lunch. The enterprise thrived as the 1960s progressed, and his parents eventually moved out of the neighborhood to New Rochelle, New York.

The cultural and societal changes that swept much of America during the 1960s worked their way onto the tradition-bound streets of the Bronx. President John F. Kennedy and Dr. Martin Luther King Jr. were the heroes, and then martyrs, for Seidenberg's generation. As the decade unfolded, Seidenberg found himself much more interested in the goings-on outside his window than what was in the classroom. His grades reflected his divided attention.

After graduating from high school in 1964, Seidenberg attended Hunter College in New York City for one year, but his academic performance didn't warrant his return as a sophomore. In 1965, he enrolled in night school and at age 18 found a full-time day job in elevator maintenance as a member of Local 32B in Manhattan. He worked at the Harry Rothman building at Fifth Avenue and 18th Street in a gray uniform, operating a freight elevator and mopping up.

## "PEOPLE ARE WATCHING"

What initially seemed like a dead-end job turned out to offer an important learning experience. His supervisor was a man named Mike, the building superintendent. He was a hard worker but rarely spoke with Seidenberg. If his boss was such a hard worker, Seidenberg decided that he had better be a hard worker, too. During his breaks, he would pull out one of his college textbooks. Mike saw him reading one day and asked him what he was doing. He nodded at the explanation and moved on.

Mike walked up to Seidenberg after he had been on the job for nearly eight months. "You know, there are companies that will help you pay for college while you work full time," he said, mentioning New York Telephone and Consolidated Edison, the power company. When Seidenberg asked him why he waited so long to share the tip, he responded, "I had to watch you. I think you passed the test . . . you'll do a good job."

Years later, Seidenberg would recall, "It doesn't matter if you're the janitor or the CEO, values and performance count—people are watching."

Seidenberg took Mike's advice and started with New York Telephone in June 1966 as a cable splicer's assistant, working mostly in manholes. There was nowhere to go but up. Barely six weeks after joining the phone company, he was drafted into the U.S. Army. Even though he had hardly learned his way around the phone company garage, the phone company treated him like one of the family. He received newsletters and periodic raises throughout his military service.

In May 1967, he landed in Vietnam as a member of the 1st Air Cavalry, stationed in I Corps more than 200 miles north of Saigon. Seidenberg never discusses his Vietnam service, even though in February 1968 he and his unit served in and around Quang Tri and Khe Sanh during the Tet Offensive, which sparked some of the most ferocious fighting of the war. Like many veterans, he would prefer that the focus remain on those who weren't fortunate enough to come home.

# PASSING INSPECTION

A few non-combat anecdotes, however, convey the life lessons learned about people coping with bureaucracy and serendipity. Seidenberg, at one point, was stationed at a landing zone that U.S. Army Gen. William Westmoreland was scheduled to inspect. Some of the bullet-riddled helicopters clearly weren't going to pass muster. One, for instance, needed a new door. Seidenberg's sergeant major from Kentucky, who had the Bronx native pegged as a wise-guy Yankee, told him to take some men and jeeps and drive to the port of Qui Nhon to get a new door and pick up the company's rations at the same time.

They arrived and collected their rations, but there were no spare helicopter doors to be found. Seidenberg finally connected with a soldier who said he could let them have a door. But they would have to give him their fresh meat rations in return, leaving them with just canned Spam. Seidenberg, not wanting to disappoint the sergeant major, made the trade. When he got back, he told the sergeant major about the exchange. The sergeant major just stared at him for what seemed like a long time and didn't ask any questions, saying simply, "Put the door on." But he had Seidenberg's back from then on.

Now that Seidenberg was known for his connections, he was sent on a second trip to Qui Nhon to bring back some supplies. He took two jeeps with two men in each jeep, including himself, in case one of the vehicles broke down in what could quickly become hostile territory. They stayed too long enjoying the port town and were barreling along the dirt tracks between rice paddies in order to get back to base before dark. Suddenly they came under fire. The jeep in front of Seidenberg accelerated and threw up such a cloud of red dust that Seidenberg's vision was obscured, but he kept driving to get out of the hot zone. The cloud of dust dissipated abruptly a few minutes later, revealing a huge water buffalo in the middle of the road. Seidenberg slammed on the brakes and the jeep skidded into the water buffalo, delivering a non-lethal blow to its enormous hindquarter and ending up halfway in a rice paddy.

He and the accompanying sergeant scrambled under the jeep from different sides to avoid getting hit by gunfire, which by then sounded as if it had moved on to a different area. The sergeant was moaning, however, and Seidenberg feared he had been wounded. When the first jeep returned and found them, everyone soon discovered the source of the sergeant's complaint. The water buffalo, shocked by the impact, had relieved itself on the sergeant's head. The sergeant, widely disliked by the troops, eventually was able to wash his hair. However, he was stuck with an unfortunate nickname for the remainder of his tour.

# GANG BEHAVIOR

By the summer of 1968, Seidenberg was back in the Bronx working for the phone company for $95 a week. His Vietnam experience gave him an in with the older men in the garage, many of whom had served during World War II or the Korean War, even if he didn't share their ethnic background. Many could see their younger selves in him.

Seidenberg was now a member of his first and only gang, as the teams of six to 12 union workers were known. The gangs would assemble every morning and head out to whatever job needed doing. Do the work, do as you're told, don't stand out. Beers after work, and softball. It was a good life. These were good family men.

Life changed for Seidenberg one day when he spotted Phyllis Maisel, a girl from the neighborhood he had known since the eighth grade, walking down the street. She was wearing a bright yellow miniskirt and walking home from the subway after work. "It was a picture right out of a movie. I was hooked right then," Seidenberg said. With her career as a schoolteacher in the South Bronx well underway, she encouraged Seidenberg to see that there was more to life than drinking beer and playing softball. At her urging, Seidenberg refocused on night school and began considering his career options. "Looking back, that was the single most important moment of my life. Phyllis has always been the most caring, well-grounded and loving person I know. She sees the best in people and sees the greater opportunities in life, never dwelling on the negative," Seidenberg said. They were married in 1969 and moved into their own apartment not far from their old neighborhood.

# MANAGEMENT RANKS

Seidenberg enjoyed the work, which often involved reading blueprints and required learning the network architecture and design as well as physical labor. But even his fellow gang members knew he was on a different career track. His first management assignment was working at 38th Street in Manhattan. In 1971, a manager helped him transfer to a job with AT&T in its headquarters building at 195 Broadway in Lower Manhattan. The august structure, with its columns inspired by Greek temples, conveyed the best of Western civilization—backed by corporate power.

Seidenberg, having exchanged his overalls for a suit and tie from Barneys Warehouse, joined a multidisciplinary team that had been created to work with engineers from Bell Labs. They wanted to further improve the reliability of the outside plant. While still working toward his undergraduate degree, he was brought on to the team to provide some frontline feedback, offering his insights on which set of testing equipment worked best under particular circumstances and how accurate it was. The effectiveness of signal repeaters serving underground canisters in manholes was a particular focus at the time as engineers at all levels constantly worked to increase the efficiency and durability of the system that was still based largely on copper wire.

During the early 1970s, the company also taught Seidenberg the ins and out of management behavior and leadership. He traveled to visit operating company facilities in Ohio and Pennsylvania, the first time he had visited either state. "The people I looked to, they taught me a lot about how to conduct myself," said Seidenberg. "How to accept criticism, how to give criticism. I wasn't really good at that, you know? Because when you grow up in the Bronx, you argue—and sometimes you just fight."

An extended strike in 1971 further separated him from the gang back in the Bronx. As a member of management, he was required to perform strike duty. That meant throughout the seven-month strike, he was working when his friends back in the union weren't. At the same time, the work exposed him to a much broader range of experiences than he had had earlier, including working on high-speed transmission lines that were much in demand by Wall Street and other financial services firms that called New York City home.

Seidenberg developed a lifelong appreciation for the complexity of the phone systems in the city but also wasn't willing to admit that working in the city, with all of its unique characteristics, was an excuse for not performing at your best. He had seen that the right people working on the right solution could get the job done. New York Telephone's substandard performance rankings compared to other operating companies could not simply be shrugged off as being the price of doing business in the world's most dynamic urban center. It was a stubbornness born of Bronx pride that would serve him well.

# "YOU DID GOOD"

The phone company gangs had their own code of behavior. A few weeks after Seidenberg was back on the job, his gang was told that they were pulling a second shift. A cable had been cut in the South Bronx, and they were going to fix it. No one questioned the assignment. It was part of providing the always-on level of service that the public expected of the phone company.

At the job site, Seidenberg was sent to take sandwich orders from the 12-man crew as midnight approached. He was paired with a giant of a phone company veteran named Ollie who didn't talk much but made an impression wherever he went. The two of them drove around the riot-torn South Bronx at length before finding an all-night diner.

Seidenberg learned later that the crew had given him particularly detailed requests as a way of testing the newbie. Before he could start reading down the sandwich list, Ollie reached over with a hand as big as a frying pan and crumpled the paper into a ball. "Twelve ham and cheese on rye. Twelve coffees with cream and sugar on the side," he told the cook. As far as Ollie was concerned, requesting customized carvings for each sandwich order would waste time. They had work to do.

The crew berated Seidenberg nonstop for botching their dinner orders. Is this what they were teaching in the Army these days? He shrugged. In fact, his sergeant major had demonstrated the importance of being willing to take one for the team. When one worker asked Seidenberg what happened, he said ham and cheese was all they had.

The next morning his foreman took him aside. Seidenberg was expecting another dressing down. Instead, the foreman said, "You did good last night." Seidenberg asked what he meant. "You didn't turn in Ollie."

Seidenberg returned to the Bronx garage where his phone company career had started 45 years later as retirement neared to say goodbye to those who were still there. He was presented with a plaque reading "Bronx Boy Done Good," which remains one of his most cherished gifts.

"I never accepted this idea that New York was too complicated, too noisy, too rude, too many unions, too many regulators, too much government. I just never accepted that that was a logical result of if you lived in New York, you have to accept a lesser standard," Seidenberg said.

Fred Salerno also pulled strike duty as a district manager working in Brooklyn, including climbing poles in freezing cold weather to restore telephone service. Even in the toughest neighborhoods, even with drug deals going down in plain sight and evidence of abject poverty around every corner, people respected the phone company personnel for the service they offered. And neither he nor Seidenberg begrudged anyone for exercising their right to join a union. On the contrary, organized labor was as New York as a bagel or a slice.

"The labor disputes were very indigenous to New York but not just totally related to the telephone company," Salerno said. "New York was a city of immigrants. And the labor unions were needed. And my father certainly, and I certainly, benefited by unions." And if labor issues were a New York problem, then Salerno, just like Seidenberg, was convinced they could find a New York solution. Working separately, the two came to the same conclusion: While they held the union members in high regard, they felt that the union leadership was not always acting in the best interest of the phone company employees.

## CARTERFONE CALLING

By 1972, Seidenberg had completed his undergraduate degree in math and was looking at his options. He had developed a reputation within AT&T as someone who was good at explaining complex technical issues in easy-to-understand terms—maybe even terms that regulators could understand, his managers joked. He applied for and got his next post as a regulatory liaison, traveling often to Washington, D.C., to meet with FCC staffers and explain AT&T's point of view.

Such skills were much in demand at the time. In 1968, the FCC had ruled that the Carterfone, built by the Carter Electronics Corporation, a private company based in Dallas, could be connected to the Bell System and could not be disconnected by the phone company. The phone company did have the right to install a protective device between the Carterfone and its system. That decision upended more than a half-century of AT&T's monopolistic control of the equipment used on its system and cleared the way for other non-Bell phones to be attached as well. In 1970, the FCC went further and said it would work toward a system of "certification" that would create agreed-to standards that, if met by device makers, meant that their phones and equipment could be connected directly to the phone system.

Starting in 1972, Seidenberg spent a great deal of his time on the Eastern Air Lines shuttle between New York City and Washington, D.C. He'd fly to and from meetings with FCC staff to help create the standards. They needed technical specifics for whatever princess phone, answering machine or automatic dialer companies wanted to create and sell to the public. The standards had to ensure the technical integrity of the phone system, but not be so strict as to act as an unfair hurdle to competition.

He began to appreciate that AT&T's point of view was not always the best path toward a solution that worked for all parties. The FCC staff were lobbying him hard for as minimal a set of standards as possible to spur competition and presumably increase choices and reduce costs for the public. AT&T engineers, on the other hand, feeling as if the FCC had forced this decision down their throats, demanded that AT&T's interests were best served by making the standards as strict as possible.

In the mid-1970s, Seidenberg began attending night school at Pace University to pursue an MBA. At the same time, he was developing a reputation as a young manager who may not have had the educational background of the typical AT&T officer, but who had a unique set of outside connections, many with the FCC. And as some, at least at AT&T, saw the company moving inexorably toward a world in which it was likely to compete more frequently with other enterprises, someone with outside connections brought a new and much-needed perspective.

## SHUTTLE DIPLOMACY

Seidenberg, still in his mid-30s, was riding the Eastern shuttle back to New York one evening with several working papers spread out on the tray in front of him. A man sitting next to him glanced at the papers and said, "Oh, you're from AT&T." He introduced himself as Dick Wiley and asked Seidenberg if he was allowed to talk about his work. Seidenberg obliged, and the two talked about some of the challenges Seidenberg was facing in working with the FCC on the standards issue. He told the man, "I want to get all the friction out. I want it to work."

When Seidenberg told his supervisor the next morning that he had a nice chat with this Dick Wiley on the shuttle, he felt as if he had pulled every smoke alarm in the building. The supervisor made a flurry of calls, and soon Seidenberg was being interrogated by one AT&T vice president after another. He had to repeat exactly how he phrased his statements, and exactly how Wiley had responded and what his body language was saying. It quickly dawned on him that Dick Wiley was Richard Wiley, then chairman of the FCC. When the furor had died down, Seidenberg's supervisor looked at him and shook his head. "Next time, look at the organization chart."

# MCI

Seidenberg's next assignment had him working closely with FCC staff yet again. This time, his work stemmed from an FCC ruling from 1969, one year after the Carterfone ruling. In 1969, the FCC had approved a small company called Microwave Communications Inc. (MCI) to sell private long-distance service between St. Louis and Chicago for companies with offices in both cities. The wrinkle MCI introduced was that its system used microwaves beamed from a series of towers to carry the phone calls. The proposal won over the FCC in part because MCI asserted that its microwave-only system could undercut AT&T in price and result in savings to its business customers. The technology, in one of the industry's more ironic twists, had been developed by Bell Labs.

Seidenberg's job was to hammer out interconnection charges that AT&T would be able to assess from MCI for connecting calls using its system back into the phone company grid. If anything, these negotiations made the Carterfone certification wrangling seem like gentlemanly discussion. Even his fellow AT&T staffers would joke about his loyalty. "They used to say, 'OK, he's in the room. Shut up. So, whose side are you on today?'" Seidenberg said. "I used to respond, 'No, no. I'm on the side of getting things done.' I used to have fun with it because while I couldn't compete with the big guys on their terms, I developed my own space." He described himself as working "behind the scenes, pulling the strings, and learning how to solve problems, build consensus and ride beneath the radar."

From his vantage point, both MCI and AT&T were taking extreme positions that weren't tenable and really weren't in their long-term interests or those of the public. They needed to find a workable solution. "The issue is we're in a new world," Seidenberg would argue with anyone who would listen. "The issue is AT&T is not going to be the only place that you can go get service from. And you're going to have to accommodate other people." His advice to FCC staff? "Don't accept MCI's approach, but don't accept ours either. Let's carve out the middle." The solution he and others developed worked as well as anyone might have expected, given the contentious relationship among the parties. But even this was not enough. Eventually, the myriad litigations brought by MCI would set the stage for the private antitrust lawsuit and the $1.8 billion decision against AT&T in 1980 that weighed on Charlie Brown's decision to propose that AT&T divest itself of its operating companies.

During this period, Salerno and Seidenberg met for the first time when Salerno, who outranked Seidenberg as a senior operating executive at New York Telephone, was getting to know the New York congressional delegation during a visit to Washington. "You've got somebody special down here named Ivan Seidenberg," Salerno kept hearing as he made his rounds. "So now I'm saying to myself, it's probably a good idea to meet this guy." The two got together and clearly had a similar view of the phone company's strengths and challenges, though they didn't have any immediate projects on which to work together. It was the beginning of a lifelong, special working relationship.

## CRUCIAL CONNECTIONS

With this growing amount of regulatory and connection fee experience to his name, it was no surprise that a few years later, Seidenberg was chosen to support the divestiture committee on interconnection charges that led to his face-to-face meeting with AT&T CEO Brown in 1982. Everyone on the committees carried out their existing jobs, and then prepared for monthly meetings around the country with the 22 Bell operating company presidents and a group of senior executives from AT&T's headquarters. It was no surprise the interconnection committee meeting process was tense. They were rewriting decades of history.

"Before divestiture," Seidenberg said, "all the revenues came in and then we split them up between the long-distance AT&T and the local companies. It was called a division of revenues process. And it was based on formulas and things like that, but it was wholly controlled by AT&T."

After divestiture "all of that had to be recast as tariffs. OK. So, we had to write the tariffs. My job was to write the tariffs so that AT&T, MCI, Sprint and the others knew what they would pay to interconnect to get their calls completed" into the local operating companies.

It was exhilarating work and the highlight of the first phase of his career. "It was great. A lot of fun. Meeting all over the country. Task forces all over the country. I ended up meeting hundreds of people outside of the New York area. These connections were extraordinary," Seidenberg said.

## NYNEX-BOUND

As the committee work wound down, Seidenberg's connections paid off, and he did entertain competing job offers from a handful of senior leaders among the seven RBOCs. But he recalled Bud Staley's offer and went to visit him at NYNEX's headquarters in White Plains, New York. Staley, a World War II veteran who went out of his way to give hard workers opportunities to get ahead, made it clear that he wanted Seidenberg as NYNEX's man in Washington, understanding the value of being able to see the regulators' point of view. Also vital was the ability to craft new, nontraditional solutions for a new, competitive world. "We don't have your skill in the company, and we need someone who can speak for us in Washington," Staley said.

Although Seidenberg's Washington experience landed him a senior post with NYNEX in the nation's capital, it would soon become apparent to the leadership of the Baby Bell that his skill set was needed closer to home. NYNEX, in step with Bell Atlantic and the other Regional Bell Operating Companies, would experiment—and at times struggle—with the right mix of businesses and leadership strategies to survive and thrive in a newly deregulating world. During its first decade of independence, it would increasingly rely on its rising, next-generation leaders to find workable solutions for the future of telecommunications that it was creating in real time.

# CHANGING MINDSETS:
# C-SUITE INSIGHTS FROM
# RAM CHARAN

___ **IMAGINE AND SHAPE ALTERNATIVES.**
Break the frame of conceiving what the industry needs to be. Play offense. Position the company in the new era not just to survive but thrive. First, focus, and help create a healthy and sustainable industry, and then define a strategy to fix the company.

___ **WALK A MILE IN THEIR SHOES.**
Work with regulators, legislators and other stakeholders to learn their points of view. Don't be bound by it. Develop win-win outcomes to limit future regulatory or stakeholder backlash.

___ **IT'S ALL ABOUT THE CUSTOMER.**
Reframe your and regulators' thinking on the customer. Markets change faster than statutes. Identify businesses that are artificially sustained or restrained by regulation, and manage over time for the increasing impact of market forces. Regulatory processes are almost always behind the customer trend. Give regulators the analysis and insight they need to catch up.

# CHAPTER
# 02
# COMING OF AGE

—

1984-1994

"**W**hat's NYNEX?" That was not a question anyone at the newly created Baby Bell wanted to hear in 1984 as the company worked to establish its identity as one of seven Regional Bell Operating Companies created out of the breakup of AT&T. That was especially not a question Ivan Seidenberg, NYNEX's man in Washington, wanted to hear as he escorted NYNEX CEO Delbert "Bud" Staley on a visit to Capitol Hill. That the questioner was none other than Thomas P. "Tip" O'Neill Jr., the larger-than-life speaker of the House of Representatives, whose congressional seat sat squarely in the heart of NYNEX's New England Telephone coverage area in Boston, only added to the phone company officers' sense of frustration. On the way out of the speaker's cavernous office, Staley turned to Seidenberg and said dryly, "The next time we come, he ought to know who we are."

Defining themselves and getting others to understand who they were would drive much of the decision-making at NYNEX, Bell Atlantic and the other Baby Bells during their first decade as independent companies. From day one the Baby Bells, jointly and independently, strained against the tight leash on their activities otherwise known as the Modified Final Judgment (MFJ) issued by Judge Harold Greene. Wanting to enter the broadly defined information services business with as few restrictions as possible was at the top of the Baby Bell wish list—as was getting out from under the control of the judge and instead having their activities overseen by the Reagan administration's more market-oriented FCC. At the same time, each Baby Bell rushed to expand its array of businesses that were not regulated, often taking the phone companies around the world to more lightly regulated communications and other business markets in the process. And cellular would become an increasingly important, and profitable, business segment.

The strength of the U.S. economy throughout the balance of the 1980s helped the regional phone companies produce positive financial results. Yet, this period of relatively robust growth masked some serious weaknesses in the Baby Bells' business plans, as well as those of their parent turned rival, AT&T, that would continue into the early 1990s. Meanwhile, GTE, the leader among the phone companies that developed independently of the Bell System, also struggled at times to thrive in this increasingly competitive

# ALEXANDER GRAHAM NYNEX

NYNEX continued to be rooted in the past and its Bell System heritage while still stepping somewhat tentatively into the future. Its initial marketing spokesman for business systems was Alexander Graham Nynex, a fictitious character dressed in 19th-century attire. The marketing campaign, lampooned by the widely read *New York Times* columnist Russell Baker, was quietly retired in the mid-1980s.

As for the NYNEX name itself, NY stood for New York. NE stood for New England, and X marked "the unknown," or as detailed in a company press release, "the unknown and exciting future of the burgeoning information market whose outer reaches will be determined by tomorrow's science and technology." Chairman and CEO Bud Staley, who understood that the company had to grow and change, defended the name choice in the fall of 1983 to a *New York Times* reporter by asking, "You remember it, don't you?" Maybe not.

It turned out that Tip O'Neill wasn't the only one having trouble with the name. In the fall of 1987, four years after confronting the journalist from the *Times*, Staley gamely embraced humor as a foil for deflecting lingering concerns about nomenclature. As he told an audience of business executives in Manhattan, "Some of you may not be entirely clear as to what a NYNEX is. It is not something you take to go to sleep at night. It is not the bottom line of the eye chart."

world. By the end of their first decade as independents, the more pre-cocious Baby Bells, including NYNEX and Bell Atlantic, were coming to the conclusion that in order to survive they would need to think bigger.

## RUSH TO DIVERSIFY

Judge Greene's continuing interpretation and implementation of the MFJ following the launch of the Baby Bells concluded that the phone companies could not generate more than 10 percent of their revenues from a non-phone business. Annoyed by what he termed the Baby Bells' "rush to diversify" and the attention they lavished on non-regulated businesses, as opposed to their "relative lack of interest in basic telephone service itself," he reserved the right to sign off on their specific non-phone expansion plans. The Baby Bells kept his pen very busy.

All of the Baby Bells pushed as hard as they could to expand beyond their regulated phone businesses. Jim Cullen and his strategy team developed a strategic vision statement for Bell Atlantic at a May 1983 planning retreat in Princeton, New Jersey, months before the company had even started operating as an independent entity, not to mention the actual divestiture. Bell Atlantic's small, money-losing wireless business was not featured in the original strategic plan.

The vision statement, in abbreviated form, was featured on the cover of Bell Atlantic's first annual report to shareholders, for 1984: "Our mission is to meet the requirements of our customers for high value communications systems and services by building on our reputation, the character and capabilities of our people and the strength of our technological resources." Conveying the "Brave New World" tone adopted by most of the Baby Bells, the cover design didn't feature local phone service or mention the word "telephone."

Cullen's team urged CEO Tom Bolger, Vice Chairman and Chief Financial Officer Raymond "Ray" Smith and the rest of senior leadership to "keep their powder dry" and wait for the right acquisition to come along. Smith, who spent much of his time during the mid-1980s focused on strengthening Bell Atlantic's core phone network and service, agreed. The advice proved prescient for most non-phone investments, as profits were hard to come by, and the attention required to manage the businesses far exceeded their contribution to revenues. But the advice also fell mostly on deaf ears. Bell Atlantic and all of the other Baby Bells went on a cash-flow-fueled spending spree in their first few years as independents. At one point, Bell Atlantic held an ownership stake in one of the world's largest independent computer maintenance businesses called Sorbus Service. Equipment leasing, commercial property development, systems integration, beeper and cellular resale services,and, a few years later, a New Zealand telephone company were also part of the Bell Atlantic portfolio.

NYNEX made its share of non-phone investments in the mid-1980s, but at first it kept its focus closer to home. One key reason was that NYNEX's concentrated base of business customers—25 percent of New York Telephone's revenue came from just 1 percent of its business customers—made it vulnerable to poaching by the competition. As William Burns, NYNEX vice chairman and CFO, told *The New York Times* in October 1983: "The large customers are easy for us to serve, but they are also easy for the competition to go after." Burns added, "When we look at the management challenge we have, it is to try to manage so we provide a fair return to our shareholders, and that isn't necessarily going to happen with new businesses."

# AT&T STUMBLES

It didn't take long for AT&T's prospects to dim. While the company in 1982 had been widely viewed as the winner of the divestiture process—a slimmed-down, new-technology dynamo freed from outdated regulations—the phone company quickly discovered that competing in new markets was tougher than it looked. In 1984, its first year as the new AT&T, profits fell roughly $1 billion shy of projections, while most of the Baby Bells were exceeding profit projections. Fourteen thousand AT&T employees were cut or took early retirement as part of the transition. In addition, AT&T's rate of return on capital in its traditional phone business was well below the 12.75 percent rate approved by the FCC.

As for finally being able to compete in the manufacture and sale of computer products, AT&T's first foray resulted in a line of gear that was dogged with operating glitches and simply wasn't viewed as able to rival most market leaders. To take a second shot at the market in 1985, AT&T shuttered four factories in an effort to slash production costs by 25 percent.

AT&T's new headquarters opened at 550 Madison Avenue in Midtown Manhattan in 1984. In the pre-divestiture days when the building was on the drawing boards, the 37-story tower was to hold at least 1,500 employees. By the time the new, smaller AT&T took possession, only 600 moved in, while others were transferred to cheaper space in the Basking Ridge, New Jersey, office complex. Much of the space in the Madison Avenue location was leased to Sony Corporation of America, which eventually bought the tower in 2002.

# SIBLING COOPERATION

In Washington, the Baby Bells formed the MFJ Task Force in the early 1990s to channel their pooled efforts to push back against the limits on their activities as defined by the MFJ and Judge Greene. The heads of each company's Washington office met once a week, and the CEOs met in Washington every two months. Over time each company anted up $3 million a year, giving the group a $21 million annual operating budget, a hefty sum at the time, with which to lobby regulators and members of Congress. To pool their telecommunications research efforts, the Baby Bells formed Bell Communications Research (Bellcore for short) in 1983 as part of a consent decree.

An early legal challenge led by Bell Atlantic that benefited all the Baby Bells was decided in their favor in August 1986. A federal appeals court panel in Washington, D.C., ruled unanimously that the Baby Bells did not need Judge Greene's prior approval before selling services outside of their original regional boundaries. It was a relatively modest victory but an important one in establishing that the judge's interpretation of his own rulings could be successfully challenged in the courts.

Despite the ruling, the Baby Bells continued to complain that, thanks to Judge Greene, the public was not getting the full benefit of the information revolution that was transforming global communications. As NYNEX's Staley told a business group in October 1987:

> Problem is, though, that we can't compete effectively as we need to because of that theory which says the local networks are monopolies, bottlenecks. It's because of that theory that the judge who presided over the breakup of the Bell System recently ruled that no, we can't manufacture phone equipment; no, we can't compete in long distance; and yes, we can transmit information; but no, we can't process it, at least not right now. Those markets are where the growth is.
>
> . . . There's also a lot more your phone could do now if we were able to unleash the computer capability of the local network. Right now, you have call waiting, abbreviated dialing, and call forwarding—but your phone could be much more versatile than that with today's technology. It could do everything a computer can do, if only it were permitted to do so.

While its initial focus was to bolster its key business segment, NYNEX also joined the other Baby Bells in adding non-phone enterprises. It bought a chain of computer retail stores from IBM, giving it a retail presence in 33 states. NYNEX also opened offices in Switzerland and Hong Kong, and was doing business in Thailand, the Philippines and Indonesia. In 1987, NYNEX was in talks to run a new transatlantic, fiber-optic cable to Great Britain, with connections to continental Europe.

In 1997, the fiber-optic cable system went worldwide and was called FLAG, for Fiber-Optic Link Around the Globe. It also invested in a handful of cable television companies in the U.K. and had a strategic alliance with Japan's Nippon Telegraph and Telephone (NTT), and similar agreements with national telephone administrators in France and the Netherlands.

# PUT A NEW WING ON THE BUILDING

While NYNEX was ratcheting up its non-phone expansion plans, Staley called Seidenberg—who still was responsible for Washington affairs—back to New York. He wanted to test Seidenberg's management acumen and tap his people skills with an expanded portfolio of duties. In 1986, Seidenberg was named vice president of external affairs and put in charge of external and internal communications, advertising, community relations and state-level regulatory efforts. "My role was to bring the company forward and lay the groundwork for what NYNEX might become in the future. This was the role that Staley and Bill Burns, vice chairman, thought would help the company move forward," he recalled.

Late in 1987, Staley wanted to enhance Seidenberg's operating company leadership experience by moving him to the Boston area to serve as the chief operating officer of New England Telephone, the No. 2 officer of the operating company. That position would've put Seidenberg on the traditional operating company ladder to more senior-level management in the future. He also would've been following in the footsteps of Fred Salerno, who became the first New York Telephone officer to move into a senior leadership position at New England Telephone in 1985, in an effort to break down some of the cultural barriers separating the two operating companies. Rising through the ranks, Salerno was promoted to president of New York Telephone in 1987 and transferred back to Manhattan, vacating the No. 2 spot in New England.

Seidenberg told Staley that he considered the offer a "great honor." But he had a counterproposal: NYNEX had several officers with more operating experience who were better qualified for the New England post. Rather than send him on the same path, Seidenberg offered, why not put him in charge of finding a way to "put a new wing on the building"? Seidenberg wanted to oversee the unregulated businesses. He told Staley that he understood that taking this path might limit his chances for promotion to the top echelons of the company, but he was willing to take that risk. Staley didn't respond immediately.

A few months later, Staley told Seidenberg that he had a new job for him. Seidenberg asked if a relocation to New England was pending, but that wasn't the plan. Staley explained that he was now in charge of all the unregulated businesses, just as he had requested. In addition to the title of senior vice president, which he was given in July 1988, Seidenberg said, "I had an indescribable title that included mobile, international, software companies and a real estate business."

Seidenberg's business card should have read, "Be careful what you ask for." As he recalled, "I knew nothing about any of this, and the combination of all these activities was that they were losing a lot of money." Lessons that would serve him well in years to come included the ins and outs of mergers and acquisitions, managing a profit and loss (P&L) for a business line, creating value for and dealing with shareholders and negotiating commercial deals across disciplines. According to Seidenberg: "We bought a few things, expanded a bit more in Asia, but sold more than we bought and generally improved the overall bottom line, even though we were still not profitable."

"The key lesson for me is that broad-scale diversification is hard," Seidenberg said. "It is best to manage what you know, but there clearly is a value in integrating new skills into your business. We also tried to build out our mobile business but had only limited success during this period."

# JUST LISTEN TO THEM

After a few years in business, the other Baby Bells also started to reorganize their operations and shuffle executives to new positions as they began to see what worked and what didn't. Even though Cullen had argued against creating such a corporate grab bag of non-regulated phone businesses, in January 1987 he was named president of Bell Atlantic Enterprises, which comprised these non-regulated operations. Included was the Yellow Pages directory service for the region Judge Greene had given to each of the Baby Bells. Cullen, in 1987, also was named a member of Bell Atlantic's eight-person Corporate Development Council and was clearly being groomed for more senior positions.

Like his colleague Larry Babbio, Cullen grew up in densely populated North Jersey. Delivering the Newark *Star-Ledger* by bicycle every morning and trying to collect weekly payments from his tight-fisted customers, Cullen developed a taste for business and an understanding of people during his childhood. His parents were proud that he was the first in the family to attend college but told the Rutgers University student he would also be paying the bills, which he did by supplementing a scholarship with playing billiards on the weekends. A summer job tending the asbestos ovens for Johns Manville, his father's employer, provided a steadier stream of cash. Fortunately, it did not result in any lung-related ailments.

Cullen had a two-year Reserve Officers' Training Corps (ROTC) commitment to fulfill with the U.S. Army after graduating from Rutgers in 1964 with a degree in economics. He was stationed in Fort Polk, Louisiana, and in a matter of months, 1st Lt. Cullen had 150 soldiers working for him and using computer punch cards to process the hundreds of new recruits passing through the system each week. Had he entered the military a year later, he might have been shipped out to Vietnam as part of the massive troop buildup ordered by President Lyndon Johnson in 1965. With barely a year left to his military commitment by that point, he remained stateside.

The military structure and discipline prepared Cullen well for the Bell System. He had started with New Jersey Bell shortly before entering the service and returned to an office in Cranford, New Jersey, a few weeks before turning 23. He entered the Initial Management Development Program (IMDP) in computer operations, and like most young managers found himself supervising teams who were older and more experienced than he. A few years later, Bill Davidson, vice president of New Jersey Bell's northern area, imparted advice that stuck with Cullen: Leadership isn't just about telling people what you want them to do. "You would be amazed what people will tell you if you just listen to them," he told Cullen.

# WIRELESS GROWTH

It was advice Cullen would put to good use throughout his career. And as he listened in his role as president of Bell Atlantic Enterprises, he liked what he was hearing about the cellular, or wireless, phone business. After being too incidental to even warrant a mention in Cullen's Bell Atlantic strategic planning document in 1983, the wireless business, while still losing money, was beginning to look like it had real potential by the late 1980s.

During this period, Babbio moved from Arlington, Virginia, where he was vice president overseeing various technology initiatives, to a small office in Basking Ridge, New Jersey, to take over as president of the wireless business, which reported in to Cullen's Enterprises group. Babbio retained his oversight of the cellular business when he moved up to serve as president of Bell Atlantic Enterprises International in 1991, a newly created position that opened up after Cullen moved over to serve as president of New Jersey Telephone.

As a lifelong visionary and innovative engineer, Babbio had a natural inclination to focus on improving the company's wireless technology by building the best network. Higher-capacity digital technology at Bell Atlantic and among most wireless carriers across the country was gradually replacing the old, limited analog wireless technology used by the Advanced Mobile Phone Service (AMPS) system developed by Bell Labs. That meant wireless capital budgets, while still modest compared to the multibillion-dollar annual capital budgets at each of the Baby Bells' landline businesses, were set to increase dramatically.

In the fall of 1989, Babbio and others recruited Dick Lynch, a Bell of Pennsylvania engineer Babbio had known for years, to lead the digital buildout of the wireless system. Lynch, who had spent his career working on the traditional wireline side of the business, realized he would have to learn on the job. He inherited a wireless system that had increased its customer base by 88 percent year over year in 1989, but still had only about 100 employees and 160 cell tower sites.

Lynch, who was named Bell Atlantic Mobile chief technology officer (CTO) in 1990, discovered that Bell Atlantic, like most wireless providers, had been building cell towers to serve population centers. That was the traditional approach to capital spending taken the length and breadth of the old Bell System. What Lynch and his team were quicker to understand than most competitors, including their wireless peers at NYNEX, was that the key to success in the wireless business was to improve the customer experience of calls being handed off from one cell tower to the next. That meant building cell towers between population centers, even if there weren't that many potential customers in the immediate range of the cell tower itself. Customers at the time were putting up with having 5 to 10 percent of their wireless calls regularly being dropped. Driving down that number with more efficient cell tower handoffs was sure to be a competitive advantage.

## FOCUS ON THE CONSUMER

As Bell Atlantic Mobile was building out its wireless system to improve the quality of customer calls, it was also helping to improve the look and feel of the cellular business. In 1989 it began selling a cellular phone that, compared to the cumbersome models sold a few years earlier, weighed less than 11 ouncesand could be "tucked away in a shirt pocket or a purse," the company said in its annual report to shareholders. The new phone was a "model for the cellular phone of the future and, as such, it signals our intention to be a leading provider in the business of personal wireless communications."

That effort took another step forward in 1991 when Denny Strigl was named president of Bell Atlantic Mobile. The previous year, he had been serving as Cullen's No. 2 at New Jersey Telephone as vice president and chief operating officer. His focus was "trucks and tools," as Strigl said. When Anton Campanella, Bell Atlantic president, offered Strigl the chance to run the small wireless business, he wasn't sure Strigl would want to make the change. But Strigl jumped at the chance.

Strigl started with New York Telephone in Buffalo, New York, in 1968 after a stint in the Army. In light of the fact that his father had twice declared bankruptcy, Strigl was attracted to the phone company's job security and service ethic but was frustrated with the bureaucracy and

# DRIVE TESTING WIRELESS

To test the quality of their rapidly expanding wireless network, Bell Atlantic Mobile CTO Dick Lynch and his team incrementally developed what became known as drive testing. "We had a couple of guys who were pretty good at computer control testing. And we actually took a vehicle . . . a station wagon . . . and we put into it a computer, and we put in a bunch of phones," Lynch said.

They started testing their own wireless network in the Philadelphia area and quickly determined that they were not alone. "It wasn't too long after that before I realized that we have competition here. This isn't the Bell System anymore. There's somebody out there with this, competing with us." In fact, the independent competitor, Metro Phone, based in Philadelphia, was building out its system faster than Bell Atlantic Mobile was. So, Lynch decided his team would measure the quality of their rival's service as well as their own:

> What we ended up doing was creating a very objective, methodical process and equipment set for going out and continually measuring not only our improvement from month to month but our competitor's improvement from month to month, and our comparison between ourselves and our competitor at any given geographic point. . . . I think that's one of the key points because once we began doing that, it really didn't take more than a year, year and a half, before our network in every geography we serve was better than our competitors.

That early effort at network testing helped identify the quality of the wireless network as a key competitive differentiator for Bell Atlantic Mobile. Within a few years, the station wagons would be used as part of the wireless business' public relations efforts and appeared in numerous articles and local TV segments in the early 1990s. That was just a hint of the concept's potential. In the following decade, the idea of testing the quality of the network would evolve into the single most memorable ad campaign in the history of wireless—one that customers would hear loud and clear.

bureaucratic thinking. Later he moved to New York City for a position with parent AT&T and then moved into sales with AT&T in Morristown, New Jersey. He left the parent company for a sizable promotion—general manager of sales and marketing for Wisconsin Telephone.

As divestiture loomed, Strigl—like Cullen, Babbio, Seidenberg and many next-generation phone industry leaders—was caught in the talent tug of war that preceded the January 1, 1984, breakup of the Bell System. AT&T wanted him back. But he stayed in the Midwest, and became a manager for regional Bell Ameritech. Then in 1983, Ameritech CEO Bill Weiss and President and COO Jim Howard took Strigl out to dinner.

"We have this company that is brand new. We're going to call it Ameritech Mobile. It's cellular communications," Howard said. "If you take this job, it's not going to amount to much." Strigl wasn't exactly bowled over by the offer. Then the two sweetened the deal. "We have introduced it and we're having trouble selling it," Howard said. "If you would go run this place for a couple of years, I can almost guarantee we'll make you president of Indiana Bell, Ohio Bell, Michigan Bell or Wisconsin Bell." Sold.

With a career mostly spent in sales and marketing, Strigl had to learn about wireless technology on the job. He quickly realized, as Babbio and Lynch would several years later, that the mobile division needed to spend much more on building out the system to reduce the number of dropped calls. "To the customer, you're only as good as your last call," Strigl said. Fights with company management to increase capital spending were never-ending.

Those fights were nothing compared to the pushback Strigl got when he and his leadership team cut the price of cellular service by 50 percent—from 50 cents to 25 cents a minute—without getting board approval. Howard, the chairman of Ameritech Mobile, called

Strigl and told him it would be his last day on the job. Strigl, who had a commercial pilot's license, went home that night and told his wife he might give one of the airlines a call. The next morning his chairman called back. He was willing to give the new price a try for 30 days, as the damage had already been done. Within a month, the discounted price plan had nearly doubled the number of subscribers, and Strigl kept his job. He also learned that to make cellular a success, it had to be kept as far away from the tradition-bound approach of the phone company as possible.

By the latter part of 1986, Ameritech Mobile had growing mobile operations across much of the Ameritech footprint in the Great Lakes states. Strigl was asked to take on a new responsibility in early 1987, moving to Princeton, New Jersey, to serve as president and COO of Applied Data Research (ADR), a software company that Ameritech had acquired in 1986 when, like the other Baby Bells, it ventured into nonregulated businesses. Within a year, the company discovered that a new database software product from IBM, DB2, was competing directly for about 50 percent of ADR's business. Meanwhile, Strigl took over as chairman and CEO and successfully sold ADR for a modest profit.

He commuted back to the Midwest to work for Ameritech's Illinois Bell unit in a marketing position, but he felt like he was treading water in his career. He had wanted to be named head of Ameritech Mobile, but that position was already taken by Richard Notebaert, a fast-rising star who would later be named Ameritech's CEO. Strigl and his family really wanted to stay on the East Coast. Someone at a party recommended that he meet Jim Cullen. The two connected immediately. Strigl took a job in Arlington, Virginia, for Bell Atlantic in product marketing for less than a year until Cullen could bring him in as his No. 2 at New Jersey Telephone. Once Strigl was named president of Bell Atlantic Mobile in 1991, he finally felt that he had landed his dream job.

Even though the position was ideal for the new president, the business side of Bell Atlantic Mobile was something of a nightmare. The Pittsburgh wireless operations were under-performing so consistently that they were actually on the auction block, Strigl said, when he took over Bell Atlantic Mobile. In many other markets, sales were conducted in the very plodding, incremental fashion of the Bell System monopoly days of old. Strigl would spend the next few years driving a top-to-bottom business, and more importantly a cultural transformation of the wireless business. He and his team built a platform that would redefine wireless success as the 1990s progressed.

# GTE GROWTH

While all of the Baby Bells were building out their wireless businesses with varying degrees of success by the early 1990s, the nation's second-largest wireless provider was the largest U.S.-based provider of local phone service—their independent phone company rival GTE. In the fourth quarter of 1992, GTE Mobilnet passed the 1 million customer milestone and accounted for 10 percent of all wireless customers in the nation. Its subscriber base had more than doubled in 1990 to 511,000 and then received an added surge in wireless customer growth the following year, to 811,000 from its $6.2 billion purchase of Contel Corp., the third-largest independent phone company, in 1991.

That wireless growth outpaced all of the Baby Bells and ranked second in size only to McCaw Cellular Communications' Cellular One, with roughly 1.3 million customers. McCaw Cellular was one of many independent cellular companies that were encouraged to compete with the Baby Bells in wireless via the freeing up of cellular spectrum by regulators in markets across the country. As a clear indicator that wireless was viewed as a technology with a bright future by the early 1990s,

AT&T, in order to re-enter the wireless business in the post-divestiture era, bought one-third of Cellular One in late 1992 for $3.8 billion. Two years later, AT&T bought the balance of the company for $12.6 billion.

GTE had started its wireless business in 1982. Similar to Strigl, the early GTE wireless executives realized that they needed to create their own wireless culture if the business was going to thrive. "It [is] more like the Wild West when you're starting up a company," said Marc Reed, who transferred from another GTE office to lead HR for the wireless group in Houston. "You played ethically, and you played by the right employment rules, but from a corporate perspective, you were left alone to do the things with a lot less bureaucracy."

While managing its soaring growth rates, GTE researchers developed widely adopted wireless technologies during the early 1990s. Those included "Follow-Me Roaming," which facilitated the handoff of cellular calls among towers. Dan Mead, who ran GTE's Mobilnet operations in Ohio and Pennsylvania beginning in the mid-1990s, said that one of the keys to success at GTE was the competitive instinct ingrained in every aspect of the business that was part of GTE's highly competitive manufacturing heritage: "You need to make sure that you're doing the best job for your customers. You're beating the daylights out of your competitors in terms of growth. And you make sure you're doing it with the highest level of integrity. And you make sure you're the most profitable in the industry."

In September 1991, GTE made the strategic decision to concentrate on the telecommunications industry, reflected in the purchase of Contel, and divest its Sylvania lighting business and its precision materials operations. GTE Mobilnet was a key part of that strategy. Charles "Chuck" Lee, who was named chairman and CEO effective May 1, 1992, was the driver of the reorganization and had served as president and COO since December 1988. He had joined GTE as CFO in 1983. Lee believed that GTE needed to continue to expand to thrive in the telecommunications realm, and he would soon be back on the hunt for his next acquisition.

# THE BELL ATLANTIC WAY

Ray Smith, who had been named president and chief operating officer of Bell Atlantic in 1988, succeeded Tom Bolger as CEO and chairman in 1989. Smith was the son of a steel mill worker and was born and raised in Pittsburgh as a member of a close-knit Catholic family. He attended Carnegie Mellon University in Pittsburgh and graduated with a degree in industrial engineering in 1959. (Smith received an MBA from the University of Pittsburgh in 1967 after taking night school classes for seven years.) He went to work for Bell of Pennsylvania in downtown Pittsburgh right out of college as part of the IMDP management training program.

For the next two decades, Smith worked his way up the management ladder, first with Bell of Pennsylvania and then with parent AT&T, all the while scoffing at the mind-numbing bureaucracy. His generation of Bell executives, Smith later quipped, built their careers on the idea that "the future would look much like the past, except with nicer carpeting." As AT&T budget director, he produced the first five-year budget plan for AT&T. Then-CFO Charlie Brown greeted him the first time they met by saying, "You're the inventor of the Smith Plan!"

By the early 1980s, Smith was back at Bell of Pennsylvania serving first as vice president of operations and then as president of both Bell of Pennsylvania and Delaware's Diamond State Telephone. As president of Bell of Pennsylvania, he pushed through an unprecedented $350 million rate increase that enabled the operating company to at least partially catch up with the impact of 1970s-era inflation on the cost of maintaining its infrastructure. With divestiture looming, he served with Seidenberg on the rate-setting national committee. (Seidenberg's deep understanding of the intricacies of interconnect tariffs, and his beard, earned him the nickname "Ivan the Technical" among his fellow committee members, Smith said.) When Bolger formed his Bell Atlantic leadership team in 1983, Smith was an obvious choice.

As Bell Atlantic CEO, Smith initiated a review of company practices and goals after five years in business. He wasn't about to develop another five-year plan, as he had for AT&T's budget department. This was a new, rapidly evolving business that required a new way of thinking and operating. He championed what he termed The Bell Atlantic Way. It was a new way of thinking about phone company operations that emphasized looking outward instead of in. Smith encouraged leaders to develop more of an external focus based on competitors in the marketplace as well as customers, rather than the focus on internal competition that had evolved as part of the Bell System. All of the Baby Bells wrestled with similar attempts at redefining their businesses and corporate cultures during this period, with mixed results. To Smith's credit, the Bell Atlantic Way most likely helped his leadership team see the value in linking their fates to that of another Baby Bell a few years hence.

## MIXED MEDIA

More so than his predecessor, Bolger, Smith emphasized the public, external-facing role of the Bell Atlantic CEO. That was made all the easier for him because he had two highly able lieutenants in Jim Cullen and Larry Babbio running day-to-day operations. While Babbio remained in charge of the nonregulated enterprise businesses, Cullen assumed oversight of all phone operations as president of Bell Atlantic in 1993. Both would be named Bell Atlantic vice chairmen in 1994.

The role of "Mr. Outside" at Bell Atlantic fit Smith's multitude of talents, which included being a published author, playwright, actor, poet and painter. More so than many telecommunications industry leaders, Smith focused incessantly on the convergence of media in the form of voice and video or television that was being driven by digitization and related technological advances. He was determined that Bell Atlantic was going to be in the vanguard of this telecommunications revolution. As early as the company's 1990 Annual Report, Bell Atlantic was using "broadband" to refer to fiber-optic cable as the "high-capacity—or broadband—highway for transmission of digital signals."

In a prescient prediction, long before anyone had reason to coin the terms "Verizon" or "Fios," the 1990 report ventured that "within 15 years—given a favorable regulatory climate—Bell Atlantic's deployment of digital and optical technologies will reach homes and businesses region-wide, providing a virtually limitless number of high-speed, high-quality channels capable of transmitting such services as high-definition television and full-motion, interactive video."

In July 1991, when Smith described the nascent internet as "the collection of high-speed public and private computer networks that links more than 175,000 computers in 35 countries to serve the needs of the research community," he was thinking bigger. Ten to the power of 100 times bigger. In a speech titled "The Googolbit Network" delivered at the Symposium of Gigabit Networks in Washington, D.C., Smith said: "So the term 'googolbit' is simply a reminder of the potential of the network we can create if we aggregate our collective resources—a touchstone in the series of imaginative leaps that will provide the conceptual impetus we need in this country to pull political consensus and private capital and personal genius toward the notion of a universal broadband network."

# TCI LETTER OF INTENT

As part of his embrace of a broadband future, Smith in 1992 had Bell Atlantic file suit in federal court to challenge the 1984 restrictions on the company's ability to own as well as transmit video programming and content. Bell Atlantic won the suit in 1993, marking a victory for all the Baby Bells. That paved the way for the proposed deal that would shock the worlds of telecommunications and high finance.

Smith wanted something that would be truly transformative for Bell Atlantic, and he wanted more "scale and scope." He didn't want to be just one among many Baby Bells. Bell Atlantic had come of age; it was time to think big. He reached out discreetly to John Malone, the entrepreneur who had built TCI Communications into the country's largest cable TV purveyor. The two had previously met at telecommunications industry conferences and shared a common vision of a broadband future. Malone, who also controlled cable television content provider Liberty Media, realized that his nationwide agglomeration of cable companies would need billions of dollars in upgrades in the years ahead as the industry entered the digital age. He had let it be known among AT&T and the Baby Bells that he might be interested in some form of a deal.

Smith and his team insisted that for any such deal with TCI to make financial sense, it had to be a merger of Bell Atlantic and TCI, with Liberty Media to be folded into TCI as part of the transaction. After weeks of hashing out pricing and other details in secret, Smith and Malone announced they had signed a letter of intent on October 13, 1993, to merge Bell Atlantic and TCI. The combination was valued at $33 billion, making it, at the time, the largest corporate merger in history. Crucially, this was not a definitive merger agreement. There was much research and due diligence ahead before the two parties would be prepared to sign a definitive deal.

The telephone-cable deal reverberated around the world of telecommunications. It spurred several other players to propose combinations of their own as they raced to enhance their own "scale and scope." They seemed to fear being left behind as a wave of convergence appeared ready to wash over the telecommunications terrain. Their shareholders acted as if they thought the Baby Bell leaders were in over their heads.

Many shareholders of TCI and Bell Atlantic, not to mention other industry members hoping to ride the convergence trend, hated the deal. As a reflection of that displeasure, share prices of the two companies drooped in the weeks following the announcement. Many TCI holders were demanding a significant premium to the existing share price to give up a future of escalating equity values for TCI's systems and Liberty Media's programming assets. Bell Atlantic shareholders, on the other hand, balked at the idea that Smith and his team would issue new shares—diluting their holdings—and pay a special dividend.

They soon had additional reasons to complain. Other problems with the deal included the impact of earlier legislation, the 1992 Cable Act, which was driving a round of cuts in the effective rates cable companies were able to charge. Lower rates meant lower revenues for TCI and the rest of the cable industry, putting additional downward pressure on their stock prices.

And then there was the price tag attached for stepping in and upgrading Malone's far-flung TCI cable systems and integrating them with the Bell Atlantic network. No wonder the man who was considered one of the most adept allocators of capital in corporate America thought it was time to cash out. Few in regulatory or legislative circles lavished praise on Malone when talk turned to customer service—Vice President Al Gore called him the "Darth Vader" of the cable industry—so the Bell Atlantic team thought they knew what they were getting into.

Industry talk hadn't prepared them for the amount of time and money they determined they would have to invest to bring the TCI systems up to their standards. Enough was enough. Less than five months after their bombshell announcement, Bell Atlantic and TCI called off the proposed deal on February 23, 1994.

While Smith was disappointed, he also was relieved that the merger hadn't worked out, based on the deplorable state of the TCI cable networks that his teams had unearthed. Other leaders might have wanted to take some time out to review the lessons learned after such a potentially game-changing deal had so very publicly collapsed. Not Smith. If anything, the excitement generated by the TCI deal clearly demonstrated that his strategy was well-founded. Now he needed to find the right target, or targets.

Seidenberg recalled being stunned when the TCI-Bell Atlantic deal was first announced. "The sheer magnitude and audacity to do this left an impression on me about thinking big," he said. The collapse of the deal sent another message. "We had to make sure we could finish what we started."

Even as Bell Atlantic was exploring a deal with TCI, it was one of several Baby Bells joining forces to pursue video ventures. In the fall of 1994, Bell Atlantic was the first company to offer video on demand with its Stargazer trial service, offering video on demand initially to hundreds of homes in Virginia. In early 1995 it linked with NYNEX, Pacific Telesis and the talent firm Creative Artists Agency to launch Tele-TV, offering video on demand through a set-top box and transmitting video over existing phone company copper wiring. Smith captured the great expectations of industry leaders as they eyed the impact of telecom convergence. "Before the communications industry is through, your computer will speak, your TV will listen and your telephone will show you pictures."

Other joint ventures followed, but none lived up to their promise. High costs and slow consumer acceptance were formidable hurdles to clear. When Tele-TV was discontinued in December 1996, the partners had invested more than $500 million in the project and had little growth to show for it.

# SWITCHING JOBS AT NYNEX

Seidenberg watched the evolution of Bell Atlantic Mobile during the late 1980s and early 1990s with interest, and no small amount of envy. Mobile was recognized as an important service to NYNEX's core business customers, especially those working on Wall Street or in financial services. But even though wireless was adding customers at a respectable pace, he struggled to develop the right business model of service excellence and profitability to build out this sector that fell under his wing as a nonregulated business. He would later admit that he trailed Babbio and Strigl in recognizing mobile's growth potential in its early years. The buildout of the mobile business would happen at some point, but in the meantime he prioritized rationalizing the operations and stanching the flow of red ink from NYNEX's international and other unregulated businesses.

NYNEX's reputation was damaged by a 17-week-long strike in 1989, with sharing of health care costs by union members being at the core of the dispute. It was eventually settled, but not before Wall Street and industry experts had tarred NYNEX as high-cost with out-of-control labor issues and poor performance relative to its Baby Bell siblings. Salerno was consumed with strike issues as president of New York Telephone. He had a well of sympathy for organized labor, but it wasn't bottomless. He and other operating company executives had been cutting costs where they could to make the phone company more efficient. Some sharing of health care costs by workers was going to have to happen; continuing with the status quo simply wasn't an option. Seidenberg coordinated the company's media and advertising strategies during the strike as head of external affairs.

William C. "Bill" Ferguson, NYNEX president and vice chairman, succeeded Staley as chairman and CEO in 1989 as the company was still reeling from the impact of the strike. When Ferguson was named CEO, Bill Burns, vice chairman and CFO who was his rival for the post, retired. Since Seidenberg reported directly to Burns, he thought he should offer to step aside as well so Ferguson could put a team of his own choosing in place.

When Seidenberg met with Ferguson to offer his resignation, the new CEO told him to get back to work. He expected his team to focus on getting the job done, not office politics. "He kicked me out of his office and said he would decide when it was time for me to leave," Seidenberg said.

It was the first of many times that Ferguson would impart his nononsense Midwestern form of leadership. After one particularly contentious meeting of his leadership team, Ferguson turned to Seidenberg as they were walking back to their offices and asked, "Why do people here keep attacking each other rather than the problem?"

That was just one of several bits of leadership wisdom that Ferguson shared with Seidenberg. "He understood that the role of the leader was to create a vision for the future," Seidenberg said. And to act on it. "Every day we have to get better," Ferguson used to say. Ethical and principled, Ferguson built a strong foundation on which Seidenberg would build his own approach to leadership. He conveyed a sense of knowing when to listen and when to speak, when to encourage and when to deliver a sterner message. "He gave me great confidence," Seidenberg said. "I quoted him endlessly."

After more than a year of damage control and getting a better understanding of the challenges he was facing, Ferguson decided it was time to shake things up. He called Salerno and Seidenberg into his office in 1991 and shocked them both by saying he wanted the two of them to switch jobs. Salerno would take over the nonregulated businesses, and Seidenberg would be put in charge of the phone companies. They would both be vice chairmen and, by implication, contenders to succeed Ferguson. And both men continued to work closely together.

# WE NEVER, EVER FIXED THE CORE

The relatively strong economy of the second half of the 1980s enabled the Baby Bells as a group to post strong revenue and earnings growth. But this economic boom masked a deeper, disturbing trend in telecommunications. The Baby Bells were slowly losing market share. And so was AT&T. And none of them had yet developed a strategy for fixing their core businesses.

"It always bothered me that we never had an answer for loss of market share" during this period, Seidenberg said. "Our answer was, 'Well, we'll get into real estate, go international. We'll do this. Maybe wireless will give us a little bit.' We never, ever fixed the core in terms of reducing the steady loss of market share. AT&T never addressed their core. They tried to market their way around it."

For the next three years, Seidenberg's job was to fix the core. Even though he had started out in a New York Telephone garage, he had not risen through the operating ranks of leadership. He could approach the phone companies as an outsider who wasn't beholden to any one leadership team or operating unit. NYNEX had been in business since 1984, yet the company's major operating units were still known, proudly by most of their leaders and workers, as New York Telephone and New England Telephone. A separate service company coordinated related projects between the two. They had trimmed their respective workforces at the margin and made other steps aimed at cutting costs and boosting efficiencies, but neither seemed to benefit significantly from being part of a larger entity. NYNEX was corporate. They were the operating companies.

Seidenberg held a series of meetings with the heads of the two operating companies and the service company during his first several months. They clearly hoped that he would stay out of their way. He finally called a meeting and presented them with a number of studies that highlighted NYNEX's performance and service issues. "We're not modern. Our costs are too high," he pointed out. "We've got crappy relations with the unions," he said. "We've got crappy relationships with the regulators. So, I think we've got to fix that."

As part of this retooling process, he announced during a meeting with about 20 officers of the operating and service companies that their business would be called NYNEX. One of them shot back, "Over my dead body." Seidenberg paused and said, "That's not necessary." A few weeks later, Seidenberg went to the man's office on a Friday to continue the discussion. The officer said, "You're here to get my badge." Seidenberg responded, "Not necessarily." The officer insisted that he couldn't continue under the NYNEX banner. "I'll be gone Monday morning," he said. Word soon spread among the phone company officer corps that Seidenberg may not have come up through the chain of command, but he was not to be messed with.

Under what eventually became known as One NYNEX, Seidenberg began a sweeping reorganization of NYNEX's core business. He eliminated the boards of the operating companies and combined the two entities, basing the phone company in New York. Costs were cut, and capital spending budgets gradually increased. "We merged finance, we merged operations, engineering, regulatory, HR and real estate to start," he added. "We effectively wanted a full-scale merger of the two independent telephone companies."

Seidenberg was named NYNEX president and chief operating officer in 1994. Salerno was named vice chairman of the new businesses and business development. By this point, fixing the core went well beyond nomenclature. NYNEX took $1.4 billion in after-tax charges in 1993 related to business restructuring, including $700 million in severance and retiree medical costs, as well as $400 million in business re-engineering costs. These and related charges left NYNEX with its first annual net loss since it opened for business. The company told shareholders, "We're making the hard choices now to streamline and redesign our operations in order to become a new kind of company—the premier full-service communications provider in the Northeast and a force to be reckoned with in dynamic growth markets around the world."

Seidenberg looked outward as well as inward to improve NYNEX's operations. His team worked out longer-term, more flexible agreements with state regulators. And with union contracts up for renewal in 1994, Seidenberg was able to push through a five-year deal rather than the standard three-year contract. It was not cheap, but the extended duration and flexibility on other issues were well worth the price, he said.

## BELL ATLANTIC-NYNEX TALKS

As president of NYNEX, Seidenberg worked with CEO Ferguson to develop and refine strategies for growing the business. He knew that Ray Smith, following the collapse of the Bell Atlantic-TCI deal, had reached out to Ferguson. The two had talked about a range of options, including combining the two businesses. As previously stated, Smith was quick to point out that he thought NYNEX's operations were a mess that had to be significantly improved before he would consider a deal. Seidenberg concluded that Smith was not seriously interested in doing a deal at that time. "Ray thought that the New York company would be there for the taking whenever he wanted," Seidenberg said.

# CEO SEIDENBERG

In the fall of 1994, Ferguson called Seidenberg into his office in White Plains. He was turning 65 the following year, so to speed up the transition process, he wanted to name Seidenberg CEO in November, with the promotion to become effective January 1, 1995. The chairman title would follow in mid-1995. Seidenberg was stunned. He told Ferguson that he was honored but that he was convinced that Ferguson and the board of directors would go outside of the company to find his successor to provide a "dose of fresh air." He didn't think that he or Salerno was in the running.

Ferguson looked a bit uncomfortable. "It wasn't the only option I considered," he confessed. "I tried to go outside, but I didn't quite find the right fit." Another bombshell followed. "There are people on the board who think this may be a bridge too far," Ferguson said, even though they voted in favor of his recommendation. Seidenberg asked for a few days to consider the offer.

When they met again, Seidenberg accepted. Then he insisted that Ferguson hear what he was planning to do as CEO. "There are two or three things I've got to tell you before we start so you're not surprised," Seidenberg said. "We can't make it on our own," he told Ferguson. Seidenberg said he didn't know if the answer was to rekindle talks with Smith or not. "We've got to do something because we can't compete. We've got too much of our company tied up in a bad situation in New York State, and we have a no-growth situation in New England."

"Are you talking about selling?" Ferguson asked. "I don't know what I'm talking about, but we need to be looking," Seidenberg said. He then told Ferguson that he wanted to move the headquarters out of White Plains and into New York City, where New York Telephone was head-quartered. Ferguson blanched. "Do it when I leave, OK?" he asked.

Seidenberg then went to meet with Salerno. Congratulations and handshakes ensued, and then Seidenberg got to the point: "Fred, here's the deal. We've worked together for the last four years doing this. I don't know what to say other than I don't think I want to do this if you're not here to help me get started. And then if it works out, we'll keep going. If it doesn't, we will have an honest discussion about it."

Seidenberg offered Salerno the positon of CFO. Salerno protested that he was not a "financial guy" by training. Seidenberg countered that Salerno was still ahead of him in that category, and the job en-compassed more than financials in any case. In many ways, he would be Seidenberg's right-hand man. "That's a meaningful job. Let's give it a shot," Salerno said.

# COMING OF AGE:
## C-SUITE INSIGHTS FROM RAM CHARAN

---

### \_\_ LEND AN EAR.

Leaders at all stages in their careers benefit by being close listeners and observers. Leadership teams across industries consistently complain about listening deficits. Natural selection suggests humans benefit over time from having two ears but only one mouth.

### \_\_ PUT A NEW WING ON THE OLD BUILDING.

Apply yourself in a new role. Do what is needed, not what you are told. Try failing, learning and trying again; iterating is key to building leadership potential and seeding new talent that will develop the future of the enterprise.

### \_\_ FIX THE CORE.

Diversification is sexy but no substitute for tackling basic problems with a company's core business.

# 03

# RE-CREATE, REORDER, RESTRUCTURE

## 1995-2000

T here were times during his first few months as CEO of NYNEX, in early 1995, that Ivan Seidenberg felt as if he were a pawn in someone else's game. The consummate behind-the-scenes insider for much of his career, the 48-year-old Seidenberg was now corporate royalty. "I had never been a visible symbol of any organization," he said. "It was just like, how do you do this? I talked to analysts, customers, politicians. I talked to the board. But I was never a visible leader in front of employees." He had attended plenty of board meetings, of course, but he had never run one as CEO. "I had all these advisers who were telling me what to wear, how to smile, what to say. And then I quickly figured out they don't have all the answers either. So, I had to develop my own style and approach."

Bill Ferguson, his predecessor at the NYNEX helm, later confided to Seidenberg that picking him to be CEO was a risk. But Ferguson was willing to risk some "rookie mistakes" on Seidenberg's part. "As long as you continue to show the capacity for growth," Ferguson told Seidenberg, "you aren't going to fail."

That capacity for growth would prove key to the phone company's, and Seidenberg's, success for the balance of the decade and beyond. Two transformative mergers and major joint ventures would leave the regional realms of the Baby Bells far behind and position the successor telecommunications company as a nationwide juggernaut. Seidenberg made these transformations a reality by building on his strengths as a leader able and willing to position the company and his leadership team to take advantage of the next opportunity. Even if that meant stepping aside as the sole leader of the enterprise not once but twice.

That said, the young CEO was still a work in progress. Business consultant and GTE Director Sandy Moose met Seidenberg in the mid-1990s and later worked closely with him for years as a Verizon director. She counseled a rising executive intimidated by Seidenberg's track record: "Ivan didn't start off the way you see him now. It took a number of years for Ivan to grow into being Ivan."

# CHESSBOARD STRATEGY

Seidenberg was true to his word in working closely with his newly named CFO, Fred Salerno. At one meeting, they came up with a metaphor for corporate strategy that they would use for years to come. Seidenberg said, "Fred, we have to chart the future of this company. We have to figure out what we're willing to do and what we're not willing to do." Salerno, knowing they were both chess players, responded, "Ivan, this is like the chessboard. We've got to take our company, which is in the corner of the chessboard, and move it to the center so we have control over more pieces and spaces."

The two executives saw NYNEX as being boxed into the corner of the chessboard—that is, with limited options relative to the other Baby Bells—for all of the reasons that had been identified for years as dogging NYNEX: high labor costs and the complexity of operating in the country's densest urban market; restrictive state regulation, especially in New York State; a limited geographic footprint; and a heavy reliance on large business customers who rivals were tempted to poach.

They were determined to develop a strategy that would enable them to expand their options in response to each of these challenges, opportunistically moving forward on multiple fronts if needed to take advantage of the rapidly shifting competitive and regulatory environment in which they operated.

Their first move was to enhance NYNEX's mobile phone capability. Even before Seidenberg had been named CEO in late 1994, he and Ferguson deputized Salerno to meet with Larry Babbio from Bell Atlantic, whom Salerno had known for years, to explore combining their cellular businesses. Bell Atlantic CEO Ray Smith backed the effort, as did Bell Atlantic Mobile President Denny Strigl.

Many involved in the cellular project viewed it as a dry run. If the two companies could work together in cellular, more might follow. Perhaps even the first marriage of two of the original seven Baby Bells was on the horizon.

There had already been quite a bit of cellular information sharing among the two Baby Bells. Since divestiture, they had operated northern New Jersey in partnership, as many of their customers in the area worked in Manhattan but lived across the Hudson River in New Jersey. Many officials from both companies would concede at that time that Bell Atlantic, with slightly more than 1 million cellular customers, ran a more efficient cellular business compared to NYNEX, with its 900,000 customers.

Bell Atlantic had been more aggressive than NYNEX, seizing an opportunity in the fall of 1991 to buy independent cellular service provider Metro Mobile CTS Inc. for nearly $2.5 billion in Bell Atlantic stock and the assumption of Metro Mobile debt. It was the third-largest mobile deal ever at the time. That move expanded its cellular market to include Arizona, North Carolina, South Carolina and Connecticut.

# BELL ATLANTIC-NYNEX MOBILE

Bell Atlantic Mobile's Strigl was particularly outspoken in lobbying for combining the cellular businesses. He was confident his team could improve the existing customer experience. When he drove north from his offices in Bedminster, New Jersey, to NYNEX Mobile's headquarters in Orangeburg, New York, for board meetings for the northern New Jersey cellular partnership, he could predict precisely where his calls would drop: It was just opposite a McDonald's on New Jersey Route 1 that marked the dividing line between Bell Atlantic Mobile's territory and the northern portion of the state operated as a partnership with NYNEX.

Strigl wanted to make a deal because he was confident his team would end up running the combined entity. His goal was sidetracked, at least temporarily, by Smith, who called him to Alexandria, Virginia, for a meeting after the cellular deal was announced in June 1994. Smith told Strigl that since his counterpart at NYNEX Mobile, Alfred "Al" Boschulte, was equally highly regarded by NYNEX, neither one of them was going to get the top job at the combined cellular business.

Strigl thought the Baby Bell executives were making a mistake. He wrote a long letter to Salerno and another director of the combined cellular business detailing why he should be CEO. Unbeknownst to Strigl, Seidenberg was also lobbying on his behalf, questioning why Salerno and Babbio wanted to look outside of the company when they had a proven leader in Strigl in-house, even if he wasn't from the NYNEX side of the deal. After a relatively brief search for a CEO from outside of the companies, Strigl was named CEO of Bell Atlantic-NYNEX Mobile in 1995.

# "WE'RE GOING TO CALL IT OUR CULTURE"

In true phone company fashion, the Baby Bells were deliberate in creating multiple task forces to steer the cellular merger, which was finalized in July 1995. It was a painfully slow process for Strigl, given his get-it-done-yesterday mentality, as well as for Mobile CTO Dick Lynch. As Lynch said, "We did an awful lot of best-practice analysis paralysis during the merger of Bell Atlantic Mobile and NYNEX Mobile, which I never repeated again."

Months later, Strigl, after telling Salerno what he was going to do, announced that the task forces were "dead." He said, "We're going to do it the way I say we're going to do it. And the culture that we're going to adopt here is the culture that we have in Bell Atlantic Mobile. And we're going to call it our culture. Not one or the other—it's our culture."

Jim Gerace, who had been managing public relations for NYNEX Mobile, was offered the equivalent post for the combined Bell Atlantic–NYNEX Mobile business. At their first meeting in Strigl's Bedminster office, Gerace, worried that Strigl just thought of him as the NYNEX guy filling an opening, started in on a recitation of his resume. Strigl, not looking up from the pile of mail he was sorting on his lap, said, "Stop. You wouldn't be here if I didn't want you here."

Among Gerace's many duties, he served as a modern-day James Boswell to Strigl's Samuel Johnson. Directness, honesty and integrity were principles espoused by Strigl that Gerace would jot down as the 1990s progressed. These principles were at the core of Strigl's approach to leading a rapidly growing cellular business. In fact, Strigl had been keeping his own list of principles and leadership maxims for at least a decade as he rose through the cellular ranks, beginning with his role in building the mobile business for Ameritech. Other principles would follow. By the new millennium, they would help forge a unifying wireless culture that tied together disparate heritage businesses and provided a platform for further explosive growth in the years ahead.

# "SCALE UP TO 100 MILLION CUSTOMERS"

At Bell Atlantic-NYNEX Mobile, Babbio, Cullen, Lynch and Strigl obviously had their differences over time. But they were united on an essential point: They were going to build the best system possible for what was considered at the time unimaginable growth. At the time, when the newly merged cellular business was just passing the 2 million subscriber milestone, Bell Atlantic-NYNEX Mobile was thinking big. Very big. As Jim Cullen said, "We want to get big enough in wireless that we can advertise during the Super Bowl. This was our benchmark. This was our yardstick. We want to control so many territories that we'll have a national business."

Roger Gurnani, chief information officer of Bell Atlantic-NYNEX Mobile, met with Strigl less than two years later to discuss cellular systems integration. By this time, the company had more than 4 million subscribers. As Gurnani was laying out the challenges facing the growing operation, Strigl, who was not an engineer by training, said, "Well, make sure that stuff that you put together, the systems and stuff—they've got to scale up to 100 million subscribers." It was one of many such instances during the mid- to latter 1990s when Strigl, with the concurrence of the leadership team, emphasized the importance of scale in every aspect of wireless planning.

Gurnani was stunned and blurted out, "You're really nuts." As it turned out, Strigl was the more prescient technologist of the two. "Amazingly, today Verizon Wireless uses the same systems that we put in. And obviously, we've done a lot of work. We've renovated those systems and scaled them up, but it's the same provisioning system; it's the same customer management systems. The foundation was laid back then," Gurnani said. "Denny was right."

---

# PRIMECO

---

While other executives were focused on integrating the mobile businesses of Bell Atlantic and NYNEX, Larry Babbio, Bell Atlantic vice chairman, also homed in on a new wireless opportunity, in consultation with the senior leadership team. After years of planning, the FCC announced that it would conduct the first public auction of radio spectrum beginning in the second half of 1994. The spectrum to be auctioned was called Personal Communications Service (PCS). The government's goal was to free up additional capacity for wireless communications to meet the needs of the rapidly growing cellular phone industry and to introduce additional competition in existing wireless markets. Babbio wasn't worried that the PCS technology wasn't compatible with existing cellular equipment used by Bell Atlantic or NYNEX, which was a concern of Lynch's and Strigl's. He was thinking ahead about gaining footholds in new markets. As Gerace recalled:

> So, now the shot heard around the world was the FCC saying, "This business is something. This is going to be a consumer staple someday. We're going to introduce more competition." So, they awarded spectrum to two additional carriers in every market. Now, to their credit, Bell Atlantic and NYNEX together saw that as maybe not a threat, maybe an opportunity. They said, "Why don't we try to get spectrum in the markets outside the Northeast footprint?"

Looking for partners, they turned to AirTouch Communications, a joint venture between the wireless businesses of Pacific Telesis and US WEST that had most of its markets in the western United States. Bell Atlantic-NYNEX's position was: "You guys have the West Coast; we've got the East Coast. Why don't we bid on the spectrum in the middle? So, that's ultimately what we did," Gerace said. To meet government requirements, they had to create a separate entity to carry out the bidding, which Babbio christened PCS PrimeCo—a name that initially was a placeholder in legal documents.

The business, which was referred to simply as PrimeCo, was based in Dallas. The partnership invested $1.1 billion for cellular licenses in 11 cities, including Chicago, Dallas, Houston, Tampa and Miami. More would follow. Over 57 million people lived in the markets covered by the new PCS licenses.

In a matter of months, Bell Atlantic and NYNEX became partners in a cellular business that was truly nationwide. Managing the business among multiple partners at times was a challenge. But as Seidenberg recalled, "It was the basis for the beginning of going from a local to a regional to a national wireless model." And like their own cellular partnership, Bell Atlantic and NYNEX officials viewed the PrimeCo deal with AirTouch as a possible harbinger of a closer relationship to come.

The creation of PrimeCo demonstrated the wisdom of acquiring spectrum in anticipation of future growth in cellular. CTO Lynch and Babbio were constantly on the lookout for ways to increase the network's breadth and depth. Adding spectrum was key to their strategy, which Babbio communicated to the leadership team.

"Babbio and Lynch always understood the power of spectrum management" among the cellular leadership team, Seidenberg said. "They made us buy spectrum whenever it was available. . . . Most of the time, when Larry said, 'You need some spectrum,' that was good, and there

# WAITING FOR CDMA

Technology, as well as business interests, brought the Bell Atlantic and NYNEX mobile systems together. As the cellular phone industry was preparing for the transition from analog to digital in the late 1980s and early 1990s, to what was known as Second Generation (2G) cellular technology, it had agreed to adopt a technology called Time Division Multiple Access (TDMA). With TDMA, referred to as Global System for Mobile Communications (GSM) outside of the United States, systems could handle three times the number of digital calls as were carried on previous analog systems.

But even as an agreement was being reached, and billions of dollars' worth of orders were being placed for TDMA equipment, a rival technology called Code Division Multiple Access (CDMA) was being promoted as a superior option by its developer, San Diego-based Qualcomm Communications. CDMA technology was not yet available when the first TDMA systems launched in 1992. But Qualcomm executives and others argued that the payoff was worth waiting for, even if that meant waiting until 1995 in many cases. CDMA's wide spectrum technology could handle 10 or more times the calls carried by analog systems, versus the three-fold advantage provided by TDMA.

It wasn't an easy decision, said Bell Atlantic CTO Dick Lynch, who made multiple trips to Qualcomm to gauge their progress in getting CDMA to market and to harangue Qualcomm founder Irwin Jacobs to move even faster.

Lynch told Denny Strigl that he was willing to wait for the higher-quality CDMA service. Strigl didn't overrule him, but he did point out that Southwestern Bell, which was operating a cellular service in Washington, D.C., was already putting in TDMA. "And so, I then had an additional piece of pressure on me, which was that the competition was putting out digital before we were," Lynch said.

Southwestern Bell was joined in the TDMA camp by AT&T's Cellular One wireless behemoth, and the cellular battle lines were drawn. These two gained a first-mover advantage with the launch of TDMA as customers flocked to the first digital service offered. But the technology's limitations quickly caught up with them, said GTE Director Sandy Moose, who served on a GTE board subcommittee that studied the issue and came down clearly on the side of waiting for CDMA.

was always a lively discussion at the board about when we would have enough spectrum. The discussion continues today."

---

# THE URGE TO MERGE

---

Even while the details of the Bell Atlantic-NYNEX cellular partnership were still being worked out in 1995, Seidenberg gave Bell Atlantic's Smith a call. In talking about combining the two companies, Seidenberg asked, "Do you want to start over again?" He was still convinced that Smith was in no rush to make a deal, thinking that Bell Atlantic's relative strengths in wireless and its core phone business would continue to grow as time passed. In fact, Smith had put pursuing a deal with NYNEX on hold during this period, assuming it would be there for the offering when he returned to the subject. He made the rounds of other Baby Bell CEOs to discuss possible options, but nothing came of it.

Seidenberg proposed that they work through a list of secondary issues that needed to be decided in advance of any potential combination of the two Baby Bells. They would leave the potential deal-breakers—such as who would be CEO, where the company would be headquartered and the new company name—for later. "We started to chip away at things we could decide on. So, we had this body of 100 issues. We had 75 of them done. And they were done."

Seidenberg's overarching concern was that, despite improved efficiencies notched by both companies in the early 1990s, neither Bell Atlantic nor NYNEX was in a very strong competitive position. "I'd say to him, 'You're going nowhere, Ray. You have a 2 percent growth company. We have a 3½ percent growth company. You're getting better margins because you don't have New York. The bottom line is . . . you're not going anyplace either.'"

## "IVAN, YOU'RE BARKING UP THE WRONG TREE"

Prior to the merger talks with Bell Atlantic, Seidenberg had represented NYNEX as he quietly approached AT&T about making a deal. He wasn't interested in a merger but rather in creating a united front in opposition to Judge Harold Greene and the overbearing regulation of the industry. Seidenberg tried to make the case to AT&T that long-distance profits were sustained only by government or legal fiat, not market economics. Deregulation would enable them all to benefit by expanding into new businesses. He was rebuffed.

A few years later, Seidenberg explained to the board at many meetings, as part of his chessboard approach to the industry, that it was just a matter of time before all local and long-distance companies would consolidate, and AT&T would be bought by one of the regional companies. According to Seidenberg, the long-distance companies did not have a sustainable business model to survive the customer relationships, poor economics of the long-distance business and competition from both cable and local telcos. There were many directors on the board who had a longtime familiarity with the industry and thought this might be a broad overreach. The board held many lively discussions, including one director telling Seidenberg, "Ivan, you're barking up the wrong tree." Seidenberg disagreed, and would be proved right.

## TELECOMMUNICATIONS ACT OF 1996

The talks between Seidenberg and Smith weren't happening in a vacuum. For a number of years, various congressional committees had been drafting legislation that would modernize the regulation of the rapidly expanding telecommunications industry. It also aimed to promote greater competition among providers and produce more fairly priced product offerings for consumers. The Clinton administration came into office in 1993, and Vice President Al Gore led the push from the White House to get telecommunications legislation through Congress.

As the 1995 congressional session neared its conclusion, the legislation's proponents were finally able to push the bill over the myriad of hurdles set up by opponents and call a vote. The Telecommunications Act was passed by Congress in late 1995 and signed into law by President Bill Clinton on February 8, 1996; it became known as the Telecommunications Act of 1996, or the '96 Act for short. It did away with Judge Harold Greene's oversight of the Baby Bells in the form of the Modified Final Judgment.

With the passage of the Act, the Baby Bells were finally provided with a pathway to offering long-distance service, for years their holy grail. To qualify for long distance under their federal regulator, the FCC, they had to take several steps to open up their local markets to greater competition, including leasing their systems at wholesale rates for use by newly created third-party phone service providers as well as established long-distance providers. State regulators also had to sign off.

Crucially, the details of what would constitute compliance with the need to open up local markets to competition were left up to the FCC. Section 271 of the Act included a 14-point checklist of requirements that had to be met by the Baby Bells for them to be able to offer long distance. The FCC took those 14 points and promulgated hundreds of rules that the Baby Bells had to satisfy in order to bring their long-distance odyssey to an end. Those rules triggered litigation from NYNEX and other Baby Bells alleging overreaching on the part of the agency. By the time NYNEX was finally allowed to offer long-distance calling to customers in New York State, it would be part of a much larger enterprise at the dawn of a new millennium.

Though still a small slice of the overall telecommunications market, access to cellular phone long-distance service kicked in shortly after the '96 Act was signed into law. Credit for accomplishing that goal without making cellular long distance a political hot potato went to NYNEX's top lobbyist in Washington, former Rep. Tom Tauke of Iowa, and a handful of his peers on Capitol Hill.

## MARKET FORCES

In many ways, the '96 Act was an example of government regulation catching up with market forces. The wireless market was able to innovate relatively free of government intervention, thanks in part to its minuscule market share in its infancy. That enabled the Baby Bells to build their own systems, merge with others, as in the case of Bell Atlantic-NYNEX Mobile and AirTouch, and buy wireless systems outside their regions. The next logical step in response to customer demand for greater, and hassle-free, wireless access to service in major markets across the country was to create the beginning of cross-country systems such as PrimeCo.

If competition worked so well in wireless, why not in the heritage wireline business as well?

"I was convinced that AT&T, Bell Atlantic and NYNEX were too constrained by the regulatory process," Seidenberg said. "They were trying to solve everything inside of the regulatory process. And that was a real issue. To me, even though I was considered to be the expert on that, I kept breaking the frames on the regulatory process." Strigl, with his experience in wireless leading him to push back on any suggestion that their activities be regulated further, stiffened Seidenberg's anti-regulatory resolve.

Seidenberg even encouraged Tauke, who dealt more closely than anyone with regulators, to help the company break free of the regulatory mindset. Tauke said, "His perspective was—is—that this was a company that was not focused on defining its own future. And he wanted a culture where the company was defining itself, was creating its own future, and he wanted . . . leaders who would think that way."

# BELL ATLANTIC-NYNEX MERGER

All of the Baby Bells had been on cost-cutting paths for much of the 1990s in order to improve their operating performance. The new wave of competition that the '96 Act was requiring them to subsidize, in effect, also drove a new round of budget cuts. "In large part, due to the '96 Act and the unbundling of networks, and the competitors coming in and the selling your network at below cost—I mean, there was no choice but to cut expenses," Tauke said.

One way to slash costs in preparation for the implementation of the '96 Act was to pursue economies of scale in the form of a merger. That brought Smith and Seidenberg back to the negotiating table. Smith said, "NYNEX became an imperative. . . . There wasn't anything in Europe that would help us get the scale and scope in the world's greatest market in the United States."

On December 18, 1995, *The Wall Street Journal* broke the story that Bell Atlantic-NYNEX merger negotiations had been going on for months that might lead to the creation of the "second-biggest phone firm" after AT&T. The article floated the logical leadership progression of Smith, 58, initially serving as CEO of the combined company. Seidenberg, 49, would take the helm a few years later.

Smith was at the forefront of pushing the industry's technology envelope, but his ambitious reach for telecommunications industry leadership had so far exceeded his grasp. He had been searching for the next big thing since the 1993 collapse of the deal with TCI, the *Journal* article noted. "He's frustrated, and there is a perception that he's not going to go quietly into the night when he retires," an unnamed "rival Bell executive" told the *Journal*. Still, the article quoted an unnamed official as saying that the two companies were "a long, long way off from signing legal documents."

The merger talks stalled in early 1996 over numerous issues, including leadership roles. But price was also a significant barrier to progress.

## ESCAPE FROM NEW YORK

Seidenberg wasn't shy about pointing out to Ray Smith that Bell Atlantic faced its share of hurdles on its path to success. At the same time, he was honest with himself, his leadership team and his board of directors about the No. 1 issue facing NYNEX: its concentration in New York. "I looked at NYNEX, which was 65 percent New York State. New England was another 30 percent, and there was another 5 percent, like Yellow Pages and stuff." Seidenberg's conclusion? "This company can't make it."

"There is no major company on the planet that has 65 percent of its earnings tied up in New York State. So whether you look at AT&T, IBM, American Express, Manufacturers Hanover (later acquired by JPMorgan Chase), Citigroup—any of these companies, they all started in New York. And they figured out a way to be important in New York, but New York had to become a smaller percentage of the total. I started out with the idea that the merger with Bell Atlantic immediately cut the percentage of the company's earnings in New York by half. I started from the perception that if all I did in my career was to do the Bell Atlantic merger, and then I was thrown off the ship, I will have done step one of what I needed to do."

Doreen Toben, Bell Atlantic vice president and controller, was a member of the finance department team that made a covert trip to New York City to review NYNEX's financials. They didn't like what they found. "We felt that they had underinvested. Their maintenance numbers were much worse than Bell Atlantic's," she said. "Their regulatory was not good, from oversight. And we really saw a financial issue." That sort of feedback made it easier for Smith to decide he didn't need to pay a premium over NYNEX's share price to seal a deal—and dictate terms as the victor. The financial team's results supported something closer to a merger-of-equals outcome, which may have led Smith to think there was no need to rush to the altar.

Meanwhile, NYNEX employees from Seidenberg and his leadership team down to the union members answering service calls resented the leaks to the press—which appeared to come from Bell Atlantic or their Wall Street bankers—about the deal talks that typically made NYNEX appear as the junior player in any potential business combination. The leaks also appeared to bad-mouth NYNEX's financials to drive down its asking price in the event of a deal. Even New York State regulators made it clear to NYNEX that they were not happy with all of this takeover chatter.

To every question from institutional investors or security analysts about the terms of a potential deal, Seidenberg would only respond with a terse "We do not comment on rumors and speculation." He would complain privately to Smith about the leaks. "I used to say, 'Listen, Ray, you don't need to do this, you're making it harder on yourself'" by adding to the tension between the two companies. "A merger with us is the next logical play for Bell Atlantic."

# "ARE YOU IN OR OUT?"

Everything changed in early April 1996 when Southwestern Bell (SBC), announced plans to buy Pacific Telesis, whose financial performance had lagged the industry, for $16.5 billion. Ed Whitacre, a hard-charging Bell System lifer who took the SBC helm in 1990 as chairman and CEO, had been sounding out other Baby Bells about possible mergers over the previous few years and had made many wireless acquisitions. An exasperated Seidenberg called Smith. "Now that we've dillydallied with this for all these months, he beats us to the punch. So, are you in or out?" he asked Smith.

Smith said he was ready to make a deal. It was time to get down to the so-called soft, or social, issues that were often more difficult to resolve in such a situation than "hard" issues such as price. Many of the possible Baby Bell combinations Whitacre, Smith and other Baby Bell CEOs had been discussing in recent years, for instance, foundered on the issue of who was going to be in charge of the company post-merger. Morgan Stanley investment banker Paul Taubman, who advised NYNEX on the deal, pointed out that "Ivan never let the social issues get in the way of the right deal. He always put the company first."

Seidenberg always took a long-term view of what was needed to transform NYNEX into a telecommunications company with a future. He was willing temporarily to step aside as CEO and cede that role to the senior Smith. Seidenberg, in turn, would be the company's sole chief operating officer. He wanted two things in return. First, he wanted a date in writing by which Smith would retire, and he would step in as CEO. And Seidenberg demanded that his dismissal require a supermajority vote of the directors of the new company, whose board would include equal representation from NYNEX and Bell Atlantic. Smith initially balked at these conditions, which Seidenberg acknowledged were not typical merger protocol.

Seidenberg pressed his case. "You're in charge. I work for you. But there's got to be a certain date at which transition occurs," he said to Smith, who pointed out that under corporate law there was no guarantee that the board would feel obligated to honor that agreement. "That's absolutely right," Seidenberg said. "But the reason for the supermajority vote is if the board changes its mind, I want to know that it was the entire board and the NYNEX directors who agreed to make a change. If they do, Ray, I'm OK."

Smith answered, "That could happen, Ivan," which Seidenberg took as a not-so-veiled threat that Smith and his team would consider the possibility of promoting this option. Seidenberg responded, "Ray, I'm OK with that. As long as you can't fire me without a full and fair discussion with the board, I'm fine." Some industry insiders speculated that one reason Smith and his team weren't willing to pay a premium to NYNEX's share price for control was that they were assuming that over time Seidenberg would leave, and they would assume control anyway, without having to pay for the privilege.

Choosing which executives would stay and who wouldn't survive the transition "was the hardest part" of the merger, Seidenberg said. He knew that Smith would insist on Babbio and Cullen maintaining senior roles in the combined company. He made the same demand for Salerno.

The next levels involved some tough decisions. The companies brought in a consultant to make the process as fair and effective as possible. For each management position where there was an overlap, they looked at the candidate from Bell Atlantic and the candidate from NYNEX, and weighed whether it made sense to recruit from the outside or adopt a best practice from elsewhere. "I lost several guys that had been iconic leaders in their own right in our company—that I didn't want to lose, and it bothers me to this day," Seidenberg said. Others had to agree to demotions to stay on. But Seidenberg could point to his own situation and encourage them that it was worth the change in status to create a much stronger enterprise going forward.

Seidenberg was also willing to give ground on another soft issue. He agreed that the combined company should take the Bell Atlantic name, not combine it with NYNEX as the wireless business had done. That was perceived as a loss to many NYNEX workers, but Seidenberg and Salerno had never felt a strong affiliation with the NYNEX name in the first place. The Bell brand retained its allure but would be diminished by the addition of the acronym, they reasoned.

More importantly, from Seidenberg's point of view, he prevailed in having the combined company based in New York. That not only appeased testy New York State regulators, it also meant that the new company's board would be meeting on his turf. His case was strengthened by the fact that the original Bell Atlantic had something of a split personality when it came to where it called home. Corporate headquarters were in Philadelphia, yet the company had a major executive and operational presence

## "NOBODY KNOWS WHAT THEY'RE DOING"

Bear Stearns merger adviser Alan Schwartz worked shoulder to shoulder with Seidenberg and Salerno as the negotiations to merge Bell Atlantic and NYNEX dragged on. Schwartz was on a flight with another client, a NYNEX board member, during the middle of the merger talks. The client said, "I really hope these NYNEX guys know what they're doing on this one." Schwartz replied, "No, of course they don't." He explained to his shocked client:

Regulators have announced that all the rules of the game are going to change, and we'll get back to you someday as to what those rules are going to be. Therefore, nobody knows what they're doing, but that doesn't mean that standing still is not making a decision. If you ask me if this management team is making the most intelligent bet on where that future is going and trying to get in front of it, I would tell you absolutely I do [agree]. But nobody knows what they're doing.

in Arlington, Virginia. Rumored plans to build a massive corporate center à la AT&T's Basking Ridge, New Jersey, complex near Virginia's Dulles International Airport had been mothballed.

Then there was the issue of price. The two companies haggled for weeks. Seidenberg and Salerno agreed that getting the deal done was more important than the last fraction of a fraction of a share being exchanged. Alan Schwartz of Bear Stearns, who advised them on the negotiations, said, "Ivan, we've got it down to where it's a fair price one way or the other. Beauty is in the eye of the beholder." He added, "This merger is not going to later be a success or a failure [based] on whether you gave them an extra two-hundredths in the exchange ratio."

The two companies announced the deal on April 21, 1996, as effectively a merger of equals, even though Bell Atlantic shareholders would own slightly more than half of the company. The sides eventually agreed to a tax-free stock swap valued at $23.7 billion that in financial terms would be treated as a "pooling of interests," as if the two had always been combined. The NYNEX shareholders would receive roughly three-quarters of a new Bell Atlantic share of stock for every NYNEX share they held. Bell Atlantic shareholders would retain their shares, which would become shares in the new Bell Atlantic. The shareholders of both companies approved the merger in November 1996.

The regulatory approval process made the company-to-company negotiations look like an ice cream social. Bell Atlantic and NYNEX were required to get approval from state regulators in every state where they operated. New York, as the companies expected based on NYNEX's experience dealing with often testy regulators, proved the most formidable hurdle. In addition, they were required to seek and receive approval from the antitrust division of the Department of Justice as well as the FCC. Unfortunately from the phone companies' point of view, the DOJ attorneys considering their fate included attorneys who had been involved in the negotiations leading to the Modified Final Judgment under Judge Greene. The phone companies felt as if there was some lingering ill will on the part of some of the DOJ legal staff, who appeared to resent the fact that the '96 Act had nullified the MJF and as a result their role in monitoring phone company operations.

"The approval process was long, detailed and very contentious," Seidenberg said. "There had to be millions of pages of filings and proceedings to litigate and examine the issues."

Following final regulatory approval, the merger took effect on August 14, 1997.

The combined company joined the front ranks of global telecommunications leaders with $30 billion in sales, $3.4 billion in profits and 141,000 employees, reached 39 million homes in its 13-state region, equal to more than one-third of the population of the United States, and 5 million cellular users.

FCC Chairman Reed Hundt wanted to ensure that if in fact the Baby Bells were to continue to consolidate, future combinations "would have to be pro-competitive." He said, "The burden is on the companies to prove that." But Hundt stated in a controversial 1997 speech at the Brookings Institute that there was still a line he wasn't willing to cross when it came to telecommunications mergers. A merger of one of the Baby Bells and AT&T was "unthinkable," Hundt said. Critics wondered how he could prejudge any such combination without being presented with a specific transaction.

# "WE REALLY HAD A CHANCE TO CHANGE THE MOMENTUM"

Seidenberg realized that, based on his temporary demotion and the name change, in many observers' eyes, Smith and Bell Atlantic had gotten the better of him and NYNEX. He could live with that. He was confident the demotion was only temporary, despite the risks involved. "The Bell Atlantic name gave us a fresh start," said Seidenberg, who grew even more focused on the outlook for the company and the industry.

The new Bell Atlantic had significantly improved its position on the industry chessboard. Its combined geographic footprint provided economies of scale for providing certain services. And the regulatory green lights for the merger, while arduous to win, indicated that expansion going forward might be easier to achieve. "Once the government agreed to the first merger, there were going to be others. We were going to get bigger, and we really had a chance to change the momentum" among industry players, he said. "So I immediately started to think about how not only were we going to manage integration but at the same time begin to expand our scope to begin thinking about more moves."

According to Seidenberg, once the merger was closed, the new Bell Atlantic developed a strategic framework for further industry consolidation and transactions. "We made a decision to be an industry consolidator," he said. Seidenberg, working closely with Salerno, seized the initiative. Smith ran the board meetings as the chairman and CEO. When it came time for the operational report, he turned it over to Seidenberg. Seidenberg had Cullen, head of the wireline operations of the combined company, and Babbio, head of the newly created Network Group, report on their progress. Strigl often would also report on the wireless business. Then Seidenberg and Salerno would take their chessboard approach and brief the board on industry trends and where they saw opportunities for the new Bell Atlantic. They laid out a multi-year plan for industry consolidation and growth and discussed this at every board meeting.

"We slowly started to get the board focused off of the internal politics of the deal and on to what the company's going to do going forward," he said. It helped that the tremendous economic growth spurt of the latter 1990s, which propelled the telecommunications and internet sectors in particular, drove growth in their core businesses. That more than compensated for whatever merger-related hiccups the company might have suffered. In 1997, the total return to shareholders of the combined company was 46.5 percent.

Moving ahead, the leadership team was going from strength to strength. In 1998, Seidenberg had the wireless business and Yellow Pages, which had reported to Babbio and Cullen, respectively, report directly to him to give those businesses more visibility and focus. Among the original Bell Atlantic senior leaders, Babbio in particular had demonstrated a desire to dig in and make the business as efficient as possible and build a platform for future growth. Cullen focused increasingly on state and federal regulatory issues. Strigl demanded excellence from every aspect of the wireless business. Tauke and his team as well as corporate attorney Randy Milch continued to take an industry-leading role in working with regulators to create as clear a path as possible for the company to invest for an increasingly competitive future and to keep unneeded oversight from crimping the accelerating growth of the wireless business. And Doreen Toben was a welcome addition to the financial team, bringing a very detail-oriented approach to containing costs.

"The executive team that drove the business after the creation of the new Bell Atlantic was as focused, tough and hungry to continue this expansion as you could want. They accepted the challenge to be an industry consolidator and gave me and the board the comfort that we had the capability to build a new and important industry institution," Seidenberg said.

"We had whetted the board's appetite that there was a larger restructuring going to occur in the industry," Seidenberg said. "If you think about it, the board got to see this merger take on—with all of its craziness—a sense of normalcy." Over time, Smith took on more of the role of elder statesman and also talked with other industry players and strategized with Seidenberg on Bell Atlantic's options. "Ray was comfortable that we had developed an even bigger vision for the company beyond this deal," Seidenberg said.

## "WE HAD TO BE STRONG IN AMERICA"

The Bell Atlantic-NYNEX merger and the SBC takeover of Pacific Telesis, coupled with soaring stock prices for virtually every industry player in the context of the broad technology-led stock market rally of the latter 1990s, created a frenzy of corporate speed dating. Seidenberg talked with Baby Bells, wireless providers and even long-distance provider MCI about possible mergers or other combinations. Their dance cards were filled with other suitors as well. Meanwhile, Bell Atlantic bought some smaller wireless companies to continue to make progress toward filling out its nationwide network and continued to make some overseas investments.

Though it went unreported at the time, Seidenberg met with Brian Roberts, who with his father, Ralph, controlled cable industry giant Comcast Communications, about a potential merger. While such a move would not have helped Bell Atlantic solve its need to expand its wireless business, it would have given the phone company access to video services across much of its core regional wireline market. When Seidenberg broached the subject with Roberts at the Four Seasons Hotel in Philadelphia, Roberts was taken aback. "He was very gracious and was clearly surprised by the aggressive nature of the idea," recalled Seidenberg. Roberts thought about the proposition and then decided it was something he didn't want to pursue.

BellSouth attracted a constant stream of suitors, including SBC's Ed Whitacre and Chuck Lee of GTE. Seidenberg was more persistent than most in pursuing a merger that would have created a company with markets blanketing the East Coast from Florida to Maine. It seemed like an obvious fit. He and F. Duane Ackerman, BellSouth's CEO, met five or six times at the Fulton County airport near Atlanta and had what Seidenberg considered a handshake deal.

"The deal would have been a merger of the two companies. He would have moved to New York. I would have moved to Atlanta. And we actually negotiated all of the points, including the price and everything else," Seidenberg said. Their goal was to merge their companies and then make a tender offer for European telecommunications giant Vodafone. Just as Seidenberg thought they had a deal, Ackerman told him he wanted to think about it overnight. The next morning, he called Seidenberg and told him that after talking with a few of his board members, the deal was "dead in the water."

Seidenberg was itching to do a deal of significant size in Europe, beyond the relatively small investments Bell Atlantic had in Italian, Czech, Slovak and Greek telecommunications companies, among others. Many of these were good financial investments but weren't big enough to be transformative for the entire company. He knew he didn't yet have the heft he needed at home to make a game-changing deal with a foreign entity. "My view at the time was to be strong globally, we had to be strong in America." And that meant another transformative deal.

# GTE'S INTERNET ALLURE

Salerno and his wife were driving on vacation in 1998 when he took a call from Seidenberg. His CEO was asking him to come back to work; he needed Salerno to be the lead negotiator in merger talks with GTE.

Both Seidenberg and Smith had a great deal of respect for GTE Chairman and CEO Chuck Lee and his leadership of the reorganization of the company in the early 1990s to concentrate on telecommunications. The nationwide reach of its landline phone business and its ability to offer long-distance calling caught the attention of every Baby Bell leadership team. And now it sounded as if Lee was ready to make a deal.

GTE, free of most of the regulatory constraints that had dogged the Baby Bells since their inception, had in many ways been more aggressive in building out its capabilities, particularly in its focus on the broadband internet arena. The company had seriously considered, in the mid-1990s, making a bid for America Online (AOL) but decided it wasn't a good fit. "We got very close, but there was a big debate on the board about how far we wanted to go into content," Moose said.

Then, in May 1997, GTE agreed to buy pioneering internet backbone service provider BBN Corp. for $616 million. While unprofitable, the Cambridge, Massachusetts, company was doubling its internet traffic every four months. *The Wall Street Journal* quoted industry analysts as saying that buying BBN, whose engineers in 1972 came up with the "@" sign used in email addresses, "would instantly positon GTE as one of the world's most significant internet players and arm it for the day when much of the world's voice traffic moves to the internet's high-speed data network." The BBN purchase paired nicely with GTE's $465 million payment at roughly the same time for a portion of Qwest Communications Corp.'s nationwide fiber-optic network.

"We not only bought BBN, we were building a backbone network," Lee said. "We were thinking of a bundled service. Our whole goal was a bundled service, poised in both wireless and wireline, voice, data and video. People are still moving toward that vision today." Skeptics inside the company and out would later question the value of the money-losing enterprise. Yet the dot-com boom mania that seized the markets and technology sectors in particular in the latter 1990s made it seem almost as if any price was worth paying for a vital piece of the internet.

Lee and his team seriously upped the deal-making ante in October 1997 when they made a $28 billion all-cash bid for long-distance provider MCI Communications Corp. That put them in a bidding war with WorldCom Inc., which a few weeks earlier had bid $30 billion for MCI, but in the form of an all-stock offer. They were both competing with an earlier offer from British Telecommunications PLC, which wanted to buy the 80 percent of MCI it didn't already own for $18 billion. Lee could have bid for MCI a year earlier, and ahead of British Telecom, but backed away from the deal based on MCI's asking price at the time.

## "YOU'RE HANGING OUT THERE ALONE"

MCI ended up being merged into WorldCom. It was a blow to Lee and his team, although some GTE directors were happy that the company wasn't going to have to go deeply into debt to fund the offer. But it also positioned them to consider future combinations.

The failed bid for MCI led the GTE board to reappraise how the company was positioned for the future, said Moose. There was a clear mismatch between company and customer base. "The realization hit us by the late 1990s that while GTE was probably right" about the direction the telecommunications business was headed, "we ended up having the ideas and the products and some of the capabilities that were consistent with a different customer base than the one we had," Moose said.

Going it alone no longer looked like the best option. GTE's strengths "were consistent with more of a business-corporate customer base and more of a customer base that was urban-centric as opposed to suburban, because it was easier initially to build out these fiber networks and everything in cities," Moose said. "Then we realized that our customer base was both too small and not the right customer base (more suburban/rural) for where we saw the industry heading and where we had already invested in some fiber and data capabilities. That led us to Bell Atlantic, which had a more urban/business customer base."

Bell Atlantic and BellSouth would have created an enormous contiguous wireline footprint. Their wireless businesses were not quite as compatible. "The chessboard strategy relied on creating many options to pursue a victory, so we naturally turned our attention to GTE, which had much less compatibility in fixed wireline but had a terrific wireless business," Seidenberg said. Chuck Lee and Ray Smith had both grown up in Pittsburgh. Each had also worked in the local steel industry early in their careers and risen through the financial ranks of various companies to serve as CFOs before landing in the CEO's office. They had gotten to know and respect each other over the years and would see each other at telecommunications industry conferences and other events.

So, it made sense that when Bell Atlantic wanted to sound out Lee's interest in making a deal, Smith was the messenger. To establish even deeper ties, Smith showed up in Lee's office with a bound copy of Alexander Graham Bell's drawings as a gift. Lee unwrapped the present and, as Smith recalled, said, "Ray, I'm not a Bell company. We're not a Bell company." Smith said, "Chuck, we're all the children of Alexander Graham Bell. He invented the system. I know you're an independent company and not Bell. But you're hanging out there alone." By the end of the meeting, Lee agreed that he would meet with Seidenberg, with whom he had discussed different deal options over the years, to talk about a potential merger. Smith, after helping bring the two companies together, retired as Bell Atlantic chairman and CEO at year-end 1998 and stepped down from the board. Lee had a very impressive record of transforming GTE and clearly understood that industry consolidation was inevitable. He also had a very practical view that there were many ways to accomplish this. He was very open-minded and willing to explore every angle, Seidenberg said.

## TELECOM FRENZY

The two executives, who had each followed unconventional paths to the corner office, hit it off. Lee had come up through the finance ranks, but he was "very different than Ray," Seidenberg said. "He was an outsider. He was brought into GTE, and they actually picked him over a longstanding internal guy for the idea that they wanted something different. Now, GTE had done some very innovative things. They had diversified in buying some electronic companies. They had bought a long-distance company. GTE had a healthy, innovative streak in them."

Seidenberg and Lee brought together their negotiators, Salerno from Bell Atlantic and Mike Masin from GTE, to work out the fine points of the deal. The two worked together well and, unlike with Bell Atlantic and NYNEX, the process moved swiftly toward a conclusion in a matter of weeks.

Competition kept the pressure on to complete the deal. In May 1998, SBC announced that it would pay a stunning $62 billion for Chicago-based Ameritech. That positioned the combined company, which would retain the SBC name, to pass Bell Atlantic and become the largest local phone company in the country. Earlier in the year, it agreed to pay $4.4 billion for Connecticut's Southern New England Telecommunications Corp. Adding to the sense of merger mania was the pending WorldCom-MCI deal, which ended up with a $37 billion price tag.

The Bell Atlantic and GTE CEOs worked on strategic and soft issues as their lieutenants talked price. Seidenberg volunteered to step aside as the sole CEO to make the deal work. The two agreed that Lee, 58, would serve as chairman and co-CEO, and Seidenberg, 51, would serve as president and co-CEO. They also agreed that on June 30, 2002, Seidenberg would become the sole CEO and Lee would continue another two years as non-executive chairman. They agreed as well that the newly merged company would be based in New York City. With the regulatory approval process expected to take at least a year, a new name could wait.

On July 28, 1998, the two executives announced their proposed merger in New York. At $53 billion it was valued at more than twice the price of the Bell Atlantic-NYNEX merger that had concluded less than a year earlier. Wall Street was underwhelmed, at least concerning GTE's stock price. GTE shares skidded more than 5 percent the day of the announcement. The $53 billion deal actually valued GTE's shares at slightly less than the shares' closing price the day before. One securities analyst described the deal as a "takeunder," not a takeover.

Lee, back in his Midtown Manhattan hotel room after the merger announcement, called Seidenberg to his office. "He was just livid," Seidenberg said. Lee said, "We have to fix this." The Bell Atlantic team thought they had negotiated a fair price for the GTE assets and technology. Seidenberg assured Lee that over time together they would reinforce the idea that there was value in the merger that Wall Street was not appreciating at first blush.

"There was tension there," Seidenberg said. "But to his credit, it was tension internally, and with me, and with the CFO. When Chuck was outside of the business, he was very supportive. He never once ever said anything negative."

Lee was facing added pressure from his senior ranks at GTE. The company, which had been based in Stamford, Connecticut, had just opened a new corporate headquarters in Dallas, reflecting the focus on its telecommunications businesses. Senior executives had just recently closed on homes in the area when they learned of the merger and that the combined company would be based in New York City. Many of them said publicly that they wouldn't be making the move.

As a show of support for GTE and its future, Lee invested in a spacious Dallas home. "I bought one of the nicest houses in Dallas. It was a developer's showcase house," he said. "I wanted everybody to know that I was committed to Dallas if the merger didn't happen, and we were going to be fine if the merger didn't happen."

## AIRTOUCH AND VODAFONE

A merger twice the size of the Bell Atlantic-NYNEX merger carried a great deal of complexity and regulatory requirements in its own right. But Seidenberg and his team saw an opportunity to make yet another transformative move even as the GTE deal was just beginning to work its way through the approval process. And it involved talking with an existing joint venture partner about deepening their relationship.

Bell Atlantic had been involved with AirTouch in its wireless partnership for a number of years by 1998. The two companies had talked about potential mergers even before the Bell Atlantic-NYNEX merger, Babbio said. "We could never make that deal happen. It was always price issues and governance issues, and who's going to lead the company business, etc."

With GTE now in the Bell Atlantic fold, however, Seidenberg, who had his own series of talks with AirTouch, saw a new opportunity. He approached AirTouch CEO Sam Ginn, and they agreed that the wireless firm, while highly successful, had a better future as part of the Bell Atlantic-GTE team. The two companies and CEOs talked on and off through the fall of 1998. As with BellSouth, Seidenberg thought he had a handshake deal with Ginn, just as Thanksgiving week arrived.

Then another suitor appeared on the scene: Vodafone Group PLC. As the largest wireless player in Europe, Vodafone made the case that it was a better fit for Ginn—who clearly thought that wireless was the future of telecommunications and AirTouch—than Bell Atlantic and GTE.

Seidenberg had started the talks with Ginn in the fall of 1998 based on an offer of $45 a share, all cash. When Vodafone arrived, the price was in the mid-$60s. Bell Atlantic executives would huddle and see what they could justify as the price for AirTouch kept climbing. Were there savings here? Could Strigl wring additional revenue out of the wireless business there? Ray Smith was a valuable sounding board for Seidenberg as they weighed the impact on shareholders and Wall Street. Seidenberg and his team finally backed out at $89.

Bell Atlantic was offering cash; Vodafone was offering cash as well as shares in its own stock, which was appreciating in step with the broader global rally in telecommunications shares and the dot-com boom. Vodafone's final offer would equal $97 a share for AirTouch stock.

With the clock running out on 1998 and revelers already flocking to Times Square a few blocks away to celebrate the New Year, Jim Gerace and a few other communications department officials huddled in Babbio's office. They were waiting for a call from Seidenberg and the verdict on their offer. Babbio shocked Gerace with a phrase Gerace would clearly recall years later: "No matter what the outcome is," Babbio said, "this story isn't going to end here."

"Ivan's not going to give up," Babbio added. "Ivan wants a national footprint for wireless." Babbio took the call from Seidenberg. He hung up. "Well, our work is done for tonight." He said, "They went with Vodafone. It's unclear when they're going to announce it or what this really means for us, but good work." In mid-January 1999, Vodafone announced that it had won the bidding war for AirTouch and that Bell Atlantic had declined to counter its offer.

Seidenberg called Vodafone Chairman Chris Gent to congratulate him on his success and assure him there were no hurt feelings. "Chris, you won this thing, but you still have a U.S. problem," Seidenberg said. Gent responded, "I think I agree with that." AirTouch carried a hefty price tag, but it was still far from a nationwide wireless network. Seidenberg said, "When you get settled, let's chat and let's see if we can figure this out."

# 55 PERCENT SOLUTION
# FOR WIRELESS

Roughly six months later, the two were talking again about combining their U.S. wireless operations. Ideally Bell Atlantic would have bought the business outright. But that would have triggered onerous tax issues in the States for Vodafone and raised leadership questions. So, the talks narrowed to focus on a joint venture. Bell Atlantic negotiated that it would have a controlling interest in the partnership, eventually set at 55 percent, and be the operating partner. Denny Strigl and his team would be in charge, though Vodafone had the right to put in its choice for CFO in the partnership. "I thought, 55 percent of the loaf was better than zero, and that enabled us to consolidate all of the other things that we had going on," Seidenberg said.

Chuck Lee lived up to his reputation for being an innovative risk-taker when Seidenberg briefed him on the Vodafone wireless deal. "I always give Chuck credit for this—how much risk he was willing to take. He let us cut the deal with Chris Gent in the middle of the merger approval," Seidenberg said. "So, after talking to Chuck and really taking him through the compatibility of AirTouch's assets, Vodafone's assets, Bell Atlantic's assets, GTE's assets, PrimeCo's assets, and saying, 'Look what kind of a national footprint that creates,' he was really excited."

Lee said it would not have been possible to make the overlapping deals work if it had not been for the bonds of trust that he and Seidenberg had forged, along with their common vision. "This is pretty gutsy. Here we are doing post-merger deals but doing it before the merger. So, we just worked together very well, Ivan and I," Lee said. "Neither of us ever broke our word, not once . . . and that's why these things could happen. That's why the integration worked."

## PAYING THE "MERGER TAX"

The boards of Bell Atlantic and GTE also stepped up to the challenge. It was a more complex set of transactions than it initially appeared to be, Seidenberg said. "We had to negotiate these crazy conditions that if the GTE merger fails, but we still go through with the other deal, how do we do that? What do we owe them? How much do we have to pay them? And how much of a penalty did we take?" Another condition regulators set for the Bell Atlantic-GTE merger was that GTE had to set up BBN and the rest of its internet backbone business, rechristened Genuity, as a stand-alone business, of which Verizon could not own more than 10 percent. Genuity's initial public offering occurred in June 2000.

"To the credit of the boards, [they] were willing to deal with the complexity because the payoffs of these transactions were so large," Seidenberg said. "We would say to the board, 'Don't worry, we'll get this done. We're getting this done.' And I always felt that there was a price that you could pay to get it done. And, it turns out—this is a term that I used in all of these meetings—there's a merger tax that goes into all of these things. It includes financial costs but also matters of policy. And if you figure out what it is, you pay the tax, negotiate merger conditions, and you move forward."

The challenge of the "merger tax" and conditions acted to pull the teams from the multiple entities together to act as one as the approval process continued into early 2000. "The collective effort of all the people to solve the puzzle became more important than all of the secondary political fights that went on," Seidenberg said. "Because people could now see that if this deal got done, this company was a very different company." They could also see that it was time to find a name for this telecommunications industry leader.

# RE-CREATE, REORDER, RESTRUCTURE: C-SUITE INSIGHTS FROM RAM CHARAN

## ___ ENTERPRISE FIRST, INDIVIDUAL SECOND.

CEO Seidenberg and his team twice shared the lead role in order to build a better company. Next generation leaders need to understand they will get ahead and be rewarded as the enterprise excels.

## ___ CLARITY AND INTELLECTUAL HONESTY DRIVE CHANGE.

The big idea is always bigger than any one person, and everybody knows it. Not everyone will be comfortable being part of something bigger than themselves. The closer the employee is to the customer, the more obvious the big idea is, because it inevitably will be driven by the customer.

## ___ LINEAR FIVE-YEAR PLANNING IS DEAD.

Get out of your comfort zone and pursue outlier options during periods of accelerating change. Understand that one option opens up multiple, non-linear options that can't be fully anticipated. Apply algorithmic, decision-tree thinking augmented with artificial intelligence: If not A, then B, then C; reconsider A.

### ___ OUTLIER OPTIONS CARRY OUTSIZED RISKS.

Leadership teams need to understand that radically reordering the industry may put the enterprise at risk. They may lose their original goal of controlling their own destinies but open new and bigger doors.

### ___ MESSY MANAGEMENT LESSONS.

Lessons from complex and messy external situations will increase the momentum of internal change. Building new regulatory relationships concurrent with developing credibility with your board and Wall Street position a leadership team to thrive in the messy external world. Apply those external lessons internally by setting goals, defining strategies and executing all at the same time. Embrace messy ambiguity as a management team as you approach options with uncertain outcomes.

# Checkmate

By Ram Charan

The chessboard was the metaphor Ivan Seidenberg and his leadership team embraced to describe their multi-pronged approach to transforming their industry and business in response to customer needs. Move toward the center of the board to increase your options, both to attack and defend. And win. Today's born digitals think in terms of algorithms and decision trees. Metaphors change with the times, but the messages they deliver are ever more relevant: Digital discontinuity accelerates change across global industries. That means multi-year linear planning and execution is dead. And customer needs drive success—yesterday, today and tomorrow.

No piece on the communications industry chessboard circa the mid-1990s was more clearly stuck in the corner than NYNEX. Its revenues were generated in slow-growing New York, widely considered to have the most challenging union and regulatory environments in the country, and New England. Telecommunications consumers, meanwhile, were increasingly mobile and becoming increasingly connected through rapidly changing technology and communications.

The leadership team's choice was move or be a pawn in someone else's game. They saw a need for a national network, one with the capacity to serve the rapidly emerging digitization of consumer communication and entertainment. They merged the adjoining mobile phone networks of NYNEX and Bell Atlantic and set their sights on building a system to serve 100 million customers—a market that was unimaginable to most rivals at the time. Even as the kinks in that deal were still being worked out, they took another bold move and merged the two parent companies into the new Bell Atlantic. With each deal, they moved into a stronger competitive position, even at the expense of the NYNEX name. And in Seidenberg's case, at the expense of sole control of the company, at least for a time.

Another move on the chessboard involved simultaneously educating and convincing regulators that industry consolidation among legacy phone companies, and not just the creation of new entrants, would serve the public interest. At the same time, the leadership worked with its board, treating it as a valued sounding board to weigh in on the next series of moves.

The late 1990s dot-com boom turned the leadership team's strategy into a version of speed chess. Technology industry growth and consolidation accelerated dramatically. So did tech company stock prices. When a merger of mobile assets with AirTouch fell through, the team forged the first truly national wireless network a few months later through a four-member partnership that included AirTouch. The wireless deal ultimately was consummated with Vodafone, which had acquired AirTouch's interests. At the same time, when another potential merger partner, BellSouth, walked away, the team pivoted in pursuit of still another bold move, merging with GTE. Again, Seidenberg and his senior leaders agreed to share leadership, for a time, to get the deal done.

Verizon Communications was born. It was messy, simultaneous leadership decision-making and was truly a group effort. We can all learn a lot from what the original Verizon team accomplished.

As Verizon continued to evolve, it executed more key mergers to improve its competitive position at the vanguard of the communications industry. At the same time, the leadership team realized that rapidly evolving technology and consumer demands required them to add a third dimension to their chessboard. They had to look beyond the immediate competitive and regulatory environment. Advancing technologies were making mass customization possible. More clearly than ever, the customer was king and in control of the competitive chessboard, not industry players. Verizon would pivot once again, moving to meet the needs of a customer base that would number not just in the hundreds of millions but billions.

# 04

# NEW COMPANY,
# NEW INDUSTRY,
# NEW CENTURY

2000-2002

**B**ruce Gordon, a Bell Atlantic employee since 1968, was aware of the angst some NYNEX employees experienced losing their brand name when the Baby Bells merged in 1997. He learned firsthand that the controversy over nomenclature then was nothing compared to the effort it would take to brand the newly formed company in 2000. As president of the retail side of the wireline businesses, it was Gordon's job to lead the process of christening the merged Bell Atlantic and GTE. The stakes could hardly have been higher. As co-CEO Ivan Seidenberg said, "This was a transformative merger moving the company into the digital, broadband era, so we needed a transformative name."

Seidenberg, co-CEO Chuck Lee and the rest of the leadership team were in the telecommunications vanguard as they created a new company for the new century. Their actions in the first two years of the company's existence set the stage for its explosive, multibillion-dollar growth in the decades ahead. They engaged their board of directors extensively in developing the strategy that would create a company capable of surviving and thriving well into the future. Fresh challenges required a fresh approach. Even as the company won regulatory approval for long-distance service, it was already pivoting toward a future of market-oriented regulation. The new competition for the broadband future was led by the lightly regulated cable companies. To respond, the leadership team moved the company closer to the center of the strategic chessboard and prepared for their next series of moves.

"We had a growth and investment orientation," Seidenberg said. "Without a doubt, we all thought we could move this new company to a much higher level of performance and higher standards than any of us had ever thought possible." It was continue to change or die, as the long-distance companies would soon discover. "Companies have to figure out how to take risks, how to grow, where to apply their capital, and have the confidence to do it," Seidenberg said.

# TRUTH IN BRANDING

Gordon and his team brought in three outside brand consultants— Landor Associates, Lippincott & Margulies, and the DeSola Group—to help name the company. From an initial list of thousands of mostly invented names, Gordon's team whittled it down to 10 that were unique, had no copyright issues and seemed to capture the essence of what the new company was all about. One early favorite of some team members was Crossphere, though Gordon thought it was "weird." At the top of his list was Verizon. The branding advisers said it was a combination of "veritas," Latin for "truth," and "horizon," conveying the sense of future possibilities.

"Verizon was a slam dunk. Slam dunk," Gordon said. But he told the team, "The problem [is] it's just a name on a piece of paper with nine other names. You've got to get the design people to express it." The graphic designers came back with the bold-red theme, using a color not associated with Bell Atlantic or GTE. The design featured a large check mark and letter "Z," added somewhat later in the process, which remained the basis for the Verizon corporate logo for 15 years. Five names and designs were tested in focus groups with more than 2,500 residential and small- and large-business consumers across the country to get their reactions.

Gordon's office was only a few doors down from Seidenberg's in the 1095 Avenue of the Americas headquarters. He wandered in impulsively one evening to get Seidenberg's advice. "You need to guide me, Ivan, in terms of the internal sales process to get this decision made," he said. The two of them had discussed Gordon's top choices, including Verizon, earlier. Seidenberg asked Gordon whether Verizon was still his first choice and if he thought it fit the marketing and communications plan. "It's easy. It's Verizon, and we can make this work well in the marketplace," said Gordon. "I'm clear that's the right name."

Seidenberg supported Gordon's choice: "If that's what you think, and frankly that's what I think, then that should be it." But he added that Gordon had to sell it to a broader group of senior leaders, including Chuck Lee.

That's when Gordon ran into resistance. "Chuck didn't like it at first," said Gordon. "Chuck said there is a convention in our industry around telecom company names" using initials, including MCI, SBC, AT&T and GTE. Lee said, "We should take the "B" from Bell Atlantic and the "G" from GTE, and we should become BG Telecom." He also lobbied hard for retaining the Bell logo, one of the most iconic in corporate history. Lee was also perceived by other leaders as playing the role of devil's advocate in the naming process to ensure that the best choice possible would be the outcome.

Gordon couldn't get an immediate verdict from the leadership team. Gordon commiserated with a colleague, "If I can't make this sale on

Verizon, and we end up naming this company BG Telecom, I'm going to tell people that I had the responsibility for naming the company, and I named it after me" ("BG" for "Bruce Gordon").

The leadership team came together to support Gordon's top pick. The new company was christened Verizon Communications. Seidenberg brought in about 150 leaders from the combined company for a meeting in New York. The team presenting the new brand all wore Verizon-red ties. Gordon led off the meeting and then gauged the crowd's reaction. "I would say it was 50-50," he recalled. A contingent of executives from both the Bell Atlantic and GTE sides appeared to think that at least some aspect of legacy heritage should be retained. Seidenberg, who spoke last, was firm on his stance. "He made it very clear. This is the name. Own it. Sell it," Gordon said. "People walked out of the room and understood." Everyone left the meeting understanding that the new name clearly positioned the company for the future, rather than miring it in the past.

Senior Vice President Peter Thonis came from the GTE side of the company in corporate communications and might have been seen as favoring the use of some form of the GTE name. But he understood the need for a clean break. And he appreciated Seidenberg's commitment to the change process.

"One thing you learn in naming is that it isn't so much what the name is as what you bring to the table," Thonis said. "When you rename a company, you can count on 50 percent of the people in the organization, including your executive team, hating it. They will absolutely hate it. Within a year they'll go, 'Hmm.' All of a sudden, they'll like it. Then all of a sudden, two years later, they would never change it."

# VERIZON WIRELESS

The continued delay in winning final regulatory approval for the merger of Bell Atlantic and GTE would drag on until mid-2000. As a result, the Verizon name actually debuted as the name of the wireless joint venture, Verizon Wireless, in early April 2000. Vodafone, the minority partner in the wireless venture, agreed to the Verizon Wireless name. That meant the child was giving its name to, and helping to brand, one of its parents.

When Vodafone signed off on the new name, and the leadership team was poised to roll out Verizon Wireless as a truly nationwide network, Fred Salerno was "on cloud nine," said Mary Beth Bardin, the senior communicator from GTE who was named executive vice president for communications for the combined parent company. Salerno, as CFO, had been supportive of the continued expansion of wireless and was solidly behind Strigl and Babbio in the buildout of the business. It was a realization of his and Seidenberg's chessboard strategy, the dream of creating a "wireless powerhouse," that had been years in the making, Salerno told her.

The wireless business provided a strong nationwide platform for spreading the word about Verizon. Initially a patchwork of four different cellular systems (Bell Atlantic, GTE, AirTouch and PrimeCo), Verizon Wireless launched as the largest cellular service provider in the country, finishing the year 2000 with 27.5 million subscribers. It covered 49 of the top 50 markets in the United States and 96 of the top 100. Nearly 90 percent of the U.S. population lived in areas that were covered by Verizon Wireless.

Verizon and Vodafone filed with the Securities and Exchange Commission (SEC) on August 24, 2000, to offer an unspecified minority stake in Verizon Wireless to the public. The regulatory filing had been agreed to as part of the creation of the wireless joint venture. It kept an option open for the company but was not seen as a serious alternative at the time by Verizon officials, Seidenberg said.

The collapse of the dot-com boom that began in March 2000 spread across a wide sector of other industries that summer and fall. The U.S. economy tipped into a recession. That meant the public appetite for shares in a wireless phone company, even one as solid as Verizon Wireless, appeared to have cooled. Verizon shelved the stock offering on October 16, 2000, and later canceled the option permanently.

## "WE'RE ALL VERIZON NOW"

With all regulatory approvals finally in hand, the merged company started doing business as Verizon Communications Inc. on June 30, 2000. Lee may have initially questioned the Verizon name, but he supported the decision once it was made and personally helped break down some of the cultural barriers between the Bell Atlantic and GTE sides of the business.

Lee led by example at the first senior leadership meeting of the combined team. "Chuck often opened these meetings," Bardin said. "Chuck came out, and he said, 'I'd like everybody to stand who is from the former Bell Atlantic.' So, all these leaders stood up, and there was applause, and they sat down. And he said, 'Now I'd like anybody who's from the former GTE to stand and be recognized.' And they did. And then he said, 'OK, that's the last time we're going to ask what your former company was, because we're all Verizon now.'"

Some employees took longer to acclimate. Seidenberg and Lee traveled together to the former GTE offices in Dallas to introduce the new company and themselves as co-CEOs. They met with a group of young executives considered "high potentials" likely to advance far and fast, including Rose Kirk. According to Kirk, who was helping to launch a small video business unit at the time, many in GTE saw themselves as small-town, community-oriented employees with roots in the Southern and Midwestern towns they and their customers called home. The feeling among many employees, Kirk said, was along the lines of, "Then there were these Northerners who seemed to be just a little bit curt and a little bit disrespectful and a little bit—'we're taking you over, and you guys are the hicks from the sticks.'"

Most officers, including Kirk and employees from the former GTE, stayed with the newly merged company, but not all. Executives who had recently moved to Dallas to help lead telecommunications operations were reluctant to make the move. Some lost out to former Bell Atlantic officers holding similar jobs as Verizon, working with an executive search firm, carefully reviewed its options for each leadership post and had officers from each predecessor company "apply" for the position. Of course, that worked both ways, with Bell Atlantic officials being edged out by GTE officials as well.

# VURR-EYE-ZON

To help drive acceptance of the new name, the company rolled out a nationwide advertising campaign and an extended rebranding campaign that cost $500 million in 2000. The ads featured employees from a variety of divisions within the company assuring customers that even though the company had a new name, Verizon, they were still going to receive the same reliable service. "Our employees take center stage in this first campaign because they are the face of the new Verizon," said

---

## STARTING LINEUP

The Verizon executive leadership team reporting to the co-CEOs in 2000 included a mix of Bell Atlantic and GTE faces. Babbio was named a vice chairman and president of Verizon, overseeing all domestic businesses. Mike Masin, who helped negotiate the merger for GTE, held the same title as Babbio and was in charge of international, just as he had been for GTE. Fred Salerno served as vice chairman and CFO. Denny Strigl was named an executive vice president of Verizon as well as president and CEO of Verizon Wireless. Bill Barr, former U.S. attorney general under George H.W. Bush and general counsel of GTE, was named executive vice president and general counsel of Verizon. Jim Cullen retired in mid-2000 after helping the two companies clear their regulatory hurdles.

---

Janet Keeler, senior vice president for marketing services and brand management. The voice of the new Verizon was the award-winning actor James Earl Jones, who played a similar role for Bell Atlantic, greeting callers to directory assistance from Hyannis Port to Honolulu.

Gordon conceded that the company was surprised that many members of the public, as well as company employees, were inclined to pronounce the new name as VEHR-i-zon, without accenting the middle syllable. News releases incorporated pronunciation guides (pronounced "vurr-EYE-zon," or rhymes with "horizon"), Bardin said. The guides helped and were reinforced in the pre-online payment days because each month, every customer received a bill from Verizon and wrote the Verizon name on their checks to the phone company.

The company's branding campaign received another boost from unexpected quarters. As if testing the resolve of the new company, unionized workers went on strike in August 2000. The 18-day strike, with union demands centering on cost-sharing for benefits among other issues, was settled promptly enough that it caused minimal disruption to company activities. The intensity of New York-style labor negotiations, however, was an unsettling eye-opener for Lee and other GTE executives, who generally had more congenial relations with organized labor. But the strike also had the effect, especially in New York City and Verizon's other major urban markets, of putting the company's name on the local evening news night after night. "Every reporter had to say our name almost every day for the length of that strike," Bardin said.

## "FANATICAL ABOUT THE FACTS"

The telecommunications sector evolved so rapidly in the late 1990s and early 2000s, with mergers and spinoffs creating new corporate entities at a steady clip, that it was difficult for some in the media to track who was who. Inevitably, errors or opinions were being repeated as facts. Reporting during labor actions could be especially difficult to fact-check on a timely basis. Executive Vice President for Communications Mary Beth Bardin, who reported directly to the co-CEOs, decided that it was time to draw a clear line on accuracy regarding the creation of Verizon. The fact that she reported directly to the co-CEOs—and not through legal or marketing departments, as was the case at other companies in the sector—underscored the importance Seidenberg and Lee attached to communications as they positioned Verizon for the future. Her approach also aligned with the continued push for operational excellence at every level that would become a hallmark of Verizon.

Bardin gave a presentation to the Verizon board on the subject. She knew it resonated when she heard back from senior communicators who worked with many of the board members at their companies. "Yes, we want relationships with reporters, but we're not their friends," Bardin said. "We have a dual responsibility. We help them do their job, but we also have to be fanatical about the facts."

She noted that "some misstatements, because they weren't challenged, had become conventional wisdom and got repeated by other publications. So, we said we are going to have a zero-tolerance policy for errors. And we don't even care if they're small errors. We are going to demand accuracy. That's going to be the mantra."

# VERIZON PROMISE

Seidenberg met with Verizon's senior communicators as they were preparing to introduce the new company to the public and their fellow employees. He pointed out that between the two parent companies and their subsidiaries, "We must have had about 15 vision statements and 20 value statements." At the time, Seidenberg thought, "If I go out and make a speech, what am I going to say?"

His concerns dovetailed with efforts already underway in Bardin's department and led to the creation of the Verizon Promise. After polling employees across the new company, the communications staff found that "when asked to pick out the single most important value, customer commitment [service] overwhelmingly came out on top for both Bell Atlantic and GTE employees." The company defined service as "the first among equals" when it came to values, "the centerpiece of our measurement, compensation and reward systems." The other values identified in 2000 were integrity, respect, imagination and passion.

Seidenberg said that although every value is important, senior leaders tended to emphasize some values at certain times when they spoke and stress other values on different occasions. Strigl and his wireless team would develop a similar values statement. Later in the decade, combining the wireless and wireline businesses led to another iteration of the values statement. "We spent a lot of time as a group talking about what integrity meant. For instance, what it meant to show respect, not just to fellow employees, but to suppliers and regulators as well," Seidenberg said. "[These values were a] fundamental dynamic of our culture. These can't be compromised. And we spent a great deal of time building context and actions that supported our values."

## SEPTEMBER 11, 2001

The sustained effort of so many Verizon employees in the aftermath of the September 11, 2001, terrorist attacks on America reflected the company's long-standing commitment to serve "our country, our customers and each other," as Lee and Seidenberg told employees. For that reason, a detailed account of Verizon's response to 9/11 forms the cornerstone of Chapter Five, "Part of Something Bigger."

The wrenching events of that day—including the loss of three Verizon employees—also compelled company employees to forget their different corporate backgrounds and come together around a common cause. Whether an employee was ex-Bell Atlantic, ex-NYNEX or ex-GTE, "that all went away" on September 11, Peter Thonis said. "We were all Verizon. It was a great team exercise, done in the most horrendous manner possible."

As Lee and Seidenberg said in a year-end 2001 statement to employees, "In July, we celebrated our first year as a new company. On September 11, we came of age."

## DIVERSITY

Long before he worried about what to call the latest iteration of his employer, Bruce Gordon joined then-named Bell of Pennsylvania in 1968, fresh out of Gettysburg College. He was recruited into the IMDP management training program, like so many Bell leaders before him, and had his sights set on a job in middle management. And if he did well, maybe an even better position. But as an African-American in an overwhelmingly white organization, he couldn't find many role models.

"That company had 36,000 employees. Of the 36,000 employees, 800 were middle management and above. Of those 800 middle management and above, there was one African-American. One," Gordon said. And even though the company had a parallel recruitment track for women college graduates, WIMDP, which Ray Smith had helped launch, there wasn't a single woman in middle management at that point. New York Telephone and the other major Bell operating companies across the country faced similar challenges when it came to looking more like the communities they served.

Long odds. Gordon accepted the challenge, seeing himself and his minority peers in business as among the vanguard leading the next phase in the campaign for civil rights. "I had this theory . . . that the workplace would be another platform for social change. I saw myself as a social change agent. Actually, a civil rights activist of sorts," he said.

For more than 30 years, Gordon and many others helped promote diversity at Verizon and its predecessor companies. When he retired in 2003, Gordon was the highest-ranking African-American employee in the company. Among the Verizon executive leadership team, Gordon was a promoter of widespread diversity for the company and its suppliers and contractors, including the use of minority firms to manage a portion of Verizon's pension funds. Board member Hugh Price, president and CEO of the National Urban League from 1994 to 2003, promoted similar priorities at the board level, with the full support of Seidenberg and the leadership team. Gordon served as president and CEO of the National Association for the Advancement of Colored People from 2005 to 2007.

The work of Gordon and many other diversity advocates at Verizon, while difficult at times, continues to reap benefits. Right from the start, in 2000, *Fortune* magazine named Verizon one of America's "50 Best Companies for Minorities." The company, while continuing to face challenges in certain areas, has been recognized ever since for its commitment to broadly defined diversity goals. In 2016, for the 11th consecutive year, for instance, Verizon was named among the best companies for multicultural women and continued to be recognized for promoting supplier diversity. Leadership continues to realize that more needs to be done.

"It was always important to me to promote a company culture that was open to all, with an emphasis on inclusion and opportunity," Seidenberg said. "I grew up in the Bronx; our schools, schoolyards and neighborhoods were all of mixed ethnicities and races. Clearly, in the '50s and '60s, our country was in the early stages of understanding the deep racial and ethnic barriers to inclusion. In the Army, I saw first-hand the deep divisions of discrimination. In Vietnam, where I served, it was very clear that black Americans carried a disproportionate burden of combat. These facts always stuck with me, and as I progressed in my career, I wanted to do my part in making this matter of race and inclusion better for all. Looking back, Verizon has made some great progress, though there is always more to be done. I always admired Bruce for his courage and dignity, how he handled himself and the standards he set for all of us in our company."

## LEAD FROM THE MIDDLE

Verizon prepared to compete in an ever more diverse and dynamic marketplace. Seidenberg realized that he would need to rely on his board of directors even more intimately as a sounding board and strategic asset as Verizon pursued its chessboard strategy. Industry consolidation was far from over. At the same time, competition, especially from cable companies, was continuing to mount. Fortunately, the new board would bring together a collection of experienced individuals with a range of expertise that was well-suited to support, and when necessary challenge, the Verizon leadership team.

The Verizon board was formed with seven independent directors each from Bell Atlantic and GTE, as well as Seidenberg and Lee. Adopting a suggestion from Bell Atlantic board member Richard Carrion, Seidenberg asked each of the 16 independent Bell Atlantic board members to identity which seven directors they would choose to serve on the new board. They were not allowed to choose themselves. Seidenberg was surprised to find that there was agreement among the board members as to who should serve on the new board.

GTE had nine outside directors, so fewer independent directors were cut. But the cuts were still painful, Lee said. "For example, one hard conversation I had in this whole thing was telling Ed [Artzt], 'We have a retirement age of 72; you're 71. We've got to go forward.' Ed Artzt is a fabulous human being and a wonderful man. He did a great job at Procter & Gamble" before retiring as chairman in 1995.

At the first meeting of the combined board, the directors were interspersed, so the Bell Atlantic directors didn't gravitate to one side of the table and the GTE directors to the other. The two sides came together with little, if any, friction, and some of the directors developed close friendships. As Sandy Moose recalled, she was seated next to former Bell Atlantic Director Joseph Neubauer, the founder of Philadelphia-based food service giant Aramark. "Joe kind of took me under his wing and he explained who everybody was on the Bell Atlantic board." She did the same in introducing Neubauer to the former GTE directors.

As much as Seidenberg and Salerno had been effective in working with the Bell Atlantic board as they pursued their chessboard strategy during the 1990s, Seidenberg took to heart Lee's advice for engaging their combined board going forward: Lead from the middle. "Chuck came up with the concept at the board meetings, which I thought was great. He said, 'There are two ways to think about a board meeting. You run it from the middle of the room, or you run it from the head of the room,'" Seidenberg said.

Lee recalled telling Seidenberg: "We used to run [our board meetings] from the middle of the room. I notice you sit in the middle of the room, but you run the meetings from the head of the room; the presenter goes to the screen and makes presentations." Seidenberg replied, "Chuck, usually when we want to teach and explain a complicated subject, we go to the head of the room, and when we want to have a conversation, I sit in the middle of the room." Lee's suggestion? "Sit in the middle of the room more often." Seidenberg conceded that the simple strategy paid dividends in the form of board engagement. "Our team acclimated to this right away, even though at first it was unnatural for us to give presentations from our seats as opposed to going up there. Chuck was right; we had deeper and livelier conversations."

# MEMBERS OF THE ROUND TABLE

Seidenberg took another of Lee's and GTE's practices, meeting with board members socially before scheduled meetings, and over time made it his own, again to the benefit of company leadership and board engagement. Moose said, "One of the key differences between the GTE board and the Verizon board in terms of social dynamics was we probably spent more time with each other. Because the GTE footprint was a nationwide footprint, we had people from different parts of the country coming in from out of town. As a result, we would have a dinner the evening before the board meeting, and then we'd have lunch after the board meeting. We also had an annual strategic planning retreat meeting for two to three days."

Seidenberg said that the Bell Atlantic board, reflecting the company's more compact regional footprint, took a one-and-done approach to board meetings. "Our directors hated dinners because they flew in late at night, and they left after the meetings. They didn't have time for dinners."

He reflected on his own experience serving on several corporate boards. "On all the boards I served on, dinners were always a big investment of time," he said. "It usually is a big production with a lot of people. I was OK with that, but I really wanted to talk to the other directors. I wanted to know what they were thinking. I wanted to talk to the CEO."

Lee pressed Seidenberg to adopt the dinner model. Seidenberg acquiesced, shaping the process to fit his evolving view of board leadership and participation. "Somewhere along the line, we developed the idea of having a round table, only having the board members there and making it mandatory," Seidenberg said.

"We would pick a good restaurant, get a private room with a round table. Had to be a round table. If there was no round table, we didn't go," he said. An owner of one of Manhattan's trendiest restaurants assured Seidenberg that his food would taste just as good on a rectangular table. "I said, 'Nope. Get a round table, we'll come. If not, we're not coming.' He got a round table," Seidenberg said.

A round table involved everyone equally in the dinner conversation and left no place to hide. "There are conversations going all over the place. One of the things I learned is we made everyone participate. Everybody had to say something . . . what do you think about this? What do you think about that?" Seidenberg said.

He would send advance reading material to the directors. He turned the dinners into forums for a wide-ranging discussion of trends affecting the country and the company, as well as asking his board members for input on the most important issues facing their companies and industries. "What we became is a mini-presidential cabinet, so we would solve the world's problems for an hour," Seidenberg said. They also engaged in some private wagering over everything from sports to elections.

Seidenberg would then share his thoughts on the following day's board meeting, and what he hoped to accomplish. He didn't think he was putting his thumb on the board's scales to try to influence their decision-making. "I learned that when you are chairman and CEO, you have two distinct roles and you must help the board," he said. Seidenberg also suggested questions the board might frame for the management team when they presented, for instance. And he told his direct reports that he would be discussing their presentations with the board ahead of time.

## "WE BUILT GREAT RAPPORT"

By the time the board assembled for its official meeting, members were highly engaged and willing and able to delve into key topics at considerable depth. More importantly, they were prepared to commit billions in capital expenditures as needed to long-term projects (such as the continued buildout of Verizon's wireless and Fios networks) that they understood were key to maintaining the company's competitive edge. "We built great rapport," he said. "Our directors were informed about what we did."

When Seidenberg felt that directors were going "off on a tangent," he would rein them in by suggesting the answer to their question was the subject of an essay. But he would direct one of the company officers to follow up and be sure that an answer was distributed to all board members. Once or twice a year, Seidenberg asked the corporate secretary, "Are there any questions that have been asked in the last three or four meetings that haven't been answered?" The answer was always no.

## ALL-STAR GOVERNANCE

Some corporate leaders have tried over the years to pack their boards with friends or yes men and women they can rely on to support their agendas. Even recently, as the function of corporate boards has become more robust in the wake of serial corporate scandals, some boards remain open to criticism that they too often are independent in name only. Not so the Verizon boards of directors, beginning with the first group of directors assembled in 2000.

The boards of Bell Atlantic and GTE each had impressive rosters of corporate leaders. The directors from these groups who combined to form the inaugural board for Verizon Communications could go toe to toe with any board in America. One of those directors, John Snow, the former chairman and CEO of CSX Corp., would step off the Verizon board from 2002 through 2006 to serve as U.S. treasury secretary. Involved in some of the country's most elite decision-making circles, Snow credited the relationship of Verizon CEO Seidenberg and the

# THE VERIZON BOARD OF DIRECTORS IN 2000

**James R. Barker** Chairman, Interlake Steamship Co.; Vice Chairman, Mormac Marine Group Inc. and Moran Towing Corp.

**Edward H. Budd** Retired Chairman, Travelers Corp.

**Richard L. Carrion** Chairman, President and CEO, Banco Popular de Puerto Rico

**Robert F. Daniell** Retired Chairman, United Technologies Corp.

**Helene L. Kaplan** Of Counsel, Skadden, Arps, Slate, Meagher & Flom LLP

**Charles R. Lee** Chairman and Co-CEO, Verizon Communications Inc.

**Sandra O. "Sandy" Moose** Senior Vice President and Director, The Boston Consulting Group Inc.

**Joseph Neubauer** Chairman and CEO, Aramark Corp.

**Thomas H. O'Brien** Chairman, The PNC Financial Services Group Inc.

**Russell E. Palmer** Chairman and CEO, The Palmer Group

**Hugh B. Price** President and CEO, National Urban League

**Ivan G. Seidenberg** President and Co-CEO, Verizon Communications Inc.

**Walter V. Shipley** Retired Chairman and CEO, The Chase Manhattan Corp.

**John W. Snow** Chairman, President and CEO, CSX Corp.

**John R. Stafford** Chairman and CEO, American Home Products Corp.

**Robert D. Storey** Partner, Thompson, Hine & Flory LLP

board with elevating Verizon's leadership and corporate governance to best in class:

> Ivan is extraordinarily persuasive, and one of his great gifts is bringing the board into his thinking, using the board as almost a seminar, like a continuous running seminar on the industry, on options. I think he has ideas, but he frames them through the board. He really uses the board as well as I've seen any CEO. That's one of his great strengths.
>
> When you have the sort of people on the board that he had, he knew that there's a lot to be gained from drawing all these people in. And I always had the sense he knew where he wanted to go, but he wanted to get it validated by the board, and he led us into places we undoubtedly never would've gone because we couldn't have seen around the corners the way he did.

# LONG-DISTANCE MARATHON

Looking back, there were times in the late 1990s when Randy Milch, one of the company attorneys leading the marathon race to enter the long-distance market, might have doubted they would ever cross the finish line. A Bell Atlantic lawyer in charge of litigating state regulatory matters, he volunteered to spearhead the long-distance relief process from New York City following the merger with NYNEX. The NYNEX regulatory lawyers were perceived within the company as having a strained relationship with the public utility commissions in the states where it operated. The plan was to concentrate the combined company's long-distance efforts in New York State. The theory was that if they could please the notoriously tough state regulators there, other states would fall in line.

To Milch's dismay, he realized that many of the company's sharpest business leaders, including Seidenberg, Cullen and Babbio, didn't fully appreciate that the company wasn't as prepared as it thought it was to meet the requirements to win long-distance access. Nor were they aware of the mind-numbing complexity involved in the roughly 380 steps to winning such approval generated by the rule-making staff of the Federal Communications Commission, based on what turned out to be a 14-step outline provided by the Telecommunications Act of 1996.

The NYNEX team thought they could show their readiness for long distance by holding a major public hearing in New York City. Milch didn't think the strategy would work but agreed to lead the NYNEX team in any case. He was proved right. NYNEX's failure to persuade public utility commission officials that it had cleared the hurdles necessary to offer long distance set the stage for a more focused meeting in which Milch hoped company executives would get a clearer picture of the stakes involved in winning approval for long distance.

Seidenberg, Cullen and Babbio traveled with Milch to Albany, New York, in 1998 to meet with the head of the commission and get a clear understanding of the scope of the work involved to meet all the requirements needed to win approval for long distance. Seidenberg came away committed to Milch's idea that the company required the equivalent of a highly focused, and expensive, Manhattan Project if it was going to attain this goal.

By late 1999, Bell Atlantic's team had cleared the last legal and regulatory roadblocks preventing them from offering long-distance calling in New York. State residents started getting access to long distance in 2000, and within about 18 months, long-distance calling was available across the Verizon region. Milch got a T-shirt that read "Bell Atlantic Long Distance, January 1, 2000." He also was promoted to become the first general counsel of the combined wireline businesses of Bell Atlantic and GTE.

Ironically, by the time Verizon demonstrated to state and federal reg-ulators that it had opened its local markets to competition and could offer long-distance service to its customers, the product was increas-ingly being packaged with local and regional service and marketed at discounted prices. Verizon quickly accounted for a significant if still minority percentage of the long-distance traffic in its wireline regions, which drove revenues higher. But there was no pot of gold at the end of the long-distance rainbow.

As Seidenberg and others had predicted, long-distance profits had only been sustained by government barriers to competition. Wireless competition also drove down long-distance prices. "We never made a dime on long distance," CFO Salerno lamented.

Milch and others felt that the long-distance marathon in fact gen-erated long-term gains for the company's wireline business regardless of whether there was a direct contribution to the bottom line. The pro-cess forced the company to re-examine, and price, all the components of its local networks as the networks were opened up to competitors as required by the '96 Act. That in itself made Verizon more competitive.

"It was transformative," Milch said. "This was the process requiring the business to break things apart all the way down to the network level so they could be made available to our competitors and to then enter into agreements with our competitors and to have to treat them as customers," he added. "It made us much stronger because we had to undergo those sorts of gut-wrenching changes at the most basic level of our DNA, which is the network."

# AT&T STUMBLES; WORLDCOM FALLS

The long-distance picture was worse for AT&T, which still derived 56 percent of its revenues from long distance as the new decade began. In the late 1990s, under newly arrived CEO Michael Armstrong, AT&T spent $70 billion to diversify into new businesses, buying cable TV provider TCI, which accounted for $48 billion of the total, and local phone and global data networks. The bursting of the dot-com bubble in 2000 cratered its stock, and the ensuing recession dampened demand for its products and services. The company struggled to find a winning strategy, as would other long-distance providers.

WorldCom completed its takeover of MCI in 1998 for a stunning $40 billion and changed its name to MCI WorldCom. Its strategy was to dominate global internet communications as the world's largest internet "backbone" provider of bulk communication cable around the globe. Unfortunately, easy financing enabled a rash of competitors to enter or expand further into the internet communications sector and produce a glut of fiber-optic cable. The phrase "dark fiber" was coined to describe the millions of miles of unused optical fiber around the world. And that was before the dot-com bubble burst in the spring of 2000, the same year WorldCom dropped MCI from its name. The recession that followed led experts to trim their optimistic projections of internet traffic growth.

WorldCom's leadership team failed to reverse the company's declining prospects and share price throughout 2001. In April 2002, the WorldCom board ousted Chairman and CEO Bernard Ebbers in the wake of an SEC investigation of $400 million in personal loans the company extended to its CEO, replacing him with Vice Chairman John Sidgmore.

That June the company's prospects veered from bleak to pitch black. The company fired CFO Scott Sullivan and revealed a $3.85 billion fraudulent accounting scandal. Financing dried up as a result, and the company was bleeding cash. On July 21, 2002, WorldCom, with $107 billion in assets, became the largest company in U.S. history to file for bankruptcy. Customers continued to receive service as the company reorganized operations under the protection of the bankruptcy court. Multiple lawsuits and investigations followed. In March 2005, Ebbers would be found guilty of fraud and conspiracy tied to what by then was determined to be an $11 billion accounting scandal.

# VERIZON RAISES THE BAR

Coming on the heels of the highly publicized bankruptcy of energy trader Enron Corp. in December 2001, the collapse of WorldCom the following summer cast a long shadow over corporate America, and the telecommunications sector in particular. These two events would also lead to a new wave of federal regulations pertaining to corporate behavior and oversight. Verizon took note.

Fortunately, the company and its employees had taken the Verizon Promise and its values to heart and had the sense of working as one dedicated team reinforced by the tragic events of September 11, 2001. So, when the collapse of Enron and WorldCom clouded America's view of corporate ethics, Verizon was determined to clearly demonstrate that it stood apart.

At the same time, Verizon remained grounded in its long-term service ethic rooted in the Bell System and its tradition of meeting the day-to-day needs of its millions of local wireline and wireless customers.

"Verizon's core values of integrity and respect are a fundamental part of our culture," said Seidenberg. "The myriad mergers and acquisitions we did gave us the opportunity to create one of the most rigorous codes of conduct in corporate America, which applies to all employees worldwide. We train and certify all our employees on their understanding of compliance and ethics issues." The company also tightened even further some of its standards for outside directors and eventually eliminated employee stock options.

Verizon wasn't immune from the drop in valuations that rocked the telecommunications industry and much of corporate America. Preparing its course as the telecommunications industry started to recover from the early 2000s downturn, Verizon took some write-downs on investments that didn't pan out. It also began restructuring its international investments to focus future investments closer to home on enterprises in North and South America that might benefit from synergies with Verizon's domestic businesses. Many of the international investments, such as Telecom New Zealand, produced strong financial returns for Verizon but did not fit with its operating strategy going forward. In October 2002, Vice Chairman Mike Masin, who had been in charge of international businesses, resigned to join Citigroup, where he was already a board member, as a vice chairman.

Fred Salerno retired as vice chairman and CFO in mid-2002, while continuing to serve on a number of corporate boards. Seidenberg publicly thanked Salerno for his service to the company in the 2002 annual shareholders report: "His strategic vision and moral fiber are part of our foundation and constitute a lasting legacy to Verizon's shareholders and employees." Doreen Toben succeeded Salerno as executive vice president and CFO.

Chuck Lee stepped down as co-CEO in April 2002, a few months ahead of the schedule agreed to at the time of the Bell Atlantic-GTE merger, while remaining chairman until year-end 2003. He served as a consultant to Verizon through June 30, 2004. Seidenberg credited Lee and the rest of the Verizon board for their "steadfast ethical guidance and insistence on sound governance practices." As seen in 2002, according to Seidenberg, "even sound business models can be undermined fatally if they are not based on a foundation of strong values and ethical management."

Verizon was simultaneously consolidating its identity as a new company while preparing for the next transition by shedding non-core businesses. At the same time, the company put in place the leadership team that would keep the company in front of the real and enduring trends driving the business—wireless, internet data and converging technologies. "Verizon has achieved a position of leadership in communications," Seidenberg said. "We have assembled the assets and established a record of performance that others in our business have yet to match. Now we must do what leaders do—raise the bar for ourselves and the industry."

# NEW COMPANY, NEW INDUSTRY, NEW CENTURY: C-SUITE INSIGHTS FROM RAM CHARAN

---

### __ FACTS MATTER.

Attention to and a commitment to detail and accuracy boost company standing with customers, investors and regulators.

### __ VALUES SUSTAIN CORPORATE CULTURE.

Values are identified and sustained early on and from the bottom up. Industry crises underscore the importance of living strong values rather than giving them lip service. Values form the basis of a working credo that must be practiced every day as part of everyday business to remain strong.

### __ DIRECTORS OF THE ROUND TABLE.

Engage your board of directors like a genuine leadership resource, not a governance requirement. Build rapport and relationships to foster long-term thinking and sustain performance.

# CHAPTER
# 05

---

# PART OF
# SOMETHING
# BIGGER

—

2001-Present

**H**uman nature tells us to flee from danger. The decades-old service credo of the Bell System compels Verizon employees to drive toward it, doing what it takes to meet customer needs in a time of crisis. The company was barely a year old when the response of thousands of employees in the wake of the September 11, 2001, terror attacks in New York, Washington, D.C., and Pennsylvania—and the tragic loss of three employees—helped forge a common identity and break down lingering pre-merger identities and mindsets.

That's not a coincidence. "During emergencies, we run to a crisis," said Gabe Esposito, Verizon's former director of corporate security, business continuity/disaster recovery. "It's built into our DNA." The events of September 11 and their immediate aftermath touched a relatively small portion of Verizon's total employee base and lasted for a relatively short period of time. But the effect of the event was to reinforce the ethos of serving the customer across the company. And as with the country at large, 9/11 underscored for the broadly defined Verizon family that it is good to be part of something bigger.

## SEPTEMBER 11, 2001

Everyone remembers that sunny Tuesday morning in September. Verizon CFO Doreen Toben was on the phone and looking out of her window south from the 39th floor of Verizon's 1095 Avenue of the Americas, or Sixth Avenue, headquarters. She had a clear view straight south about four miles and clearly saw the first plane fly into the north tower of the World Trade Center at approximately 8:46 a.m. She ran down the hall toward Babbio's office overlooking Bryant Park to the east to alert him.

Babbio and two lieutenants, Paul Lacouture, president of network services, and John Bell, senior vice president of northeast network services, and other executives gathered in the conference room at the southeastern corner of the floor. They watched in horror as flames and smoke billowed out of the tower. Seidenberg quickly returned from an early morning meeting a few blocks away in Midtown to join them, as did head of corporate communications Mary Beth Bardin.

The second plane pierced the south tower about 17 minutes later. Like much of America, the executives couldn't quite accept that this was happening. The nation was under attack. Bardin remembers looking from the television in the corner of the room to the actual towers burning to their south. "Somehow seeing it on TV made it more real. We could not believe what we were seeing," she said.

They quickly kicked into operations mode. The towers were in the heart of Verizon's densest telecommunications network, if not the most tightly wired telecommunications node in the world. Four massive computerized switches connected 300,000 Verizon landlines to the outside world. In Lower Manhattan, Verizon also provided nearly 3.6 million data circuits to serve the world's largest financial center and the thousands of financial services and other businesses, as well as 20,000 residential customers. Most of those copper wires and optical fibers fed into Verizon's two switching hubs at Broad Street and the 32-story art deco fortress of an operations center completed in 1927 at 140 West Street. It stands adjacent to the complex of World Trade Center buildings that were erected beginning in the 1960s. Ten cellular phone towers were also providing Verizon Wireless service in the area.

Bell turned to Babbio. "You're an engineer. How long do you think that fire can last?" Earlier than most observers, Babbio understood the structural significance of the flaming structures. "I can tell you this. If it burns for more than an hour and a half, we're in big trouble here," Babbio said, "because that steel will melt in an hour and a half." And that meant the towers were coming down.

Calls were already coming in to Verizon from city, state and federal officials, including what became known as the Department of Homeland Security. They wanted Verizon's assessment of the integrity of the communications grid serving Wall Street as well as hundreds of thousands of residents and businesses. The New York Stock Exchange, certain that the terror attacks would spark panic selling, had already announced that it would not open for trading that day. At the same time, the Verizon team was getting word that a plane had crashed into the Pentagon just across the Potomac River from Washington, D.C., and that yet another had crashed in rural Pennsylvania, apparently en route to strike the nation's capital.

## "GET THOSE PEOPLE OUT OF THERE AS QUICKLY AS YOU CAN!"

Bruce Gordon was president of Verizon's retail business, and his response was the same as if he were sporting a tool belt in the field. He headed toward the problem. In his case, he was only six blocks north of the Twin Towers near his home in Lower Manhattan, having just returned on an early morning flight from Washington, D.C. He was practically jogging toward 140 West Street as he reached Babbio on his cellphone. Gordon realized that he was the senior-most Verizon executive in the area.

"Bruce, those towers are not going to stay up," Babbio said. "That jet fuel is going to drip down that infrastructure, it's going to melt that steel, and those buildings are going to collapse. Get those people out of there as quickly as you can!" There were roughly 1,700 employees at 140 West Street, including Gordon's wife, whom he was having trouble contacting. In order to keep the wireline, computerized call-switching systems running as long as possible, Babbio told Gordon to "tell the switch people to put the switch on automatic and let it run."

It didn't take long for Gordon and officials onsite to get most of the employees out of the building. The few who remained were standing in the imposing vaulted lobby that runs through the building from west to east, making sure they weren't missing anything. Then at approximately 10 a.m. the south tower collapsed a few hundred feet south from where they stood but beyond their range of vision. "The earth shook. The sky went from blue to black. But we didn't know that, in fact, it had collapsed," Gordon said. He reached Babbio on his cellphone. Babbio told him what had happened. Then gave him a concise order: "Get the hell out of there!" Babbio confirmed that Gordon and the rest of the employees at 140 West Street were out of harm's way. In far too short an interval, the second tower fell.

The scope of the crisis was beginning to hit home for the Verizon leadership team. They would not know definitively that the company had lost three employees in the terrorist attacks for several days or that the total lives lost in the tragedy that day would approach 3,000. Three employees of Genuity, the former GTE subsidiary that regulators had required be spun off as a separate company as part of the creation of Verizon, also perished.

Several hundred employees worked in the Twin Towers themselves. Two did not survive the attacks, nor did one employee working in the Pentagon (see sidebar).

Verizon would later create a "Share Your Story" website for employees to post comments about the disaster and their personal experiences. "I went running for my life with many Verizon people and others on 9/11. We were there and saw the planes crash into the building, the towers above us in flames, the people jump from a 110-story building . . . the towers collapse and all the rest," said one employee identified only as John. "I am truly lucky and blessed that my entire team is among the group who made it out safely. For thousands of others, this is not the case. It is those individuals and their families that have been in my thoughts and prayers."

# IN MEMORIAM

For the first few days after the September 11 terrorist attacks, Verizon—like many businesses affected by the tragedy—scrambled to account for all employees known or thought to be in the areas hit that morning. It would not be until the start of the following week that Verizon could confirm that it lost three employees.

Donna Marie Bowen worked 22 years with the company. She was promoted in 1995 to communications representative with responsibility for billing procedures for federal employees, including those at the Pentagon. On September 11, 2001, she arrived at the Pentagon at her typical start time of 4 a.m., planning to leave at 3 p.m. as usual to spend time with her three children, two stepchildren and husband.

Derrick Washington had one of the best views in the telecommunications industry, manning a switch 110 stories up on the World Trade Center for Verizon's Global Networks division. His enthusiasm for the job and for life was infectious among his fellow technicians. He left behind a wife and three children.

Leonard Anthony White's proficiency as a systems technician for Verizon was such that he was lured out of retirement to work as a Verizon consultant in the World Trade Center. The Norfolk, Virginia, native was known for his love of New York City, music, and his extended family of siblings, nieces and nephews.

# THE PENTAGON

About 40 Verizon employees on September 11, 2001, were working on-site at the Pentagon. Verizon managed the communications system for the Pentagon under contract with the Department of Defense. One Verizon employee, Donna Marie Bowen, didn't survive the terrorist attack.

Others' lives were forever changed by the experience. One Verizon employee named Kathy later shared a story on the internal Verizon website created for that purpose. She had a customer in the Pentagon paying her monthly phone bill with a check-by-phone transaction that morning. Suddenly the customer shouted, "There has been an explosion in my building. I have to go!" The customer service representative could hear a roar in the background and people screaming, and then the phone line went dead. It was not until 10 days later that she was able to confirm the customer had survived.

Defense Secretary Donald Rumsfeld's office praised quick thinking on the part of Verizon staff on site. Two Verizon employees, by following emergency procedures and quickly reporting on the spread of the fire in the Pentagon, were able to save the telecommunications switch. That kept the military command onsite from losing a key communications link that was vital in responding to the crisis.

# SHANKSVILLE, PENNSYLVANIA

Verizon service employees were among the first responders to reach the site near Shanksville, Pennsylvania, where United Airlines Flight 93 crashed on the morning of September 11, 2001. The jet had been hijacked by terrorists and was on a path that apparently would have taken it to Washington, D.C., if passengers had not overtaken the terrorists in mid-flight.

Verizon supervisor Lisa Jefferson took a call that morning from Flight 93 passenger Todd Beamer on a GTE Airfone. He confirmed that terrorists had taken control of the cockpit. He told Jefferson that the passengers were aware of the earlier attacks in New York and Washington and were determined not to let their plane be used as an instrument of terror.

On the ground at the crash site, a Verizon team that had been on a service call nearby switched to emergency response mode. They set up communication terminals in a nearby abandoned metal shack. They then ran three miles of cable to provide communications to the site for the first responders and investigators who swarmed the area as the day progressed.

# GROUND ZERO

Babbio wanted a firsthand look at the damage at 140 West Street. Seidenberg had to intervene to keep all of his top 25 people from hopping in cars and heading to the site of the terrorist attacks with Babbio. He understood the impulse to run toward the problem, but as the senior officer, he had to think about his lieutenants and the unknown but very real risks they might face. "This wasn't a hurricane," he said. "This was an act of war."

New York City Mayor Rudy Giuliani said he would send a police escort and transportation for Babbio and operations leaders, including Lacouture. When the cars arrived, Babbio asked the driver how they were going to get downtown. "Sixth Avenue," he said. When Babbio protested that Sixth Avenue traffic ran uptown, the driver said, "Not today." In a testament to how dramatically the attacks altered everyday life in Manhattan, the normally bustling avenue was virtually deserted. After stopping to confer with the mayor at a police department facility on the way downtown, the Verizon team was dropped off a few blocks from what would become known as Ground Zero.

By late afternoon they had worked their way around debris, fire trucks and emergency vehicles and were just coming up to the front of their building at 140 West Street when they saw a line of firefighters running toward them, waving their arms. "It's going, it's going," they shouted. The Verizon team didn't have time to get further details and knew that when firefighters say run, you run. As they sprinted north up West Street they looked over their shoulders and saw a storm cloud of black smoke and dust billowing after them as the 47-story 7 World Trade Center building collapsed onto the back of the Verizon building with a rumble. They ducked into an alley to dodge the cloud of smoke.

When the smoke had subsided somewhat, they huddled with the firefighters. They identified themselves and said that 140 West Street was a key Verizon facility and that they had to get inside. The firefighters said they didn't even know if there was a fire somewhere in the building or if it was even structurally sound. There was no way they were letting Babbio or anyone else in that building at that point. Babbio thanked them and said the Verizon team would be back first thing Wednesday morning.

Giuliani had asked them to report back to him after their trip downtown. They met him at St. Vincent's Hospital in Greenwich Village. The mayor went to the hospital expecting to meet with and comfort victims of the tragedy. When the Verizon officials drove up, they were greeted by the unsettling prospect of a line of empty wheelchairs outside the emergency room entrance. "They had nurses behind all these wheelchairs and doctors," Lacouture said. "There just wasn't any activity, because either you survived, or you didn't."

Giuliani was aware that 7 World Trade Center collapsed onto the Verizon building at 140 West Street. "He explained that he didn't want to lose any more firemen so they let 7 World Trade Center go," Lacouture said.

# EMERGENCY LOCKDOWN

Even before Babbio and his team headed down to try to inspect the Verizon building at 140 West Street, the leadership team in Midtown Manhattan adopted emergency procedures. They closed the building and sent employees home, hoping they could avoid the gridlock that was already slowing traffic in and out of the city to a crawl and taxing every form of available mass transportation that wasn't immediately affected by the terrorist attack.

Attorney Randy Milch was checking the upper floors to be sure they were evacuated. He came around one corner, and there was Seidenberg doing the same thing. Milch said, "He's looking at me going, 'Get the hell out of here,' and I'm looking at him saying, 'You get the hell out of here. You are way more important than I am.'" They both finished checking the floor.

The leadership team had immediately activated a sub-basement vault set up for managing crises. This center was four stories below ground level and served as the command center for all communications with the outside world, as well as with the Verizon team. There was no way of knowing at that point whether theirs or other nearby buildings in Midtown might also be terrorist targets. Once in the below-ground command center, the leadership team opened a bridge phone line. That enabled employees in offices or facilities across the country to call directly into New York. The open communication is typically used to coordinate the response to a hurricane or other natural disaster.

Verizon locations from Massachusetts and upstate New York to Indiana, Texas and California kept employees on staff to answer phones and step in to fill other duties that would have normally been handled by employees in the New York City area. The crisis center and the cross-country support network would remain active for months as repair work continued in Lower Manhattan. "They acted as if they were all at Ground Zero," Seidenberg said. "You could call at 2 a.m. and someone was there answering the phone. Nobody had to be told to do anything. Every one of our people was extraordinary, willing to do whatever was necessary."

Virginia Ruesterholz realized she wasn't going to be going home to Long Island, New York, the night of September 11, 2001. She had a wireline team working in 140 West Street. She was in constant contact with team members in the early hours of the crisis, first over their landline phones and then their cellular phones, so she knew everyone got out of the building and was uninjured, if more than a bit shaken up. Like so many thousands of workers in Lower Manhattan that day, they started walking uptown to get away from the chaos and danger surrounding Ground Zero. The subway lines that passed under or near the World Trade Center site were knocked out or taken out of service.

After they walked nearly four miles to Verizon's headquarters in Midtown, Ruesterholz said they all needed to huddle, get a bite to eat and figure out what had to be done next. Dinner was a somber affair as they contemplated the still-unknown number of workers who perished a few hundred yards from their offices. "As a group," she said, "I think we were numb, but we knew we had to be ready for the next steps."

Later that evening Seidenberg was making the rounds of the Verizon offices at 1095 Avenue of the Americas, taking a break from the subterranean command center. He ran into Peter Thonis in media relations. "Peter, you and your team can go home," Seidenberg said. "We really can't; we're getting blitzed" by media calls from around the world looking for you-are-there comments from Manhattanites as well as updates on the telecommunications network, Thonis said. Thonis understood that Seidenberg was trying to take care of his team, but in this crisis, the team needed to stay on the job.

Seidenberg nodded in agreement and continued his tour of the upper floors. When he finally left for the night, it was with a terrific sense of unease. The team had spent the day fielding questions from the mayor, governor, Washington officials, the military, the press, customers—just about everyone. "As a guy who served in the military, it was scary to go home and not know what was going to happen tomorrow. Nobody knew if there would be more planes or other attacks," he said.

# THE NEW YORK STOCK EXCHANGE

The day after the terror attacks, Babbio and Lacouture returned to 140 West Street. Smoke was still billowing from the site of the collapsed towers just to their south, as it would for weeks. Milch also went to 140 West Street that morning to get a firsthand view of any liability or related issues as general counsel and to support Babbio. The damage was overwhelming. When the Twin Towers collapsed, they drove steel beams down through the pavement and surrounding buildings as if they were toothpicks spearing a marzipan miniature of Lower Manhattan. Power and water lines were severed in multiple locations, as was equipment in 140 West Street itself, which had a gaping hole in one side.

"We went down to the [cable] vault, which was in the basement of the building, and that was penetrated," Lacouture said. "There was a beam that came right through, there were wires hanging down. I've seen hurricanes, and I've seen damage from tornadoes. This was a combination of the two, with the damage and the water and everything. Water was just rushing down the stairway."

Water flooded the five sub-basements of 140 West Street from these water lines. By late afternoon Tuesday, the flooding shorted out the automated switches the Verizon employees had set on automatic when they evacuated that morning. Little if anything appeared salvageable below street level. West Street also served as the river crossing for most of the southern Manhattan cables that crossed the Hudson River.

More water came from the fire department. After the collapse of 7 World Trade Center, firefighters realized that the now-abandoned 140 West Street, built like a Mayan temple with multiple setbacks, provided a solid platform for mounting hoses in upper windows to use in dousing flames and smoke billowing from the piles of debris at Ground Zero. The south and east facades of 140 West Street sustained considerable damage, but the stout reinforced masonry construction protected the steel frame of the structure, which remained sound. The art deco lobby

# CELLULAR SERVICE STRENGTH

It would be four months before the famous Verizon Wireless Test Man commercials would redefine cellphone advertising beginning in January 2002, but Babbio's call with Grasso the morning of September 12, 2001, would have been a perfect cameo for the campaign. Wading through a flooded basement a few hundred yards from Ground Zero less than 24 hours after the terrorist attacks and being able to complete a cellular call underscored the quality of the company's wireless network. All of the cellular service providers' systems were temporarily overwhelmed by the unprecedented volume of calls on September 11. Verizon's service outlasted rivals serving the area, and it was back in service faster across a broader portion of Lower Manhattan than its competitors.

One of the first steps Verizon took in Lower Manhattan to restore service to customers was to deploy 21 temporary cellular towers. Ten cellular towers had been disrupted or destroyed in the attacks. It also brought in 220 free, wireless "no pay" phones on trailers that were deployed throughout Lower Manhattan. And the company distributed 5,000 free cellular phones to emergency workers and businesses in the area within a few days of the disaster.

of 140 West Street, while not flooded, was covered in soot, including the murals decorating the vaulted roof celebrating the development of long-distance communication over the eras.

Babbio was standing in an upper basement with water coming halfway up his hip boot waders that morning when his cellphone rang. It was Dick Grasso, the chairman and CEO of the New York Stock Exchange. The Big Board had already said it wasn't going to open on Wednesday. He wanted Babbio and his team to come to Midtown to join a meeting of financial services and government officials. They wanted to reopen the stock exchange on Thursday of that week. The NYSE was a symbol of New York and the global financial system. It was important that the world witness that the terrorist attacks had not broken America's spirit, and getting the stock exchange back up and running was a vital part of that message.

Babbio, Lacouture and Milch walked into the bank conference room on Park Avenue, where Grasso was holding the meeting that morning. They immediately realized that they were the odd men out. With the exception of two entrepreneurs who had recently purchased the small American Stock Exchange located a few blocks from the World Trade Center, they were the only ones with soot and ashes covering their trousers and the only ones, frankly, who smelled as if they had been walking through a smoky sewer. "Nobody wanted to sit next to us," Babbio joked. Clearly the rest of the room, mostly the heads of banks and brokerage firms (though Consolidated Edison officials were also present), had not been near Ground Zero, they realized. The industry leaders might not have a true picture of just how extensively their own facilities, the city's financial services and other infrastructure had been uprooted. An official representing the Bush administration in Washington was on the speakerphone.

Milch had prepped Babbio on the way to the meeting, concerned that they might face pressure to make unrealistic promises. "Tell the people your honest opinion about how long it will take to get things up and running," and then leave, Milch advised him. Babbio had too much to do to be stuck in a meeting, Milch said. Besides, if the executives wanted to take shots at anybody, they could zero in on him as the company lawyer.

Babbio listened closely to the comments as the executives spoke. Each was more intent than the next that his firm was ready to resume trading and show the terrorists and the world that America means business. Babbio and Milch, confident they had a better understanding of the situation downtown than anyone else in the room, were not about to let Verizon be positioned as the fall guy if the NYSE could not resume trading the next day, Thursday.

Babbio wasn't going to address Verizon's capabilities just yet. He spoke to the brokers and bankers in turn. He told them that they couldn't get their employees anywhere near their of-

# MIRACLE ON SECOND AVENUE

There was no precedent for the terrorist attacks of 9/11. But there was a precedent of sorts for a massive Bell System service outage. In late February 1975, fire engulfed the lower floors of a New York Telephone switching center at Second Avenue and 13th Street. The fire started in the cable vault sub-basement and spread upward. By the time it was put out, the flames had knocked out service to 300 city blocks and 104,000 subscriber lines. Included in the area without service were six hospitals, 11 fire stations and New York University. It was the Bell System's largest such service outage ever. The Bell System companies sent out a systemwide call for support and equipment. Thousands of workers put in 12-hour shifts, night and day. Operating from a temporary command center nearby and being able to take over an unused floor in the switching center, New York Telephone managed to restore service to nearly all customers in the area in 22 days. The feat was referred to as the Miracle on Second Avenue.

fices in Lower Manhattan. No transportation, no food, no water. No power. If they wanted to resume trading the following day, Thursday, they had to tell him by 2 p.m. Wednesday afternoon—in about four hours—where their traders and trading equipment were going to be located. And if not everybody could meet that deadline, then some firms were going to be trading, and some were going to have a lot of very angry customers.

Grasso called a timeout. OK, so Thursday was not a possibility. Many in the room wanted to open the exchange on Friday, in two days. Grasso and his team vetoed that idea, pointing out that opening the exchange with just one day before the weekend, when the exchange would be closed, was almost a guarantee that the exchange would be swamped by panicked sellers dumping shares.

Grasso inquired about Monday. The exchange and the city were prepared to give Verizon whatever assistance it needed. Babbio said yes, with an understanding that the trading firms would have to identify where their primary trading locations were going to be by that Wednesday night. "I had a feeling that we could make Monday," Babbio recalled.

Milch was stunned, not having thought such a quick turnaround remotely possible. What was it about five flooded sub-basements that Babbio didn't understand? Milch had been thinking weeks, not days. The attorney kept his own counsel, however. As did Lacouture, who was also skeptical of being able to meet the timeline. Once the meeting ended, the Verizon team got to work.

## "I DON'T KNOW WHAT WE NEED, BUT SEND ME TWO"

Within 24 hours of the attacks, Verizon operations managers working out of a conference room at 1095 Avenue of the Americas were already on the phone with suppliers and coworkers across the country and in Canada, where key equipment supplier Nortel was based. They weren't sure exactly what they needed in the first day or so of the crisis. But they were sure they were going to need it fast, and a lot of it. Their job was made all the harder by the fact that the federal government had grounded all air traffic as of the time of the attacks. Anything Verizon needed in Lower Manhattan was going to have to be shipped in by truck. And that would require special teams on call at the tunnels because the government had shut down all traffic connecting Manhattan with the outside world.

"We had guys at the Canadian border getting these trucks through. We had shipments coming from Georgia and Texas. We had guys at the other side of the Lincoln Tunnel, because the tunnels were closed, clearing the trucks through," Babbio said. The company even received special permission, while all commercial and private flights were still grounded in the States, to fly computer experts into Teterboro Airport in New Jersey and then drive them into the city.

There was nothing in the 140 West Street sub-basement Verizon could use to make the Monday deadline. There was some equipment in upper floors of 140 West Street that was salvageable, but it was tied into a damaged network. And, of course, there was no power in the building. So, Verizon ordered and installed emergency engines and put them on platforms running along a side street to power the building for a month on their own.

Engineers initially had tried to snake cables from 140 West's upper floors back into manholes to connect with the underground vault. Babbio grew frustrated as the effort was getting nowhere. "Just throw the damn cables out the window," he said in exasperation.

Voila. Babbio and his team realized that they would not only have to think outside of the box. They had to think outside of the building. They realized fairly quickly that they were going to have to replicate the inner workings of the building on the outside to create a new telecommunications network for Lower Manhattan in five days. They essentially turned the operations at 140 West Street inside out, not to mention their standard budgeting and permitting processes.

Verizon ran cables up the outside of 140 West Street to access equipment on upper floors that was still in working order. Babbio conceded that the process was being engineered on the fly. "So, one guy said to me, 'How many cables should we put through this window?' I said, 'When the window sill collapses, move over to that window," Babbio recalled. "That's what we're doing. Just move over a window."

The team made some quick back-of-the-envelope calculations to get the process moving. They were going to rebuild or reroute more than 2 million voice and data circuits in five days. That meant they were building a telecommunications network as big as the one that served Cincinnati—above ground, with much of it snaking past Ground Zero, which was an active quarantine site patrolled by National Guard soldiers and New York Police Department officers.

"We kept saying to people, 'I don't know what we need, but send me two,'" Babbio said. Verizon ordered two giant electronic switching systems. "Send me 20 DACs [digital access cross-connect frames, which help manage traffic flow on high-capacity fiber-optic lines]. We know they're damaged. We saw them when we walked through the building. We don't know how many we need," he said. "Just put them on a truck and send them here."

Verizon placed an open-ended order for fiber-optic cable. "Send me lots of cable; all the cable you have in the country I will take," Babbio told suppliers. Virtually every foot of cable that was beneath ground was unreachable and unusable, even if it hadn't been destroyed in the collapse of the Twin Towers.

## "WE'RE COMING BACK"

Before anything else could be done at 140 West Street, the company brought in Verizon cleaning crews late Wednesday to clean up as much of the ground floor as possible. When Babbio returned to the building the morning of Thursday, September 13, he strode through the lobby toward the stairs leading to the equipment areas on higher floors. What he saw in the lobby stopped him in his tracks. "The lobby of that building has two medallions," Babbio said. "Fairly good-size medallions, probably a good 6 feet [in diameter], round, solid brass. One of them is a lineman on a pole, and one of them is an operator. And they're right on the center floor. When I got there on Thursday morning, the medallions were cleaned. And they had stanchions put up around."

"These guys said, 'We're coming back. We're coming back.' Now, we still had holes in the side of the building, but they had the medallions cleaned on the floor."

As the work progressed downtown, it was being monitored closely in Midtown. "We had a huge task force right there in the conference room at 42nd Street. I had every organization that had anything to do with inside plant and outside plant there. And we knew literally by the hour what was going on, how much we needed," Babbio said.

## "WE'VE GOT TO BE IN THIS TOGETHER"

Local workers and those who could drive in from the region pulled together to get the job done. Three thousand Verizon workers and technicians were assigned to the job full time, and for many that meant almost 24/7 for the rest of that week and through the weekend. Union, non-union, that was a distinction without a difference in the push to get the Big Board up and running—and in the weeks that followed.

"We said to the union, anybody that doesn't want to do this, they do not have to do it," Seidenberg said. "We gave them all zoot [protective] suits; we protected them the best we could. We said we don't know what's going to happen here, but we've got to be in this together." He added, "They were great. I used to go down there; the guys would see me. They would say get your splicing tools on."

Larry Cohen, who was executive vice president of the Communications Workers of America union at the time of the 9/11 attacks, agreed that the organized labor force and company leadership worked together very closely in the days, weeks and months following the terrorist acts. "I remember several meetings with top management" in the days following the attacks, Cohen said. "There was a total spirit of cooperation." Seidenberg agreed. "All of our employees were spectacular." He added, "There were so many brothers, sisters, friends and family members of our employees in the police and fire departments, not to mention the World Trade Center itself, that this was a very personal situation for our company."

Despite the dangers of working in and around the highly unstable area, going above and beyond was the new normal for workers in Lower Manhattan and across the Verizon network. Among the must-have equipment that needed to be salvaged from 140 West Street was a group of computer servers that contained the software used to transmit stock quotes from banks and trading firms around the world to the floor of the NYSE. The problem was that the servers were housed in a space more than 20 flights above the lobby, and Verizon did not have generators large enough onsite to power the elevator banks. So, 10 employees suited up in hazmat outfits with respirators and walked up the stairs and back down carrying the servers. As it turned out, the software on the servers was so old that the programmers who designed it had retired. They jumped at the chance to get back in uniform and serve the effort to get the stock exchange up and running.

# "WE SAW THE TRUE MEANING OF PARTNERSHIP"

The NYSE, while the immediate priority in terms of restoring service, was hardly the only Verizon client in Lower Manhattan. There were roughly 34,000 other businesses and residences in the area. Verizon officials and staff worked shoulder to shoulder with large corporate customers in the area to restore service as rapidly as possible. There were daily meetings, and progress was monitored on an hourly basis. By late September service was restored to many of the largest financial services customers in particular, including American Express and the major banks and brokerage firms in the area. Co-CEO Chuck Lee told a meeting of CEOs in New York in late October that the crisis brought out the best in the Verizon culture, from the senior leadership to the rank and file. "Late last month we got a letter from Bill Harrison, chairman of JPMorgan Chase," Lee told the group. "He said, 'Inside our firm, we refer to Verizon as our business partner. We saw the true meaning of partnership over the last 10 days in your employees' every word and deed.'"

The company-wide esprit de corps was genuine and didn't need prompting, said Thonis: "Nobody wanted to go home. Nobody wanted to do anything but work there. I mean, everybody just wanted to fix the problem. It was amazing." Having a sense of purpose and an ability to serve was an incredible boost to company morale, he said. "You had the advantage of having something to do while everybody else in America was feeling helpless. We were actually trying to do something. Our Verizon badge was like an FBI badge. You could get in anywhere."

To communicate with employees nationwide, Seidenberg recorded a series of "blast" voicemails that were sent to employees' inboxes. He and Mary Beth Bardin huddled each day to pull together notes that Seidenberg himself read to staff worldwide. Many would later tell Bardin that they kept those messages on their answering machines for months as a reminder of what the company collectively went through during the crisis.

"Many, many of you have asked, 'How can I help?' said an early email message to Verizon employees from Seidenberg.

> First, take care of our customers. Our network has been strained with record levels of phone calls and Internet connections. We are still at peak levels in many locations across the country—not just on the East Coast—but in our markets nationwide.

> The absolute best thing you can do to help people affected by this tragedy is come to work every day. Do your job and do it well. It's that important. Believe it or not, people watching this tragedy on TV envy our ability to be out there, making a real difference. So, don't ever forget how much the work that you do matters.

Verizon employees contributed $3.5 million, and combined with the company matching funds, Verizon contributed a total of $16 million to a national telethon that raised more than $100 million to aid victims of the September 11 attacks. More than 6,000 Verizon employees volunteered for the telethon, helping to create call centers and answer phones, among other duties.

## "THE WEIGHT OF THE WORLD"

The Verizon crews in Midtown and downtown coordinated around the clock as the Monday morning opening of the exchange approached. Onsite power, police and fire crews also went out of their way to lend a hand to ensure that the Verizon teams remained on schedule. The media and local and federal officials were asking for almost constant updates. Everyone was assured that the company was on track to get the NYSE up and running as of 9:30 a.m. on Monday, September 17.

The official air of confidence wasn't always shared internally as the inevitable snafus arose and were just as quickly dealt with. Babbio said, "We had guys working up until the time the exchange was open. We had guys testing at all different locations. Every place where there was a JPMorgan office or some call center where they were taking orders, we had our people there. But every bit of effort was focused on making sure that it would work."

Lacouture recalled the repair process continuing almost down to the wire. The Verizon teams worked all Sunday night and into Monday morning. At 4 a.m. the NYSE system looked good, but at 5 a.m. it wasn't working. As late as 8:30 a.m. Monday morning, the system was still down. Then at 8:45 a.m., just 45 minutes before the scheduled NYSE open, they had the last bugs out of the system, and everything was good to go. The ringing of the opening bell that morning was aired on local and national news that evening and heralded as a sign of New York City's and America's resilience in the face of terrorism. Lacouture didn't wait for the opening bell. He went home to bed.

An avid investor, Babbio was usually focused on which way stock prices were moving. Not that Monday morning. "It was one of the few mornings that I really did not care whether the market was going up or down," he said. "All I knew was that I could see that tape," which meant that the stock exchange was open for business. "I was not at the stock exchange. I did not go down there, but it was just like the weight of the world had just come off the whole organization, because it was such a huge amount of pressure," he said.

NYSE Chairman and CEO Dick Grasso praised the Verizon effort. "It was a Herculean job on the part of the men and women of Verizon. I can't say enough about the wonderful Verizon people on the line who worked continuously, 24/7, from September 12 until the New York Stock Exchange reopened September 17." Seidenberg added, "What was amazing to me was how poised, smart and effective our people were in not only getting our own facilities up and running but also in helping the hundreds of trading partners of the stock exchange get back in service."

The immediate pressure was lifted, but the job was far from over. Months of work lay ahead as Ground Zero and the surrounding areas were stabilized and then cleared of debris. The temporary network Verizon constructed to run the Big Board was taken down weeks later, once existing and new cables and circuits were in place and connected.

Despite absorbing the impact of the collapse of the North Tower and 7 World Trade Center, 140 West Street's massive foundations required only relatively modest amounts of shoring up. Other repairs would

## SERVICE CALL

On Saturday evening, as the effort to reconnect the NYSE and other major clients was in full swing, Seidenberg, Chuck Lee, Babbio and Fred Salerno stopped off at the Pierre Hotel in Midtown and removed their work boots. This was a service call of a more personal nature. Seidenberg's daughter Lisa had booked the date and location months earlier for her wedding. The family decided to go ahead with a scaled-down event rather than reschedule. "In the midst of so much heartache and suffering, we decided it was the right thing to do to celebrate such a life-affirming moment," Seidenberg said. He handed his flip phone to Babbio to take his calls as he walked his daughter down the aisle. They both placed their own calls to Lacouture to get updates on the work while they were at the service. After a champagne toast of the bride and groom, the Verizon officials donned their boots and went back to work.

take years. The company decided to restore the murals and other period details of the art deco gem to their original glory, far exceeding the condition they were in on the eve of the terrorist attacks, and at a final cost exceeding $1 billion for the entire structure. As a sign of its commitment to New York City and the post-9/11 recovery, Verizon made 140 West Street its corporate headquarters in 2005.

# LADY LIBERTY

As the first anniversary of 9/11 approached, Seidenberg and Gordon discussed ways to commemorate the sacrifices of so many, as well as the incredible commitment of Verizon's staff in getting the NYSE up and running, and similar efforts in New York, at the Pentagon, and in Shanksville, Pennsylvania. It was a highly sensitive subject, since they did not want to appear to be wringing any commercial benefit from the tremendous loss and sacrifice of so many on that day. But Gordon was convinced that if executed properly, it could be an important tribute to the heroic recovery of the city and country in the year since the attack, a recovery to which Verizon had made a significant contribution.

Meanwhile, John McGarry, an ad executive with whom Gordon had worked, was in the process of starting his own agency and asked Gordon to give him a challenge and let him and his partner demonstrate what they could do. Gordon talked it over with Seidenberg, and they agreed to present the issue to the ad team and see what they came back with. McGarry and his partner, Gordon Bowen, returned a few weeks later. They said that they agreed that Verizon should pursue the idea and presented some initial concepts.

Seidenberg and Larry Babbio, who was brought into the decision-making process, were lukewarm at best and indicated they thought it was something they should pass on. Gordon felt that he had a commitment from Seidenberg to at least explore the concept some more before killing it for good.

Following typical creative fits and starts, Gordon and the ad team developed a 90-second TV ad spot they called "Lady Liberty." Seidenberg's first reaction was to tell Gordon that he had thought the idea was dead, but then he promptly fell in love with the subdued but highly emotional tribute, featuring black-and-white images of children at play, as well as the iconic Statue of Liberty. To dilute fears that they were appearing to profit from the tragedy, Verizon brought in the NYSE and American Express as co-sponsors, but those two backed out at the last minute. Verizon sent the ad to the major networks, but only CBS was willing to run it, and only once. The placement could not have been better. Following *60 Minutes'* signature tick, tick, tick . . . it was the lead-in ad to a special hour-long program devoted to 9/11.

Seidenberg's voicemail inbox exploded with messages of thanks from Verizon employees around the country. "I can still remember Ivan coming into my office that Monday morning, early," recalled Gordon, who fired his ad agency and became McGarryBowen's founding client. Seidenberg said, "You have no idea how many calls I received from employees thanking me for doing this." All three networks ran the ad the following day as part of their news coverage of the anniversary.

# LESSONS LEARNED

In the years since September 11, 2001, Verizon employees have rallied in response to the devastating impact of Hurricanes Katrina and Rita in New Orleans and the surrounding areas, to hurricane damage in Florida, wildfires in California and across the West and the crippling damage suffered by East Coast customers from the impact of Hurricane Irene and Superstorm Sandy. And season after season, Verizon employees pour into neighborhoods ravaged by the hundreds of un-named yet punishing weather systems or other calamities across the country. When anxious customers look out their windows, they see the Verizon Credo and commitment to service at work.

Verizon applied numerous 9/11 lessons learned about upgrading and hardening networks and strategically distributing assets and facilities to its operations across the country in the years that followed. That applied to the wireline as well as the wireless sides of the company. Verizon Wireless alone would invest more than $65 billion over the following decade to boost network coverage, capacity and reliability, including backup power systems that are vital to maintaining service during and after storms.

The Verizon Credo is refreshed daily across the country and around the world. Every employee who joins the company across its different business lines is united in a shared sense of purpose. At Verizon, "when you have a crisis," said Lacouture, "with or without a hurricane or fire or something like 9/11, motivation, desire to work, willingness to cooperate is never an issue."

# PART OF SOMETHING BIGGER: C-SUITE INSIGHTS FROM RAM CHARAN

### ___ MAKE SOCIAL PURPOSE AN AUTHENTIC CORE VALUE.

Companies with an authentic, social-purpose core value are intimately engaged at multiple levels with their communities in good times—and especially in bad.

### ___ DO WHAT IT TAKES.

A strong customer service ethos is an organization's muscle memory in times of crisis.

### ___ RUN TO A CRISIS.

Engage with a crisis and its implications fast to find the best solution for those most affected and for the good of the enterprise.

### ___ EMBRACE EMOTION.

Leaders understand that an organization hurts during a time of crisis, and expressing pain is not a sign of weakness. Communicate honestly, and reward steps to help and heal, not deny and cover up.

Seidenberg as a member of the 1st Cavalry Division (Airmobile)
during his service in Vietnam

Ivan Seidenberg and his wife, Phyllis

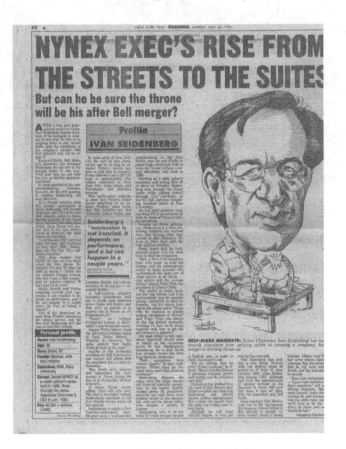

*New York Post*, May 26, 1996

Charles Lee, Chris Gent and Ivan Seidenberg announce the joint venture between
Bell Atlantic and Vodafone Airtouch, to be named Verizon Wireless,
at a press conference in New York on September 21, 1999.

Charles Lee led the transformation of GTE into a wireless phone and telecommunications pioneer from 1992 to 2000 as chairman and CEO and served as co-CEO of Verizon with Seidenberg from 2000 to 2002.

Ray Smith, who served as chairman and CEO of Bell Atlantic from 1989 to 1998, was a phone industry leader in telecommunications and architect with Ivan Seidenberg of the 1997 merger of NYNEX and Bell Atlantic.

Fred Salerno assumed positions of increasing responsibility for New York Telephone and later NYNEX, working closely with Ivan Seidenberg to develop strategic options for the Baby Bell. He was named NYNEX CFO in 1995 and retained the title following the 1997 merger with Bell Atlantic. From 2000 to 2002, he served as Verizon vice chairman and CFO.

Dick Lynch led Bell Atlantic's mobile technology effort beginning in 1990 and developed the network testing protocol that would inspire the award-winning "Can You Hear Me Now?" ad campaign. He filled the same role as chief technology officer for Verizon Wireless beginning in 2000 and served as Verizon EVP and CTO from 2007 to 2010.

Bruce Gordon was president of the retail side of the Bell Atlantic wireline business at the time of the merger with GTE and played a pivotal role in the choice of Verizon as the name for the new company. He retired in 2003 and served as president of the NAACP from 2005 through 2007.

Joseph Neubauer, a former Bell Atlantic director and CEO of food service giant Aramark, helped guide Verizon as a director during its first 14 years, retiring shortly after the board voted to buy back the Verizon Wireless stake from Vodafone.

Denny Strigl, who led the growth of the wireless business as president and CEO of Verizon Wireless from 2000 to 2007 and served as Verizon president and COO from 2007 to 2009, speaks at Ivan Seidenberg's retirement party in 2011.

The damage to the Verizon building at 140 West Street after the September 11 attacks, and the remnants of the World Trade Center complex buildings

Verizon executives, including Larry Babbio (top), and employees worked day and night after the September 11 attacks to restore vital communication services in and around New York City, Washington, D.C., and Shanksville, Pennsylvania.

Michael Capellas, president and CEO of MCI, speaks before the Senate Judiciary Committee in support of the Verizon-MCI merger, March 5, 2005. Also pictured (from left): Edward Whitacre, chairman and CEO of SBC Communications; Ivan Seidenberg; David Dorman, chairman and CEO of AT&T.

Doreen Toben, Bell Atlantic vice president and controller, succeeded Fred Salerno as Verizon CFO and EVP from 2002 to 2009.

Former Congressman Tom Tauke led NYNEX's lobbying efforts in Washington beginning in the mid-1990s and served as Verizon EVP of public affairs policy and communications from 2004 to 2013.

Larry Babbio, an avid technologist, was an executive at Bell Atlantic, advocating for the adoption of CDMA wireless technology, and Verizon, where he led the effort to bring the NYSE back online after September 11 and then promoted the rollout of the all-fiber Fios network. He served as vice chairman and president of Verizon from 2000 through 2007.

Virgina Ruesterholz advanced through the ranks at NYNEX, Bell Atlantic and Verizon, becoming one of the company's most senior women executives by the early 2000s. She served as president of Verizon Services Operations from 2009 through 2011 and was named Verizon EVP in 2012.

William "Bill" Barr, who served as U.S. attorney general from 1991 to 1993, was general counsel at GTE Corp. from 1994 to 2000. He led Verizon's legal team as general counsel from 2000 to 2008.

Mary Beth Bardin, who held a series of positions in communications with GTE Corp. from 1988 to 2000, served as Verizon's executive vice president of public affairs and communications from 2000 to 2004.

Thomas H. O'Brien, former chairman and CEO of PNC Financial Services Group, served on the board of Verizon and predecessor Bell Atlantic from 1987 to 2011.

Marty Mislevy, one of Verizon Wireless' "test men," measuring the quality of the cellular network. These test men would become the basis of the famous "Can You Hear Me Now?" ads.

Verizon Fios takes to the streets of Manhattan to promote the release of Fios HD in 2007.

Dan Mead, executive vice president and president of strategic initiatives, with Apple's Tim Cook, announcing that the iPhone would be offered on Verizon's network, January 11, 2011.

Vittorio Colao, CEO of Vodafone, talks to Bloomberg Television after Verizon agrees to buy Vodafone's stake in Verizon Wireless, September 2, 2013.

CEO Lowell McAdam arrives at the 2017 Allen & Co. Media and Technology Conference in Sun Valley, Idaho.

McAdam talks to a Verizon worker on strike in 2016.

Tim Armstrong of AOL and Marni Walden, executive vice president
and president of global media at Verizon, speak at TechCrunch
Disrupt SF 2016 about Verizon's acquisition of AOL (top).
Armstrong unveiled Oath on Twitter (bottom).

John Stratton rose rapidly through the wireless ranks at Bell Atlantic after joining the company in 1993 and held senior positions in Verizon's wireless and wireline businesses before being named EVP and president of global operations in 2015.

Roger Gurnani served as chief information officer of Verizon Wireless from 2000 to 2005. He was named president of the wireless company's Western Area from 2005 to 2008 and then served as CIO of Verizon through 2014. In 2015, he was named EVP and chief information and technology architect. He retired from Verizon in 2017.

Marc Reed, executive vice president and chief administrative officer starting in 2001, helped Seidenberg develop and implement Verizon's multi-tiered, multi-year succession strategy as head of HR.

Business consultant Sandy Moose joined the Verizon board from the board of GTE in 2000 and played a vital role in many board decisions, including the rollout of Fios and the buyout of Vodaphone's interest in Verizon Wireless before stepping down from the board in 2014.

John Killian started with New England Telephone and held several Verizon wireline company positions before serving as chief financial officer from 2009 to 2010. He was also a contender to succeed Seidenberg as CEO.

A Verizon veteran of more than three decades, Chief Communications Officer Jim Gerace is a principal author of the Verizon Credo. He joined NYNEX Mobile Communications in 1986 as a manager in employee communications.

Joellen Brown led Verizon's executive communications team as executive director from 2000 through 2017 and served in a similar position with Bell Atlantic from 1984 to 2000.

As Verizon's head of strategic planning from 2003 to 2013, John Diercksen played a leading role in completing numerous mergers, acquisitions and divestitures for Verizon, including the purchase of Vodaphone's remaining stake in Verizon Wireless.

Verizon's longest-serving director joined the board of NYNEX in 1995. Richard Carrion has worked closely with Verizon CEOs Seidenberg and McAdam in helping them develop strategies that continue to transform the company.

Verizon Inc. Board of Directors, 2017

2000-2005

**M**arc Reed's career accelerated dramatically in February 2000, beginning with the call he took in his Dallas office one morning from Randy MacDonald, a longtime human relations mentor. MacDonald didn't have time for pleasantries. He was operating on what Reed, a 13-year GTE veteran, soon learned was Strigl time. "Can you get a suit?" MacDonald asked. "You need to be on an airplane, and you need to be in New York City by 5 o'clock to meet with Denny Strigl."

Reed hustled into a cab once he landed at LaGuardia Airport and arrived at the 1095 Avenue of the Americas offices just in time for his meeting with the CEO of Verizon Wireless, which at that point still existed only on paper. Strigl had done his homework on Reed, who had spent much of his career in HR helping to build GTE's wireless business. "We had the secret code of what it's like to work in wireless and the importance of this business," Reed said. Strigl spent an hour and a half drilling Reed on his approach to bureaucracy and his operating experiences.

Three days later, back in Dallas, Reed got a call from Strigl. "Look, I want to offer you a job to lead the HR function," Strigl said. "I don't know what your title is. I don't know what we're going to pay you. I don't really know where we're going to be housed. Currently we're in Bedminster, New Jersey, but there's the possibility of you being in Bedminster, or we could be in New York City at 1095. I have no idea. You don't have a team. You're going to have to form a team. We think we're going to launch this business in April, and I need to know now, are you in, or are you out?" Reed took a beat, while his heart skipped several. "I'm in," he said.

Reed returned to the East Coast, this time the wireless offices in Bedminster, New Jersey, with two days' worth of clothes in his suitcase for what he assumed was an introductory visit. He stayed two weeks. Strigl wanted the wireless business to be fully operational from day one. The Verizon senior leadership team was confident that the joint venture with Vodafone would be approved well before the merger of Bell Atlantic and GTE. Strigl called a senior staff meeting in his Bedminster office. "OK, today's Thursday. By Friday, you need to have your organization charts in to me. I want to see how you're building out your organizations." Reed not only had to build his own group's org chart, as head of HR he worked with Strigl in refining similar charts for the other departments. Verizon Wireless was about to become a reality.

## WIRELESS DRIVES CHANGE

Reed's experience was shared to varying degrees by leaders across Verizon Wireless business lines and across the country. Strigl and his team instilled a heightened sense of urgency and focus that extended Verizon Wireless' position as leader of the nationwide wireless pack. Continuous improvement was the company mantra as the first decade of the 2000s progressed. They worked hard, along with the rest of Verizon's senior leadership, to protect and nurture their hard-charging, entrepreneurial embrace of operating excellence.

The wireless joint venture structure—55 percent owned by Verizon, 45 percent by Vodafone—required a separate board of directors, which helped further focus the business on the competitive market as well as insulate the wireless business from Verizon's legacy operations. Facing a brutally competitive cellular marketplace nationwide, Verizon Wireless nonetheless doubled its subscriber base to 51 million by mid-decade mostly through organic growth of its existing high-quality network. As of 2005, Verizon's wireless revenues totaled $32.3 billion, closing in on its $37.6 billion in wireline revenues. Verizon led the wireless industry in customer growth and profitability, and Verizon Wireless received top industry rankings in the American Customer Satisfaction Index and the J.D. Power Customer Satisfaction Survey. Rivals, meanwhile, merged together separate systems to compete.

The Verizon Wireless team instilled a sense of almost unlimited possibilities for those who were willing to work hard and think big. Verizon Wireless' first chief operating officer and car-buff-in-chief, Lowell McAdam, used to connect with employees around the country using automobile metaphors. "Think about if you have a car. No matter how fast you go, you always know there's another gear. You can just shift into it. You can just keep going. Keep going. How cool would that be?"

## OPERATIONAL EXCELLENCE

The model of operational excellence set at the top of the company by the leadership team drove the wireless business as it entered a period of hockey-stick growth. Strigl, McAdam and their leadership team were acknowledged in real time by business friend and foe alike as the best in the business and the team to beat. To continue the legacy of engineering excellence, Bell Atlantic Mobile CTO Dick Lynch was named CTO of Verizon Wireless and Roger Gurnani was named vice president of information systems and chief information officer at Verizon Wireless. They were tasked with the immense challenge of integrating the disparate wireless systems to not only function as a single network but to achieve the best-in-business standards set by Bell Atlantic Mobile in terms of zero tolerance for dropped calls and related metrics.

The joint venture structure of Verizon Wireless, including a separate board of directors, reinforced the stand-alone nature of the business. But in many respects, that stance was a continuation of the intentional approach taken at Bell Atlantic toward nurturing its rapidly growing wireless business. Verizon Executive Vice President and President of Operations John Stratton joined Bell Atlantic Mobile in 1993 to help develop its retail strategy. He was named one of Verizon Wireless' seven area presidents in 2000. He said the strategy of insulating wireless was a very deliberate, long-standing one and that it came from the top.

"We were contained. It was a community," Stratton said. "I think Ivan was very deliberate about maintaining the separation of the new business from the existing business. That's understood today in terms of business strategy and the means by which someone grows a new incubation business," he said. "I'm not sure that was as well and clearly understood then, but Ivan obviously understood that was going to be important." Stratton added, "Even though the risk to the parent was the cannibalization of the parent by the young. It was going to happen anyway. So, we created a real separation."

Operating separately was the means to an end. And that end was maintaining and strengthening Verizon Wireless' position as not only the biggest but the most entrepreneurial player in the industry. "The value of our orientation and approach was that we were very agile as a business," Stratton said.

Strigl and the Verizon leadership team wanted Verizon Wireless to operate as Bell Atlantic Mobile on steroids. It was a tall order. Verizon Wireless was not just being created out of the four original wireless companies—Bell Atlantic, GTE, AirTouch and PrimeCo—each with its own systems and operating culture. Thanks to a handful of "fill-in" regional wireless acquisitions made between the time the Bell Atlantic-GTE merger was announced and concluded, including the purchase of a portion of Ameritech's wireless business and swaps of systems with other providers required by regulators, Verizon Wireless at birth was composed of nearly a dozen different wireless operating systems.

"We knew that we could build a great business, but it meant that we would have to manage the business at a level very close to the ground" to drive a coherent and unified approach across the businesses that were stitched together to form Verizon Wireless, Stratton said. "The exchange between our people and our customers was where the business happened. And I know that's true in every business, but it's not necessarily recognized in the management philosophy of every company," he added.

Strigl believed that every manager had to be involved and hands-on in running the business. That meant store visits, cell tower visits, many led by CTO Dick Lynch, and call center visits. And visits to competitors' stores. He wanted the company to be local in its focus and close to the market. He also believed it was necessary as a teaching tool to support employees. McAdam did the same thing.

Seidenberg said, "I observed Denny dozens of times as he sat and discussed the reasons for subpar results with an employee and watched him help employees focus on the right issues, lifting both their spirits and performance." Not that Strigl didn't have limits. "Granted, he had little patience for people who were glib or consistently underperformed. But he and Lowell clearly improved the overall effectiveness of the organization with their approach," Seidenberg said.

The wireless team improved not only its own results. Its approach drove improvement on the wireline side of the business as well. "What is most interesting to me is that in our culture, the financial, regulatory, engineering and legal functions were all well-oiled and superb," Seidenberg said. "Denny and Lowell elevated the operating, marketing and sales functions to new and higher levels of performance. And this was exactly what analysts and pundits said the former Bell companies could never do. Verizon was easily the best operating entity of any of the former AT&T companies," he added.

The idea that wireless was a separate business was helpful to the transformation of the company, Seidenberg realized. At times it was a balancing act. "My role was to nurture, develop and support this approach and not allow the traditional bureaucracy to slow progress," Seidenberg said. "As strong and independent as Denny was, he also knew the whole company had to succeed together."

When Verizon was formed, Seidenberg had Strigl report directly to him, rather than through Vice Chairman Larry Babbio, "so that wireless wouldn't be the third item on Larry's agenda." At the same time, he took pains to point out to Strigl that wireless' independence was very much a conscious decision on the part of the leadership team at Verizon Communications. Seidenberg required that wireless actively be a part of the larger company. He was happy that Strigl understood that it was important over the long term to build an integrated team. Strigl supported Seidenberg's repeated belief: "It's good to be part of something bigger."

To help attract and retain a highly motivated workforce, competitive pay packages and other incentives for eligible staff, including "phantom" stock options called value appreciation rights (VARs), which appreciated in step with the success of the wireless division in its formative years, were offered. The compensation package also aligned the interests of the employees with those of the customers and encouraged greater employee accountability. In addition, it led to a greater employee focus on customer service and the success of the company. The company took the position that, as a result, employee interests typically go beyond traditional union rules.

"Employees have the legal right to choose if they want to be represented by a union," Reed said. "Our thought process is that from a management perspective, we should run this business so there's never a question of whether or not employees would be better off with the union," he added. "The reason why wireless has not been organized is the fact that employees haven't seen a compelling reason to want to join a union." Of the 36,000 wireless employees at the time the wireless business launched, only 56 were union members. As of the end of 2016, less than 1 percent of the wireless workforce was unionized.

## OPERATING REVIEWS

Strigl and McAdam used quarterly operating reviews, which had been a key tool in driving the success of Bell Atlantic Mobile, and applied them to Verizon Wireless operating units across the country. Every quarter, Strigl took the entire senior wireless team to visit a region and conducted four different operating reviews, including meeting with customers and conducting town hall meetings with employees. These 16 operating reviews were in addition to the roughly 20 times a year the senior team visited the field to check on stores and hold sales rallies and other events. The culture of activism was and remains vitally important to Verizon.

## "WE LEARNED HOW TO EXECUTE"

Marni Walden, who had risen through the sales leadership ranks at AirTouch in the western United States, was named one of Verizon Wireless' regional presidents, based in Denver. The quarterly reviews at times were brutal for managers from AirTouch and GTE in particular, she said. They hadn't experienced as intense a focus on execution as had the Bell Atlantic leaders.

"We called it 'Survivor' because you didn't have to be the best at these operational views, but you couldn't be the worst," added Walden, who went on to become Verizon's executive vice president and president of product and new business innovation. "By God, we learned how to execute."

The important point then and now, said Walden, was for managers to recognize where they went wrong and realize what it would take to fix the problems. "It was never really about the actual result," she explained. "You have to deliver results eventually, but if you have bad results, then what you have to be able to do is talk about what you're doing to fix them. Eventually your fixes have to work, but you're never going to get fired for a bad result, at least the first time. But you've got to be able to talk about what you're doing."

Seidenberg would sit in on many wireless operational reviews around the country. He did so to demonstrate support for the wireless business and to bring back the best practices to the rest of the company. Even though the legacy business remained a successful, traditional business in most aspects, it did not yet face the intense competitive environment that existed in wireless. Seidenberg also helped reassure the rising stars of wireless that they were on the right track and that the reviews were designed to bring out their best. "Shake it off," he advised Walden after one review. "You know how you're going to fix it. Just go fix it."

Seidenberg credited Strigl for his management insights in building the wireless team, even if he did come on strong. "Denny knew how to identify the traits in leaders that would spur them to higher performance and help lead their teams. That's why he pushed them," Seidenberg said. "We were fortunate that we had Denny on our side."

Seidenberg also recalled that the momentum being generated by the wireless leadership team was attracting attention far beyond the company's network of stores. "I used to make presentations at Wall Street analyst meetings, and people would take me aside and say, 'What are you feeding these wireless guys?' I used to say, 'I'm not feeding them anything. I'm learning from them every day."

Not every lesson in wireless management had a happy ending. In the early months of building the business, Strigl fired a regional president in the middle of a quarterly operational review. As McAdam recalled, "Denny asked him what about this number? And he said, 'You know, I really have no idea; you probably have a better sense of this number than I do.' So, the answer was, 'Well, then I guess we don't need you.'"

For every one manager who washed out, there were hundreds who learned from the operating reviews and significantly improved their performance—and the service they provided to customers—from one review to the next. Verizon Wireless' senior management led by example. They demonstrated day in and day out that everyone had a hand in improving the wireless customer experience. No detail was too small, nor was it someone else's problem.

"Denny was an excellent teacher," Seidenberg said, "but Lowell was also extraordinary. Lowell was one of the best process-oriented engineers I've ever worked with. He would get to the root of problems and fix the process."

## CUSTOMER FOCUS

One of the bedrock rules of wireless management was that leaders needed to be in the stores and call centers to constantly monitor and improve upon the customer experience. McAdam estimated that he was in the field 70 percent of the time as COO. Strigl spent almost as much time visiting facilities as well. The two of them would even give Seidenberg a list of stores to visit unannounced when he was attending an event or a meeting in cities across the country. It wasn't long before store managers and their regional bosses understood that their performance was being constantly monitored and that they needed to constantly improve their game. Or they were gone.

One Friday, Strigl decided to visit stores in and around Natick, Massachusetts. He was annoyed that he couldn't see the sign for the Natick store and then was further annoyed when he pulled up and there were banners in Portuguese in front of the store. There was a sizable Spanish-speaking population in the area but few if any Portuguese speakers. The store manager couldn't explain why he had the signs up. He told Strigl that they'd been sent by corporate. Strigl called corporate marketing and was told that the manager was not supposed to use them if he didn't need them.

His anger mounting at the non-responses, Strigl called the regional president. He happened to be working out of Maine that Friday afternoon, a two-hour drive away. Strigl told him to come to the store and that he would be waiting for him. Meanwhile, Strigl toured the rest of the store and spotted dirty windows and a dirty restroom.

When the regional president arrived, Strigl made it clear that this ultimately wasn't the store manager's problem. He hadn't been properly trained or supervised. Strigl asked the president, when was the last time he had visited the store? Four or five months ago, the president said. Not a good answer, they both knew. The message spread quickly through the Verizon Wireless store network in the Northeast, and then across the country, that Strigl held regional presidents responsible for every store. Period.

As regional president, Walden was in the stores, meeting with customers, four out of five days a week. "I used to have rules for my team.

# CLEAN WINDOWS, BRIGHT LIGHTS

Store appearance was an obsession with the wireless leadership team. When district managers heard that Strigl, McAdam or another senior leader was in town, they let their store managers know that their windows had better be clean. It was like an all-points bulletin went out across the regional system, Walden said.

Once inside a store, McAdam would unscrew any burned-out lightbulb he found, sign it with a felt-tipped pen and mail it to the regional president. He then sent them a new bulb. "People hated to get a lightbulb signed by me," McAdam said. "But the metaphor stuck with them." Clean windows and bright stores quickly became Verizon Wireless' signature look. "I haven't found a lightbulb out in a store in years," McAdam said.

If you were running the stores, if you were a district manager, you needed to be in every one of your stores at least once a week. Not a drive-by. By the way, not in the back of the store, but on the floor working side by side with your employees and your customers . . . that just became a discipline that we all embraced. I think because I started in stores, that's where I always wanted to be anyway. I like that part of the business. I could run the point-of-sale systems. I knew the products. I could sell them. I would say most of our leadership inside Verizon did."

Verizon Wireless leaders insisted that the business revolve around the customer at all times and at every level. That meant, in a few cases, they were willing to make immediate management changes outside of the quarterly review process if they felt the company culture of operating excellence was being flouted. McAdam arrived at the Verizon Wireless store in Murfreesboro, Tennessee, one morning about 30 minutes before it was scheduled to open. Several customers were there as well, hoping to get in and out quickly before they went to their jobs. One of the customers knocked on the door. The manager came out and shouted, "Don't ever knock on the door again; we open at 8 o'clock."

At 8 o'clock, someone on staff unlocked the door and then disappeared into the employees-only back room. McAdam's ID literally opened every door at Verizon Wireless, so he joined the staff in the back room. "They all start yelling at me, saying, 'What are you doing back here?' And then I told them who I was, and I fired the store manager and the assistant manager on the spot and waited for the regional president," McAdam said. "I told him he was going to run the store until they got a store manager in there. And we spent a lot of time the next week or two explaining to them all the way up the chain about how stores get run and how you treat customers."

# CALL CENTERS

Call centers received as much attention as the retail store network. They were a window into what was working in the disparate collection of systems the company was stitching together to form Verizon Wireless, and what wasn't. "I used to take my team and go into a call center and listen to calls for two or three hours with the management team," McAdam said. "And we'd critique each call, and then we'd go back to say, 'OK, what about our product wasn't good? What about the network wasn't good? What about our training wasn't good?'"

In some of the worst-performing systems in 2000, 22 percent of calls were being dropped. While that was unacceptable, it was still better than the industry average, which was closer to 30 percent. Chief Technology Officer Dick Lynch and his team would get a list of locations where the most calls were being dropped and take steps to improve the service, often adding more cell tower coverage. Verizon executives from Seidenberg and Lee on down were asked to report when and where a call had been dropped as they used their cellphones across the country.

Where the problems with service and products were the most severe, the call-in rate was more than 150 percent. That meant that every customer on average was calling the company with a complaint more than one and a half times a month. In more established markets, the call-in rate was closer to 50 percent. Better, but unacceptable.

"All right, customers don't call us for entertainment purposes," McAdam would tell his staff in those early years. "The entire industry is providing poor service. Our products are messed up; our network isn't performing well; our sales and services aren't performing well; we're not billing properly." They addressed each issue using what today is referred to as the Lean Six Sigma approach. The dropped-call rate fell significantly over time, and the call-in rate, within a year or two, fell dramatically as well. Over the years, it was pushed continuously lower to the present rate of about 9 percent, though consumers increasingly use cellphone apps to contact customer service.

Verizon Wireless was also ahead of its rivals, and most Wall Street analysts, in understanding the importance of customer "churn" to its success. Anyone could sign up new customers. The trouble was that most rivals lost a high percentage of new customers over the course of a year and had to replace them with a new batch, hence the phrase "churn."

Led by David Benson, wireless vice president of strategic planning and business development, and Strigl, the leadership team focused on driving down customer churn, mainly by improving network performance and customer service. The Verizon Wireless churn rate in its first several years of existence was 5 to 7 percent a year.

"Everybody said they were managing it," but the industry churn rate was anywhere from 25 percent to 100 percent higher than Verizon Wireless' churn rate, Seidenberg said. Verizon Wireless' monthly churn rate was 2.3 percent in 2002 and just under 1.5 percent by 2005, while some competitors' rates ran as high as 3 percent. "If you look at the profitability of Verizon Wireless over the history of the company, it's explained in the fact that we have had the lowest churn in the entire industry," he said.

The focus on customers and results began to take hold, Stratton said. "Generally speaking, what you got to after the course of 15 to 18 months was the people who were running the business, the people who worked for the people who were running the business and the people who worked for them . . . had a much clearer focus on the fundamentals of the business, how we drove performance, how we grew the business, etc. So, with that, the culture of the business began to emerge."

# LEVERAGING THE BUSINESS

To get more bang for its wireless buck, in 2001 Verizon Wireless named Stratton chief marketing officer. It also consolidated handset and other buying decisions at the Verizon Wireless headquarters in New Jersey. "We said we're going to create a national business and we're going to build a national brand, and we're going to start to leverage our size, scale and scope," Stratton said.

Economies of scale deriving from nationwide footprints drove the economic models of Verizon Wireless and the rest of the wireless industry as the decade progressed. More than twice the size of its nearest competitor, Verizon Wireless ordered billions of dollars' worth of handsets at a time. "We would have, running with Motorola, a particular set of their flip phones at the time, and I'd put something on sale for a certain price, and it would be for six weeks," Stratton said. "If the sale ended on a Thursday, they might be 30 percent of my volume on Thursday, and then they'd be down to 3 percent of my volume on Friday. Because on Friday, bang, Samsung is in."

Verizon Wireless directly controlled nearly 60 percent of its handset sales through its stores or telemarketing. That helped make it the largest seller of wireless devices in the country. Rivals relied heavily on resellers like Best Buy, Circuit City and RadioShack, where their products often were one among many on display.

# "CAN YOU HEAR ME NOW?"

Strigl and McAdam felt pressured by consultants and others to launch a new advertising campaign in the first year of operations as Verizon Wireless. Strigl was happy with the Bell Atlantic Mobile campaign, "You're Only as Good as Your Last Call," with its focus on customer service and network quality. But he and McAdam had to admit that many of the campaigns used by some regional systems that were now part of Verizon Wireless, featuring everything from crying babies to possums hanging from a tree branch, were badly in need of updating. Rather than extend the Bell Atlantic Mobile campaign across the system, the leadership agreed to a new campaign, "Join In."

It didn't take long for Strigl to admit that he hated it. "It was more geared to us bragging about ourselves," he complained. "No customers wanted to be part of the team, whatever that meant. So, after a period of about six months on that strategy, we saw our sales going down," he said. "We weren't going anywhere." Out went the campaign, and the ad agency.

CMO Stratton was meeting with representatives from a new agency, a unit of the Interpublic Group of Companies, in late 2001. They grappled with how to convey differentiation between Verizon Wireless and the competition. Price wars were all the rage. No differentiation there, plus the price-cutting had a direct and painful impact on the bottom line. Cool phones, from Nokia or Motorola, attracted customers first to the phone maker's brand and only indirectly to the service provider. Besides, there was always a new phone coming soon.

One day they were going through a pile of newspaper clippings about Bell Atlantic Mobile that Gerace's communications team had generated during the 1990s. The articles that caught their attention were the ones about Dick Lynch's engineers who drove around the region in station wagons testing system quality. Most of the focus back then was on the carload of test gear and the miles driven, the findings about network quality, etc.

Then the idea hit them. Personify the process. Take the test man out of the test car. As Gerace recalled, "At the beginning, we weren't trying to communicate we were the best network. We were trying to communicate, 'We care more about the network quality than anybody else.' That's why we have these guys who test it everywhere."

Strigl and McAdam loved it. "One day they came in with this strategy that just sunk in," Strigl said. "I mean, it just hit us hard. And it was this little test guy roaming around the country saying, 'Can you hear me now?'"

The ad campaign launched on January 14, 2002. It featured New York actor Paul Marcarelli playing the role of a Verizon Wireless technician who the agency called Testman. More than 100 spots aired over the next few years as Testman traversed the country, visiting urban locations and remote fields and mountains. He demonstrated the attention Verizon Wireless paid to network quality with his signature question and parting "good." The campaign's goal, according to the ad agency, was "to position Verizon Wireless as a superior wireless company that relentlessly strives to be the most reliable national wireless provider in the country."

By 2003 Verizon Wireless was spending several hundred million dollars a year on the campaign. The tagline question "Can You Hear Me Now?" quickly became a staple of pop culture references in contexts varying from politics to parody, raising the campaign's iconic profile at no extra cost. More importantly, it had a direct and very positive impact on Verizon Wireless' results.

The campaign's focus on quality established Verizon Wireless as the champagne of cellphone service providers. Customers wanted quality cellphone service and were willing to pay for it. Verizon Wireless was able to maintain average monthly service revenue per customer of $49 and resist further price-cutting as the campaign caught fire. As Marvin Davis, Verizon Wireless' vice president for advertising, told *USA Today* at the height of the campaign, "Our brand message is important, because the market recognizes it's a higher-quality service. People are willing to pay more to get more."

During the first year of the campaign, Verizon Wireless' sales grew over 10 percent. Its subscriber base jumped from 29.4 million people in early 2002 to 37.5 million in 2003 and 43.8 million by the end of 2004. "Dick Lynch and his network team were going crazy trying to keep up with the number of new customers that were added," Strigl said. Acquisitions of a number of smaller wireless providers during this period also contributed modestly to the increase in the subscriber base.

It is hard to overestimate the impact and brilliance of the new ad campaign. The team conceived of the ad based on the organic actions and culture of the company. They tapped into the core culture of wireless, and the message rang true for customers across the country. The tag line was so memorable it dominated the telecommunications industry, and its impact has never been equaled. The "Can You Hear Me Now?" campaign and the success it generated powered Verizon to a higher gear than anyone else in the industry.

# TECHNOLOGY UPGRADES

The influx of customers added to the tension surrounding the creation of Verizon Wireless' annual wireless capital spending budgets of more than $4 billion in its early years. Wireless leadership was in a constant battle to adequately fund the business and to get the most out of its capital spending dollars. As McAdam said, "We were in the 'spend every penny you can get your hands on because you'll have a competitive advantage' mode."

McAdam added, "We probably could have spent double what we got." That led to constant pressure to wring the most out of every dollar spent. The team was constantly asking itself, "OK, how do you build it for 70 percent of what it cost you to build last year? That was part of the higher gear" approach to continuous improvement, McAdam said. "I was trying to figure out how to build stores cheaper, how to take fewer calls in the call centers and get satisfaction up." Dick Lynch wrestled with, "How do I build a tower, instead of for $250,000, for $200,000?"

Rapid growth and expansion propelled personnel costs higher as well. Verizon Wireless hired thousands of employees a year during this period as it raced to adequately staff its ballooning business. Marc Reed and his HR team excelled at creating an efficient process that brought in qualified job candidates at facilities across the country and emphasized the company's core cultural values and principles that would be enshrined in the Credo. Reed also played an important role in identifying and developing hundreds of senior managers in the early years of Verizon Wireless' growth spurt. His work was greatly appreciated by Strigl, and he caught the attention and earned the respect of Seidenberg, too.

McAdam also credited the joint venture structure of Verizon Wireless and the input from the CFOs who originated from Vodafone, which did not share Bell Atlantic's heritage of investing heavily in wireless technology, for driving ever more efficient use of capital. "Andy Halford from Vodafone was all over the cost side," McAdam said. His successor as CFO from Vodafone, John Townsend, was nicknamed "the bulldog," McAdam said. "He just ground every number into the ground until we were sure we were efficient."

Vodafone wasn't the only one cocking an eyebrow at Verizon Wireless' capex plans in its formative years. Many investment professionals had been expecting baby steps. "When we told analysts we were going to spend $4 billion a year in capex for our wireless group, they were merciless," Verizon CFO Toben told *Fortune* magazine in 2004. "They all pointed out that Sprint was only spending $2 billion a year, and AT&T wasn't spending as much. Well, not a one of them bothers me anymore about the capital budget there. The quality of the network was the strategic advantage, and it needed the investment," Toben said.

The boom in customers generated by the "Can You Hear Me Now?" ad campaign was followed within a few years by Verizon Wireless' next industry-leading upgrade in wireless technology to third-generation, or 3G, technology. New customers, in many cases, were finding that Verizon Wireless offered a broader, richer cellular experience than their previous carrier.

In September 2003 Verizon Wireless started testing 3G in markets in and around Washington, D.C., and San Diego. The service, a faster, broadband version of CDMA dubbed Evolution-Data Optimized (EV-DO), rolled out nationwide beginning in January 2004. Verizon Wireless was the first U.S. provider to launch the service in major markets. Strigl said the new service offered "tremendous speed, rich graphic content, video, music and more."

The new technology rollout carried an estimated cost of $1 billion for 2004 and 2005. But it also created new revenue streams, noted

# "PARENT COMPANY REPELLANT"

Each success and continued spurt of subscriber growth reinforced the tendency of the Verizon Wireless leadership team to keep its joint venture corporate parents at arm's length. McAdam admitted, "I was probably one of the big perpetrators of this. It was close the door, lower the shades in your office, put a chair up against the door handle, and when people knocked on the door, be quiet so they don't think you're there." While he admits to a bit of hyperbole, he doesn't apologize. "We were the shiny toy . . . everybody wants to come in, and they hug you to death." He draws a parallel to recent history and his insistence that AOL, purchased by Verizon in 2015, be operated separately.

The tension between Verizon Wireless and its parents played out across multiple levels of the organization. Verizon Communications' Public Affairs and Communications EVP Mary Beth Bardin brought together the communications teams from the company's different departments in 2002 to enable them to get to know each other better and work more effectively together. During one session, a representative from each group performed a skit intended to serve as an icebreaker and to convey a sense of the group's internal culture.

Jim Gerace represented the Verizon Wireless communications team and decided to spoof the business' intense focus on its separate culture. He took a spray water bottle and squirted it around the stage, saying the bottle contained "parent company repellant." He received plenty of laughs. Unbeknownst to Gerace, Seidenberg had quietly joined the group in the back of the room and witnessed his performance. The parent company CEO delivered a performance of his own, joking with the group that effective immediately Gerace had been reassigned to the wireline business in West Virginia.

CMO Stratton. Within a few years of the 3G launch, Verizon Wireless had built a music-streaming business. "This was the beginning of downloading technology onto a non-smartphone. Smartphones didn't exist at the time." While ahead of the crowd, the service wasn't a significant moneymaker for the company. In retrospect, the streaming business would serve as an example of how Verizon could have been more effective at monetizing services running on its enhanced networks.

# COMMON USER INTERFACE

At the same time as 3G was rolling out across the Verizon Wireless system, the company launched an additional technology in 2004 that attracted and retained even more customers. Verizon Wireless' clout in the handset market was so significant that it was able to push handset providers to include a common Verizon Wireless interface on all their phones sold through Verizon Wireless. That meant customers increasingly identified their phones as Verizon products, not those of LG, Nokia or Motorola. It also simplified the process of upgrading or switching phones if customers could focus on a common set of commands. And it greatly reduced Verizon Wireless' servicing costs, since most customer questions focused around a common set of steps, not a string of commands that were different for every phone.

Handset providers bristled at sharing their handset brand identity with the service provider, but most accepted it as the cost of doing business through the nation's largest cellular service provider. Verizon Wireless and Motorola were locked in a standoff lasting about five months over Motorola's highly popular Razr flip phones. Motorola refused to include the Verizon Wireless user interface on the Razr initially. It finally gave in and agreed to the interface in order to capture sales through the Verizon Wireless channel.

# VERIZON WIRELESS CREDO

Gerace, like many Verizon leaders, was actively involved in several outside philanthropic efforts at the same time he was helping to build the wireless business. He was attending a board meeting for a nonprofit group in 2003 that was being held at the headquarters of health care giant Johnson & Johnson in New Brunswick, New Jersey. While waiting in the company's lobby, he noticed its corporate values were literally carved in stone on the walls. He felt as if McAdam had just mailed him a new lightbulb.

Gerace had been gathering many of Strigl's management maxims dating back to the days of Bell Atlantic Mobile. Seeing the display at Johnson & Johnson and reviewing in his mind the progress being made at Verizon Wireless, he decided it was time for the wireless business to pull together its core operating principles and values in a consolidated fashion. With little trouble he came up with two pages of a yellow legal pad filled with the values that were driving the success of Verizon Wireless.

His work coincided with Strigl's mounting frustration, as January 2004 approached, that he didn't have anything new to say in his concluding remarks to the group's annual leadership conference that included more than 130 people. For three years in a row, he had concluded with a summary that became known as "Denny's What's Important." "It was always very culture-oriented. How to lead, how to cast the shadow of a leader," Gerace said.

That year he looked out at the crowd and said, "I just want to read something to you." And then he read Gerace's handiwork, what would become known as the Verizon Wireless Credo, word for word. Gerace hadn't been expecting to hear his notes read to the crowd and was more than a little nervous about what the reaction would be. His anxiety was heightened by the fact that sitting next to him was Seidenberg. As much as the bulk of the Credo dovetailed with the Verizon Promise that had been created in 2002, some of the points clearly defined wireless as a breed apart. Seidenberg nodded his head in agreement, and the Credo was in business.

Out in the audience, "you could hear a pin drop," Stratton said. Strigl "moves through this discussion about our values, what we aspire to be, and essentially articulates in this couple of paragraphs the essence of the culture that we were beginning to form and build," Stratton added. "It was really quite something."

The Credo, Stratton said, "became, for us, a catalyst to accelerating the momentum we had as a business. It sharpened our focus. It became a living, breathing set of guidelines and ideas that kept us on track, kept us from drifting off purpose and ultimately was maybe one of the most important things that we used to develop and build that business."

# THE CREDO

We have work because our customers value our high quality wireless communications service.

A dropped or incomplete call is not acceptable. Everything we do we build on a strong network foundation. The quality and reliability of the product we deliver is paramount. Customers pay us to provide them with a wireless communications service that they can rely on.

We focus outward on the customer, not inward. We make it easy for customers to do business with us, by listening, anticipating and responding to their needs.

We know our products and can explain them to customers. We plan less and execute more. We are accountable and we follow through with a sense of urgency. We know that having the highest ethical standards is a competitive advantage. We view having a clean store window as more important than having a corner office.

We know teamwork enables us to serve our customers better and faster. We embrace diversity and personal development not only because it's the right thing to do, but also because it's smart business.

We are driven not by ego but by accomplishments. We respect and trust one another, communicating openly, candidly and directly since any other way is unfair and a waste of time. We don't need witnesses or paper trails to our conversations. Our word is enough. We voice our opinion and exercise constructive dissent, and then rally around the agreed upon action with our full support. Any one of us can deliver a view or idea to anyone else, and listen to and value another's view regardless of title or level. Ideas live and die on their merits rather than where they were invented.

We believe integrity is at the core of who we are. It establishes the trust that is critical to the relationships we have.

We are committed to do the right thing and follow sound business practices in dealing with our customers, suppliers, owners and competitors. Our competitors are not enemies; they are challengers. We are good corporate citizens and share our success with the community to make the world in which we work better than it was yesterday.

We know that bigness is not our strength, best is our strength.

Bureaucracy is an enemy. We fight every day to stay "small" and keep bureaucracy out. We are more agile than companies a fraction of our size, because we act fast and take risks every day. We see crisis and change as opportunities, not threats. We run to a crisis, not away. Change energizes us. We work hard, take action and get things done. Our actions produce measurable results.

We work 24x7 because our customers depend on us 24x7. We know our best was good for today. Tomorrow we'll do better.

We are Verizon Wireless.

# IF NOT THE BIGGEST, BE THE BEST

Since its formation in 2000, Verizon Wireless proudly promoted the fact that it was America's largest cellular service provider. Network quality was a constant message as well, of course. But part of the group's cultural swagger came from the fact that wireless was the big dog in town. No. 2 wasn't even nipping at its heels. At year-end 2003, Verizon Wireless had 37.5 million subscribers, compared to second-ranked Cingular Wireless' 24 million. Verizon Wireless accounted for 30 percent of Verizon's total revenues that year, and its operating income totaled $4.1 billion, up 12 percent year over year.

Cingular Wireless was formed in 2000 by the merger of BellSouth's wireless operations into those of SBC Communications. In 2004, Cingular Wireless acquired AT&T Wireless. That catapulted the combined company to the front of the wireless business pack, ahead of Verizon Wireless.

Verizon Wireless adjusted to the new reality and doubled down on emphasizing the quality of its service and network. This was not out of character. The Credo already included the statement, "We know that bigness is not our strength, best is our strength."

Within just a few years, Verizon Wireless had established itself as a dominant industry player that was rewriting the terms of cellular communication in real time and setting new standards of quality in an emerging industry while remaining true to Verizon's heritage of providing quality customer products and service.

Verizon allocated increasing amounts of capital to the wireless business. Wireless was clearly on a trajectory to provide an ever-larger contribution to the parent company's top as well as bottom line. The success of wireless was a testament to the company's overall growth strategy and its willingness to identify and nurture nontraditional business lines.

At the same time, the success of wireless demonstrated the importance of focusing growth on segments of the telecommunications industry where regulation favored market-driven solutions. Building on that understanding, Verizon turned to its wireline business even as wireless was just beginning its meteoric growth. To revitalize its traditional wireline business, Verizon bet that it could take lightly regulated fiber-optic cable technology and bridge the so-called last mile to the customer's home. The leadership team decided it was a bet the company couldn't afford not to make. No one knew whether fiber optics would prove a successful bridge to the future for the wireline business or turn out to be a bridge too far.

# BECOMING NO.1: C-SUITE INSIGHTS FROM RAM CHARAN

___ **TECH DISCONTINUITY DRIVES DESTINY.**
Address head on the classic dilemma: Legacy dominance versus reallocating resources to build a new business. Pivot to the future.

___ **GO BIG FAST.**
Build scale and your geographic footprint faster than the competition.

___ **CUSTOMERS FIRST.**
Customers are the reason we are in business. All decisions are driven by what will meet customer needs and demands.

___ **GOOD TODAY, BETTER TOMORROW.**
Successful companies are always shifting to a higher gear.

___ **NEW BUSINESS, NEW RULES.**
Create new rules for a new business so it isn't constrained by old ways of thinking, doing or regulating.

# 07

# FUTURE-PROOF
# THE CORE

## 2001-2006

T he bell was tolling for the local phone industry's historical land-line business by 2001. That year's first quarter marked the last time Verizon Communications reported a quarterly increase in its number of copper "access lines" providing phone service and di-al-up internet access. Quarterly contractions followed. The trend re-verberated across the industry.

Rapidly growing wireless operations, while boosting revenues at Veri-zon and other parent companies, were cannibalizing the very wireline business that for years had funded their growth. At the same time, cable TV companies were taking broadband access market share from Verizon and other phone companies. Even the addition of second phone lines in homes to provide digital subscriber line (DSL) internet access, which provided added support for the wireline business as of the late 1990s, would start to slow within a few quarters as well. The downturn in the traditional wireline business was the local phone in-dustry's first sustained drop in access lines since the Great Depression. The decline showed no sign of reversing, and it would accelerate fast-er in the years to come than most could have imagined at the time.

Verizon Executive Vice President Paul Lacouture and Chief Tech-nology Officer Mark Wegleitner spent their careers building and enhancing landline networks. They were not going down without a fight. Neither was their boss, Vice Chairman Larry Babbio. Even as the landline business was peaking, they and their team were refining a plan years in the making to leapfrog the access line competition. They were determined to create a new growth opportunity for the landline business and the tens of thousands of employees serving Verizon's local phone customers. Their goal, said Lacouture, was to "future-proof" the landline business.

They proposed running fiber-optic cable, which the industry had been using for decades in high-capacity, intercity and corporate phone lines, all the way to the residential customer's house. That would enable Verizon to offer a telecommunications industry-beating package of phone, internet and video services over a single fast, efficient and low-maintenance glass fiber line. The plan would be dubbed fiber-optic services, or Fios.

It was an audacious plan that would effectively leapfrog the industry status quo, rather than mark another incremental improvement in technology and service. They were positioning Verizon for an internet-driven, video-centric broadband future that was not yet fully realized in the first several years of Verizon's existence. A radical redesign of the network was the only solution for carrying data and video traffic.

The stakes couldn't have been higher. "What our internal team realized was that the deterioration of the core business and loss of market share was such a severe issue that it could threaten the viability of the local landline business," Seidenberg said.

There were plenty of technical hurdles to clear. There was also one major business challenge involved with bringing Fios to market—its staggering price tag. They were proposing to spend more than $20 billion over five years for the fiber-to-the-home service that would reach about 18 million of Verizon's residential wireline customers. "It was a bet the ranch" investment, said John Diercksen, senior vice president of investor relations, who would assume the top strategy role at

Verizon in 2003. The fiber buildout was among the largest planned private sector capital expenditures in the United States at the time it was announced.

# MAKING THE CASE FOR FIBER

Verizon wireline engineers had been studying extending fiber-optic cable further into the phone system network, meaning closer to the customer, since even before the breakup of AT&T. Cable company rivals were using high-capacity fiber in portions of their coaxial cable networks as well. Optical signal compression and other technological advances over the years made the extension of fiber deeper into the system more realistic and cost-effective.

The advantages of fiber were considerable. Glass fiber, even in its early iterations, was roughly 10 times faster than cable broadband connections and 20 times faster than copper-wire connections, making it perfectly suited to internet access use. For the same reason, tests showed it was ideal for bringing video to the home. It also proved more resilient in many situations and required less maintenance once installed than copper lines.

DSL lines were an interim solution with limited appeal. "We had been trying to compete in broadband by using DSL, which was a service that you offer over copper wires," Babbio said. "You really couldn't get the speed much above a megabit and a half. Maybe if you really worked at it, you could get up to 2 or 3 megabits. But we knew that the cable companies could beat that all the time," Babbio said. Plus, in many cases cable modems were much easier for consumers to use compared to the connections required for DSL lines.

Babbio had his team at Bell Atlantic testing different scenarios during the 1990s to determine what benefits could be derived from fiber under different conditions and buildouts. Cost remained a stumbling block to bringing fiber all the way to the home. Then-rival NYNEX had proposed taking fiber all the way to customers' homes as early as 1993 but never went forward with the concept, for cost and other reasons. Two years later Bell Atlantic's Stargazer service had used fiber-optic lines to carry video offerings to homes in a limited, short-lived test in northern Virginia. "We could never get to the point of the installation costs being equal, but we could get to the point where the fiber was economical," said Babbio. "Economical means maybe we'd be willing to spend 10 or 15 percent more for the fiber than we did for a normal installation. And we would try to recover [the cost] other ways."

## SIEGE MENTALITY

Their work was being followed, somewhat anxiously, by Verizon's senior wireline officials. Virginia Ruesterholz rose through the NYNEX and then Bell Atlantic wireline management ranks to serve as one of Verizon's top wireline officers, and one of the most senior women, in the company as of the early 2000s. The business was under siege from the cable industry, and leadership was keenly aware that they needed to have a new competitive weapon, Ruesterholz said.

"I think that we might have looked at something like Fios four or five times prior to finally launching it. We were really starting to lose a lot of market share," she said. Cable companies "were stealing our customers. They had the bundle. We couldn't compete. They were cleaning our clock." Babbio was meeting with Lacouture one day when he said that enough was enough. "We need to do something about competing in the 21st century." After all their tests and false starts, "don't you think we might as well take fiber all the way to the home?" Babbio asked. Lacouture agreed, noting that they could make a clear case that the cost savings of stopping at the curb were outweighed by the greater speeds and bandwidth realized by taking fiber all the way to the home. That would give Verizon a clear competitive advantage. "We kept getting closer and closer, and eventually we said, you know, I think we can get there" in terms of total costs, said Babbio.

Babbio was also insistent that this would have to be an all-in commitment on Verizon's part. "If we're going to do it, we can't do another trial. We can't do 20,000, 40,000 lines," Babbio said. "We should do a million the first year. The only way we can get enough momentum and seriousness around this is to put that stake in the ground and do a million lines," he added.

Cost was only one of several key issues around the use of fiber that needed to be resolved. "There's a lot of other work that needs to be done because you just can't build a fiber network. You must have something to put over it. And the only way we're going to make this work is that we have to actually provide just not voice and data. We need to provide TV as well,"

## GANG OF SIX

In the early days of considering taking fiber to the home, Verizon, SBC and BellSouth— SBC and BellSouth had yet to merge—worked together to try to formulate common standards among suppliers of optical fiber and related equipment who would be needed to support the fiber-to-the-home effort. Two officials from each company met as what Lacouture, one of the Verizon representatives, dubbed the Gang of Six. They made some headway, but the other two companies' enthusiasm for taking fiber all the way to the home cooled, apparently for cost and other reasons. That left Verizon as the industry pioneer in beating a new path to the customers' door.

Babbio said. "But to get into the TV business, you just can't say 'OK, I have a network. Now I have to have the rights to all the different channels for all the different products and everything else.'"

So, the fiber team created a business case to prove that Fios would be a viable investment. Their first stop was Verizon's senior wireline leadership. It was not an easy sell. Jim Cullen, the head of the business until he retired in mid-2000, and Doreen Toben, CFO of the wireline business at the time, initially were among the skeptics when it came to whether Fios would ever produce an appropriate return on investment.

As Toben recalled, "The engineers, there was no doubt in their minds—now they didn't pay a whole lot of attention (this is an understatement) to the cost—that Fios was a better product. And it is. I mean there's no question."

The problem from the point of view of Cullen, Toben, John Killian and others, was that AT&T was known to be advocating a plan to take fiber to the neighborhood, not all the way into the customer's house, at a cost estimated at roughly $4 billion to $5 billion. That was still a hefty price tag, but only a fraction of what Babbio's team was proposing to spend. SBC, which would buy AT&T in 2005 and take the AT&T name, was also taking fiber to the neighborhood during this period.

Was the higher-quality Fios approach worth the difference in price? Might it be a better investment to take at least a portion of the money they would spend on Fios and buy back their company's stock instead? As Babbio recalled, "there were a lot of people in finance who thought that we were crazy."

Seidenberg sided with the engineers over the financial planners. He was convinced from his early years working on the copper-wire network that copper wires were not the future, no matter how much AT&T planned to tweak the classic twisted pair. "I worked on the outside plant, I fixed copper lines and I knew that wouldn't work," Seidenberg said. "AT&T came out with the full pair, bonded . . . and we said, 'Eventually, it's going to run out of gas.' And both Larry and I from our Bell Labs days knew that fiber was not an untested technology. It would work and work well. The issue was the cost to install and the operations challenge to rebuild the entire outside plant. So to us this was a decision of conviction and a bet on the future. Interestingly, the naysayers were all focused on the financial case. No one ever challenged the technology vision."

The Fios team won over the financial skeptics, though it took detailed analysis, major interactions with suppliers and months upon months of meetings with every stakeholder. One of the key arguments concerned long-term operating costs. They persuaded the operating leadership that over several years the lower projected maintenance costs would make the numbers work in Fios' favor, despite the hair-raising initial investment. The key was scaling it across a large number of customers. "There was no question this was a gut-wrenching decision for the company," Seidenberg said. "Looking back, this is a clear example of balancing the short-term versus the long-term interests of the company."

## INVOLVING THE BOARD

Babbio began the process of educating and persuading the Verizon board about Fios. It would be a multi-year effort—sidelined for months by the company's all-hands-on-deck response to the terrorist attacks on September 11, 2001—and one that engaged the board members in the intimate details of the present and future operating plant. In terms of both scale and scope, the process also provided a template for the board's active engagement in the growth and evolution of Verizon in the years ahead.

The Fios team asked the board to make certain assumptions about the future. "We presented the case to the board by explaining, look, we're here in 2001. Does anybody think 10 years from now we're still going to be putting in copper wires?" Babbio said. "And most people would say probably not. That was 2010. OK, 20 years? And everybody would say no, no, no. Ten? How about five?"

It was a question of when Verizon and the industry would upgrade much of the wireline plant to fiber, not if, Babbio argued. "We're not talking about spending extra money. We're talking about advancing money," he said as he made the case during repeated meetings with the board in 2002 and into 2003.

Director Sandy Moose, who played a lead role while on the GTE board in researching and advocating the use of CDMA wireless technology, was once again out front in grappling with the issues surrounding Fios. While other directors were skeptical at first of Babbio's pulling the capital expenditure forward argument, Moose was quick to grasp the stakes involved. In fact, she became so deeply involved in the Fios strategy that she began presenting it as a case study at MIT's Sloan School of Management a few years after Fios was introduced.

## CAPEX REDUX

Moose estimated that the cost of Fios was about $4 billion more than the projected cost of maintaining the wireline plant over four to five years. A large number to be sure, and in excess of merely "advancing" future expenditures, to use Babbio's term, but directors understood that such figures fell within the range of multibillion-dollar annual expenditures they were accustomed to considering.

# FIBER UNBOUND

Verizon was motivated to take fiber all the way to the customer's home to build the best-in-class wireline network, just as it had created the best wireless network in Verizon Wireless. But there was another reason to make fiber the "last mile" connection between Verizon and its broadband customers. Unlike the requirement to share its copper access lines with telecommunications rivals, new rules of the road meant Verizon would have its fiber customers all to itself.

Seidenberg, EVP Tom Tauke and EVP and General Counsel Bill Barr in Washington, as well as Randy Milch and other attorneys, had been pushing back on what they considered heavy-handed FCC and state-level regulation of their networks for years. They focused on the use of fiber as a key differentiator. Running fiber to consumers' homes fostered competition for the last mile of access, one of the FCC's major concerns since the passage of the '96 Telecommunications Act. It didn't stifle it. In 2003 the FCC essentially agreed, saying that companies would not have to allow competitors access to "mass-market fiber to the premises loops." That gave the Fios team a green light, knowing that once they set the fiber table, their rivals would not be able to swoop in and enjoy a free lunch with their customers.

"The cable companies were going to completely obliterate the telephone companies, if we let them, by upgrading their coax [cable] to carry video," Seidenberg said. "The only way to do this would be to put as much fiber as we could and return to the regulatory people and say, 'Can you get the regulators to regulate fiber differently than copper?' And they did."

"Fiber was all about creating a [new] wing to the company," Seidenberg said, using the phrasing he had applied to running the unregulated businesses at NYNEX while still a young executive. Then as now, he said, the value of the strategy wasn't immediately clear, especially to Wall Street and investors. "That was a way for me," Seidenberg said, "to put in motion the strategies that would, in effect, make the telephone company a valuable asset over time."

For instance, in 2002 and 2003, while weighing Fios, the Verizon board approved annual wireline capital expenditures of $8 billion and $6.8 billion, respectively. Domestic wireless capital expenditures came to $4.4 billion in 2002 and $4.6 billion in 2003.

Director Tom O'Brien, former chairman and CEO of PNC Financial Group, appreciated the diligence displayed by the Fios team. "They brought us along, so to speak. They never just came and said, 'Hey, we have a nice new program we want to talk to you about,'" O'Brien said. "This would occur over many meetings that were sort of in preparation that this was something that they really think they may want to do," he added. "There were a lot of discussions about whether it was going to work. And who's going to buy it? And why do you think we can offer this and outcompete cable companies and other people? I think they felt very strongly that their technology was superior and . . . their customer service was superior."

O'Brien and other directors were concerned that customers might not appreciate or be willing to pay for the value Fios was going to deliver in terms of quality and quantity, or speed of video and internet services. Not only was AT&T's solution cheaper to install than Fios, so was existing cable service. What if these competitors launched a price war in the midst of Verizon's Fios rollout? That would likely reduce demand for Fios and make it harder for the venture to ever earn a return on the capital deployed to build the fiber system.

The Fios team readily admitted that there was a risk involved in making such a major investment in Fios. But, as with every major decision Seidenberg and his team proposed over the years, there was a significant risk in doing nothing as technology, consumer tastes and the competitive landscape continued to evolve. The board understood that the threats the company faced, especially from cable TV, were too great to ignore.

Babbio said two key arguments swayed the board:

> Number one, it was a lot more reliable. Number two, we'd get into the TV business. And everybody knows that the only way that we were going to keep the landline and internet was to keep the cable company out of the house. And you only keep the cable company out of the house if you can offer TV service. If cable is in there with you, their incremental cost of providing phone and

broadband is so small that they could knock you out of the house immediately. On the other hand, our incremental cost of providing TV is a little higher, but if we don't do it, cable's in the house.

So, that was the entire focus of the strategy: Get cable out of the house. And when we did the business case, we said if we could keep cable out of the house, if we could get penetration of one-third of the homes that we equipped, and one-third of them take TV, then we have a good business case. As a matter of fact, TV makes the case.

## "THE CONVERGENCE REVOLUTION"

Seidenberg, Babbio and the engineering team were consistent in their view that Fios was an investment in the network of the future. In the fall of 2003 the Verizon board approved the phased-in launch of Fios, to begin the following year. Verizon Director O'Brien called the approval of Fios "one of the most courageous decisions that the management and the board made." He described the investment in Fios as "a massive, massive risk. It was a considered risk. And it was looking at the long term, and it's worked out quite well for them. But that was no easy decision."

Seidenberg formally announced the plan in January 2004 at the annual Consumer Electronics Show (CES) held in Las Vegas. To launch the first phase of the rollout, the goal was to run Fios past 1 million homes by year-end 2004 and another 2 million in 2005. He said that Fios catered to the burgeoning consumer demand for an "all-broadband, all-the-time lifestyle."

# VERIZON JOINS THE DOW JONES INDUSTRIAL AVERAGE

Verizon EVP of Corporate Communications Mary Beth Bardin focused intently on helping establish the Verizon brand in the company's early years. Verizon had tremendous visibility among investors as the 10th largest U.S. company as ranked by Standard & Poor's, with revenues of $67.8 billion for 2003. Among consumers it had very high recognition thanks to its ubiquitous advertising, including the famous "Can You Hear Me Know?" wireless campaign.

But Bardin had been lobbying intently yet unsuccessfully to have Verizon included in a very exclusive corporate club: the 30 stocks that comprise the Dow Jones Industrial Average. Adding to her sense of frustration was the fact that rival Baby Bell SBC, with $43.1 billion in revenues, had been added to the Dow in 1999. And former parent AT&T remained a fixture among the 30 Dow stocks, as it had been since 1935, even though it was barely half Verizon's size, with $34.5 billion in revenue.

Finally, in early 2004, Bardin received the call she had been waiting for. Verizon would be added to the DJIA. She tracked down Seidenberg in Babbio's office and interrupted a meeting to share the good news. "We were so happy, just congratulating each other," she said. "That, for me, was the day that Verizon got on the map."

Their sense of accomplishment was made sweeter by the fact that Verizon was replacing AT&T. Ma Bell would return to join the Dow 30 stocks in 2005, when SBC bought the company and took AT&T as its married name. Verizon remained the last Bell standing after Apple Computer Inc. replaced AT&T among the Dow 30 stocks in 2015.

"Our broadband networks will be uniquely capable of unleashing the full potential of convergence to the marketplace," Seidenberg told the CES attendees. "Unlike cable networks designed for broadcasting, Verizon's networks are designed for communicating. As we deploy more and more broadband, we will bring all the power of true, two-way multimegabit capability—upstream and downstream—to the mass market." That, he said, was "the key" to the "next phase of the convergence revolution."

"After the announcement at the Consumer Electronics Show, we began a round of meetings with analysts and shareowners. The reaction could not have been worse," Seidenberg said. "Investors thought this was a poor decision because we could never really compete with cable, and they preferred we use shareowner capital to invest in other businesses. No one believed that over time, fiber assets and wireless were the more powerful combination to position the company for growth. The stock took a beating. The board was not particularly happy, and the game was on."

With Fios formally approved and publicly announced, the real work started for Babbio and his team. One group oversaw negotiating agreements with video content providers. Another was "established to develop all the technology that we need. The fiber at this point is kind of the relatively easy part," he recalled.

Initially Verizon contracted with Motorola to design set-top boxes consumers would use to operate the system. Microsoft was brought in to develop the software to run the boxes. After more than six months, Verizon realized there was a major disconnect between its business partners and itself. "Microsoft developed such a complicated piece of software to run your set-top box and gave you the guide and do all your programming that it literally could not fit on the capacity of the Motorola box," Babbio said. Motorola, meanwhile, was behind schedule delivering the boxes.

Verizon decided that if it was going to launch Fios on time, it would have to take control. The company assumed development of the set-top box project. At the same time, Verizon took the software job in-house and commissioned its own IT leadership, Shaygan Kheradpir and Shankar Arumugavelu, to develop what the company needed. Hundreds of programmers working in the States and hundreds more in India worked around the clock to develop the product. "It was a huge development bet. We trusted our own people to do it, some of them here, some of them in India. And we got there," Babbio said.

# TEXAS TEST

The company needed to test Fios in real-time conditions before it was rolled out nationwide. Verizon chose the Dallas suburb of Keller, Texas, as a commercial test bed for the product. In 2004 Fios offered customers the industry's fastest broadband service as well as phone. Lacouture said that his heart nearly stopped when they turned on the system for the first time in Keller with customers hooked up, and nothing happened. A technician quickly identified the problem, reversed two leads and the system went live. Everyone exhaled.

The Fios engineers had been pushing for the system to be built with maximum capacity at the time from launch, not phase in speeds that would appear to be adequate based on the equipment customers had installed in their homes at the time. Lacouture said they felt vindicated when they observed a group of Texas teenagers playing competitive video games using Fios. The teens competing who were hooked up to Fios were outscoring their rivals using cable hookups. "The demand for bandwidth was there, and it was only going to grow," Lacouture said.

Television was added in 2005. Verizon had clearly judged correctly that consumers would pay extra for the value-added speed and reliability of the service. When TV was offered in September 2005, Verizon captured 25 percent of the Keller market in weeks, not months, well ahead of predictions.

The Verizon board had reason to be cautiously optimistic as it viewed the initial, positive consumer response to Fios. "Early on, the indications were there that it really would work," said Director Joe Neubauer, CEO and chairman of Aramark. "We looked at household conversions, we looked at usage, we looked at revenues per household. They all looked pretty good."

There were some major problems. The company had significantly underestimated the cost and time involved in installing the service in customers' homes, including connecting all of their broadband-ready devices. Babbio had initially estimated that it would take about two hours for each Fios install. Instead, the first few hundred installations were taking closer to two days each.

Babbio went back before the board to plead for patience. "You have to give us at least a little room. You can't count the first 100 people. You should count the first 100,000 people." As the rollout continued, installations improved in some areas, although installation costs continued to burden the rollout across the country. Such snags would be one of the reasons Verizon would buttress the Fios leadership team in 2006, after two years of challenges in trying to speed up the adoption of and installation process for Fios.

In an effort to control costs, Verizon often used subcontractors to do the installations. That created its own set of concerns. Jim Gerace installed Fios in his home but intentionally didn't tell the installers he was a Verizon executive, since he wanted to see the level of service that was being provided in his area. "So, I went out when they got there, and I said, 'Hey, let me know where you're going to put this, because then I'll mark where my sprinkler lines are, because I have pictures,'" Gerace said. The installer replied, "Oh, no, no. Don't worry—if we break it, we fix it." Sure enough, he cut through the sprinkler lines and control wire, costing Verizon a few thousand dollars extra to repair the damage and redo the work.

Seidenberg didn't excuse shoddy work, but he said it was hard to overstate the challenges facing the Fios team. Verizon Wireless successfully overcame myriad obstacles in building a cellular business that was second to none. But they had the advantage of essentially starting from scratch. When it came to building the Fios business, the Verizon engineers were taking technology and training that had changed only incrementally from the days of the Model T. "They were rebuilding the business from the inside out as a high-performance Porsche while accelerating down the interstate," Seidenberg said. They were bound to grind the gears more than a few times.

# WALL STREET REACTION

As Seidenberg and the leadership team discovered, the Fios announcement had certain Wall Street analysts and major institutional investors scratching their heads almost from day one. The huge investment was a significant stumbling block. Susan Kalla, a telecom analyst with Friedman Billings Ramsey, said that she thought Seidenberg's January 2004 announcement was a bluff. "He's not going to do it," she told *Fortune* magazine. "The numbers, they just don't make sense."

Many Wall Street analysts, living in Verizon's East Coast coverage area between Washington, D.C., and Boston, were anxious to try out the new product as the rollout reached their homes. They loved the high-speed broadband and video offerings. But the installation service horror stories caught the media's eye and investors' attention. The use of subcontractors to install the service in parts of the country often exacerbated the problem.

In part, as a result of Fios-related hiccups, Verizon's stock price plunged by more than 25 percent in 2005. The stock recovered somewhat in 2006 but never ventured far from the fairly flat trading range that it had occupied for much of the decade to date.

"It was a tough slog as we went through it," said John Killian, former CFO of the wireline business. "Most of the Street thought it was a dumb idea [and that] we should not be putting that much capital in it."

Seidenberg kept the leadership team, and the board, focused on the long view. "We explained to the board that while our stock price was down, we were amazingly still in line with the rest of the industry, even though our peers would challenge our approach and indicate that building fiber to the home was a bad financial idea. This will pay off," Seidenberg said. "We were willing to live with the consequence of the impact of Fios on the stock price, and our compensation was lower because of the Fios rollout. Our compensation was aligned with our beliefs," he said. Management never asked the board for a change in compensation structure because of the impact of the Fios rollout.

One of the factors that made the tremendous capital expenditure required to launch Fios palatable from the board's point of view was that "a lot of the Fios buildout was success-based," Moose said. "So, unlike the mobile network, you could stop Fios if you were concerned with the results," she added. "Let's say you built out a city and it didn't work out well, you didn't have to go to the next city."

Everyone involved appreciated that the launch of Fios was a high-stakes bet on next-generation technology. "Every consumer study, all of the internet service providers and every developer of internet-based applications knew that higher broadband speeds would produce a winning strategy," Seidenberg said. "Our challenge was to accelerate the rebuilding of a legacy platform into a new technology growth engine. We were on a mission to do something not done many times before."

## "FALLING IN LOVE WITH THE BUSINESS AGAIN"

Verizon had barely been in business for a half-decade, and it was already transforming itself into the communications networking company of the future. "As it turned out," Moose said, "the decision to go with fiber was the right choice versus AT&T, and better than cable." Betting on quality in the form of Fios also prepared Verizon to take advantage of techno-logical advances and changing customer tastes that weren't anticipated at the time the investment decision was made. "Verizon turned out to be prescient," Moose said.

"There was enormous demand for two-way communication. Back when it first started, everybody was focused on more of what they called asynchronous networks," Moose said. "It was a fat tube going into your house so you could get lots of movies but a skinny tube going out, which is how the cable companies had operated. Back when we made the decision—you have to go back to 2003—there was no You-Tube. There was no Instagram. There was no photo or video sharing, and work from home was not a big deal." Those trends were already starting to change by the time of the 2006 review, taking the form of what would become known as the Web 2.0.

Seidenberg saw his role internally, as the decade progressed, as convincing employees to be comfortable with "falling in love with the business again." They were transforming Verizon into a growth company with growth businesses, even if some of them—including Fios—were initially dismissed by industry experts. "We had to get people comfortable that what we did for a living was a good thing. We weren't a regulated utility. We were building a wireless business, a fiber business, a network business." That three-legged stool provided a solid platform for the company's growth to come.

At the same time, Verizon wireline employees' embrace of Fios tapped into a long-standing phone company tradition. The service ethic of the company was always attuned to finding the latest solution to meeting customer needs. Fios now provided a pathway to continued growth for a wireline industry and workforce that just a few years earlier might have worried that they were headed the way of the rotary phone.

"Serving customers with great networks is our heritage, our future and our daily challenge," Seidenberg said. "It's what we do."

# FUTURE-PROOF THE CORE: C-SUITE INSIGHTS FROM RAM CHARAN

**— LONG LIVE LEGACY BUSINESSES.**
Make bet-the-company technology investments to leapfrog competitive threats and rebuild and redefine core businesses. Big pivots to the future don't mean that legacies have to be left to die if the leadership team can redefine legacy businesses in the context of new technologies.

**— TAKE YOUR BOARD WITH YOU.**
Invest the time up front to educate the board on major investments and initiatives as well as industry trends long before they are up for a vote. Tap the collective knowledge.

**— LEVEL THE PLAYING FIELD.**
Work with the government to reframe treatment of customer-friendly innovations so regulations don't stifle innovation. Give regulators the industry analysis needed to make them modern customer advocates.

# Dynamic Directors

By Ram Charan

I have been consulting, often behind closed doors, with more than 50 corporate boards around the world for decades. And I have written five books on the dynamics of corporate boards. In my experience, the Verizon board of directors has developed a culture of collaboration and open communications that is among the best of the handful of top-performing corporate boards.

From its formation including key members of the Bell Atlantic and GTE boards, the Verizon board consistently helped the leadership team drive crucial bet-the-company decisions. Too many leadership teams sometimes default to treating their boards as another governance box to check to stay on the right side of standard governance practices. Only in a crisis do they fully function as directors engaged with leadership. Verizon leaders have developed a close working relationship with their board that informs and strengthens decision making across categories and at all times, not just emergencies. The wise counsel offered by Verizon Directors Sandra Moose, Richard Carrion and John Snow in particular over the years represented, in my experience, board directorship at its finest.

The two most important things for a leadership team to establish with a board: building credibility and building trust. Former GTE Chairman and CEO Chuck Lee did Ivan Seidenberg a favor when he gave him some very practical advice on running board meetings. It also serves as a metaphor for driving corporate change. "Sit in the middle." Seidenberg and his team led from the front of the board room. Lee said sit in the middle, among the directors. That demonstrates senior leadership and directors are a team. Directors' sense of buy-in soars when they are involved elbow to elbow in discussions with leadership.

Seidenberg added his own innovations over time as the chairman and CEO of Verizon. He insisted on mandatory attendance. That might seem unrealistic in today's world of remote access and 24/7 demands on directors' time and attention. Yet having the directors in the same room interacting with each other and leadership creates a dynamic that is hard to replicate, even with high-quality video screens or robust FaceTime connections.

Taking Lee's "sit in the middle" suggestion one step further, Seidenberg invited his fellow directors to dine together before board meetings at a round table. Everyone participated; no one was able to hide in a corner. In addition to the distribution of normal pre-reading board materials, Seidenberg sent a few short papers as a primer for these executive dinner discussions. They engaged in spirited discussions about current events and what was going on in their fields of expertise in order to get to know each other better and share knowledge and perspective. In my experience, most boards never quite spend enough time together as a group and alone with the CEO. When it came time for major board decisions, the directors could draw on these more casual interactions to build trust among the members of the group.

Seidenberg also walked them through what the agenda would be for the board meeting and suggested questions that might be directed at presenters from the leadership team. Faced with space constraints common to many corporate settings, Verizon settled for an oval boardroom table rather than a perfectly round one, but the impact of involving directors in the meeting dialogue was accomplished. I have seen some boards sit around rectangular tables nearly 30 feet long with a microphone at each place. Directors can barely hear those at the other end of such tables, let alone interact with them.

Seidenberg insisted that established leaders as well as rising leaders of tomorrow present to the board during meetings. That further engaged the board in the thinking behind and execution of key leadership initiatives. It also led naturally to the board's in-depth engagement in the succession process, as I will discuss further in a subsequent essay.

Lowell McAdam has put his own stamp on the relationship of the leadership team with the board as chairman and CEO. As positions have opened up, he has added directors with more experience in retail, reflecting the impact of mass customization trends on Verizon's future. For the same reason, he has involved the board more deeply in studying accelerating technology trends that increasingly shape Verizon's destiny. In so doing, he works to ensure that the Verizon board remains a front-runner in its active role, helping prepare Verizon for the challenges and opportunities ahead.

# 08

# SCALING
# FOR MASS
# CUSTOMIZATION

—

2004-2009

**S**eidenberg had been tracking the rapid growth of wireless in the early years of the company as well as the plans for developing Fios on the wireline side. He saw plenty to be optimistic about on both sides of the company. But at the same time, he was convinced that the wireline and wireless networks would have to converge around broadband technologies to meet consumers' demands in all aspects of their increasingly 24/7 communication needs. The favored trend among many industry experts then and now is to operate businesses as stand-alone operations with a single focus—easy to characterize, easy to analyze. Seidenberg was convinced that over time, because of digital convergence, the whole of Verizon would be worth more than the sum of its parts. And following Verizon's chessboard strategy, he was already thinking about adding another key "part" to the business. He believed that customers, employees and investors would gradually see that when it comes to Verizon, greater scale and scope would be a winning strategy.

# BRINGING THE BUSINESSES TOGETHER

Seidenberg called Verizon Wireless HR head Marc Reed one day in early 2004 and asked Reed to meet with him in his office at 1095 Avenue of the Americas in Manhattan. "I want to talk to you about the HR function," Seidenberg said. He told Reed that he was rethinking the role of the head of HR for the entire corporation. "People in the businesses can take care of the hiring, firing and training," Seidenberg said. "I need somebody to come over here and help me think about the bigger issues facing us: culture, talent."

"Eventually, we are going to have to replace these leaders who are very iconic today, and how are we going to do this?" Seidenberg asked. "If we do not take specific action, the wireline and wireless business groups will just perpetuate their own units and not necessarily think about the business as a whole."

Their initial talks were about the position. Reed wasn't being offered the job. But Seidenberg made it clear, in time, that he would like Reed to consider the post. Reed understood that it was a promotion, but he excelled at the operational level of building the wireless team, and he wasn't certain he wanted to leave. With small children in school in New Jersey, and having already relocated his family eight times in his career, he also wasn't sure he wanted to move into New York City.

Reed talked with Strigl and McAdam, his wireless bosses. Strigl made it clear that he would hate to lose Reed. On the other hand, "this is one of those career moments. The chairman wants you to do this." He agreed to take the job.

Seidenberg wasn't just interested in using HR to bring the two businesses closer together by cross-promoting executives up through the ranks of each business line. He wanted to physically bring everyone together. After Reed had been on the job in New York for about a month, Seidenberg dropped into his office. "You know your issue about not wanting to work here in New York? I'm going to give you the opportunity to fix this," he said, half in jest. "I think it's time we start thinking about how we have an operating location where wireless and wireline are put together."

Keeping the businesses separate for the first few years was "the right incubation period" for wireless to develop its own culture, Seidenberg said. "But if we want to get the total value out of this company," he added, "we need to at least get people in the same proximity because, let's face it, nobody from wireless comes over here unless they're summoned, and nobody goes over there unless they're invited. It ain't going to happen on its own," he said.

During 2004, the Verizon leadership team and board also decided to keep the corporate headquarters in Manhattan, but move it to 140 West Street. That move, announced in January 2005, was an important symbol of Verizon's commitment to the city. But that didn't mean operations couldn't be consolidated elsewhere.

## BACK TO BASKING RIDGE

Aware that he needed to keep the major locations of most of the company's workers in mind, Reed narrowed the field initially to three states: New York, New Jersey and Virginia. After months of negotiations with state officials over tax and other incentives and surveying prospective sites, Reed reached a decision, which would be announced to the public in March 2005. In what would feel a bit like déjà vu for some company veterans, Reed said that his choice was the sprawling former AT&T operations center in Basking Ridge, New Jersey—where Babbio heard AT&T Chairman and CEO Charlie Brown announce the breakup of AT&T in 1982. Seidenberg also worked at Basking Ridge as part of the first group of AT&T employees that moved there in 1975.

The 165-acre site, including seven interconnected buildings built for AT&T in 1975, had been sitting vacant for three years after AT&T sold it to Pharmacia, a drug company that was later acquired by Pfizer. It was notorious in telecommunications circles for the multi-story waterfall that pounded down into a pool just inside the main entrance. Reed assured everyone that an integral part of the plan was a complete makeover of all building interiors, which included losing the waterfall. The first staff moved into the building in December 2005.

Not everyone was overjoyed with the prospect of moving. Wireline employees living in New York would now have to cross the Hudson River to work. And even though most wireless employees already lived and worked nearby, they balked at the idea of interacting with the legacy side of the company.

Wireless CEO Strigl announced at one of his 8 a.m. senior staff meetings that Seidenberg wanted them to move in with the wireline business in Basking Ridge, not far from wireless headquarters in Bedminster, New Jersey. Communications head Jim Gerace said, "No, we built this culture; it'll be infected by the other culture." Strigl asked for Gerace's thoughts in a concise memo. Strigl agreed with the memo and forwarded it to Seidenberg, with Gerace's name on it.

"Ivan not only says, 'This is the way it's going to be,' but 'I want Gerace on the transition team to move into this building,'" Gerace said. "So, he made me a part of it. That was one of his ways of getting you on board," he said. "By the way, it's brilliant, because if you have people in leadership positions around the business and they continue to fight even after the decision is made, they're working against you. So, make them part of the process, and then they can't help but be for it, right? That's in the Credo, too, as constructive dissent." Seidenberg also wanted to expose Gerace to the industry beyond wireless to broaden his leadership skills.

The staffs slowly started to mix. Initially, wireless was at one end of the complex and wireline at the other, with corporate staff in the middle. At first, mixing occurred in the cafeteria and exercise facilities. Then, staff from the different businesses were being invited to each other's meetings and operational reviews. As Seidenberg told Reed, "Bringing them together doesn't mean it's one way or the other way. It's bring them together to get them to collaborate."

## LONG-DISTANCE TALKS

Even as they were planning consolidating their wireless and wireline operations, Verizon officials penciled in space for a potential new business. Seidenberg and his leadership team, consulting with their board, had been considering future options. They reasoned that since Verizon had led the way among Baby Bells in competing in long distance, it was just a matter of time before the long-distance companies, AT&T, Sprint and MCI, became acquisition targets. "Based on the chessboard strategy, at some point, somebody's going to take these guys out. And we had a big debate about that," Seidenberg said.

Their initial inclination was to pursue Sprint. "We wouldn't get the biggest long-distance company, but we'd get enough of a long-distance company to do what we needed to do," Seidenberg said. "And then, once we consolidated with one of the long-distance companies, it would only be a matter of time before the rest of the industry consolidated as well." He and the Verizon leadership believed that AT&T, with its business model dependent on the existing regulatory

# DISASTER PREPAREDNESS

While Verizon continuously focuses on disaster preparedness, it was difficult for any telecommunications provider to fully anticipate and prepare for one of the nation's worst natural disasters in recent history, 2005's Hurricane Katrina. When Katrina slammed into New Orleans and the nearby Gulf Coast, it tested the readiness of all telecommunications service providers, as well as first responders and disaster relief personnel. As did Hurricane Rita, which followed a few weeks later but directly hit the less-populated portions of southwestern Louisiana. This time, BellSouth was the heritage Bell System offspring providing most of the landline phone and data service to the area hardest hit by the disaster.

Verizon Wireless had expanded into New Orleans, however, and brought its industry-leading backup and redundancies to its systems that served it well as Katrina swept through the Crescent City. "We had a cell site in the center of town right near Bourbon Street. It ran throughout the entire thing," Lynch said. Emergency responders used the Verizon cell site to coordinate communications during the height of the storm and its immediate aftermath.

Verizon sent 100 technicians and 10 supervisors to assist BellSouth in putting its wireline system back into service. Taking a page from its 9/11 playbook, Verizon Wireless also provided more than 10,000 wireless phones or data cards, as well as free wireless service, to organizations providing disaster relief in the areas hit by Katrina. In addition, many of the responses to Katrina's aftermath had already been tried and refined during the brutal 2004 hurricane season in Florida. And the positive feedback loop continued as the refinements added during the Katrina response were shared with disaster crews back in Florida less than two months later, in October 2005, when Hurricane Wilma blew into southwest Florida.

One of the lessons learned from Katrina was to move key fiber-optic and internet backbone cables still farther away from storm-vulnerable coasts. That process had been underway even before Katrina in many exposed areas. But Verizon still suffered four optical fiber cuts when transmission towers collapsed during the storm. In addition to migrating lines farther north, away from the Gulf Coast, Verizon also accelerated a planned capacity increase for its trunk lines in the area by 12 to 18 months. This ultra-long-haul project increased capacity on the trunk lines fivefold, as well as boosted resilience and cut maintenance costs. The previous generation of cables required signal regeneration every 25 miles; the ULH cables only require such a signal boost every 1,200 miles.

framework, remained stuck in telecom's past, not its future. "I was always worried that the company who bought AT&T would turn into AT&T," Seidenberg joked.

Seidenberg met with Sprint officials a few times, but Verizon couldn't get comfortable enough with combining the two companies to go forward. Government approval wasn't impossible, but it would have been difficult. A bigger sticking point was integrating Sprint's wireless business into Verizon Wireless. The store overlap and potential culture mismatch presented formidable hurdles. Verizon Wireless was on such a strong growth trajectory that it didn't make sense to force a major integration on them on top of every other challenge with which they were dealing. In addition, Sprint made it clear that it was not that interested in a deal unless it was for a very high takeout price.

## DEEP DIVES

When the Verizon senior leadership team turned its attention to the long-distance leaders as acquisition targets, it was hardly the first time Verizon put these industry players under the microscope. In support of the continuing chessboard strategy pursued by senior leadership and the Verizon board, John Diercksen in 2003 moved from head of investor relations to lead strategic planning. He worked directly with Seidenberg, and he and his team researched potential purchase or investment options for Verizon across numerous businesses. "Ivan would come in one day and say, 'Hey, did you ever think about looking at this company? Did you ever look at that? Did you ever look at this?'" Diercksen said. Seidenberg considered Diercksen and his team an indispensable part of the strategic planning process in that they were constantly evaluating acquisition targets and digging into the financials and company reports of these potential targets. Diercksen said, "We always looked at companies. At one point through the '03, '04 and '05 periods, we probably looked at 300 companies. And when I said looked at them, we did deep dives."

# "A BRIDGE TOO FAR"

With Sprint out of the running, Verizon's leadership team agreed they had to seriously look at buying AT&T, despite their concerns about the corporate culture and outlook. Seidenberg knew that AT&T Chairman and CEO David Dorman had been talking with Ed Whitacre, his counterpart at SBC, about combining forces. But SBC had yet to close on its acquisition of BellSouth and couldn't expect regulatory approval for another purchase, so there remained a window of time for Verizon to sweep in and woo AT&T as well.

Seidenberg met with Dorman, whom he had known for years, and discussed a merger of their companies. "Dave, the problem that you guys have is that you're trying to solve your problem by getting regulations imposed on us, like sharing our network and all that kind of stuff. You've never decided you should spend any money and build a network, a local network, or buy a local company," Seidenberg said.

"Now, your predecessors bought the cable guys. Your predecessors had wireless, and then they spun them all out, which to us was not the right approach," he continued. "But now you're here, and you're still trying to get the FCC to regulate our prices, because you don't think they're fair. That's a bad way to think," Seidenberg said. "You are going to fail."

Seidenberg also made it clear that if AT&T merged with Verizon, it would have to adapt the Verizon way of doing business. "I'm just saying you have to change your attitude, because if you come in with a company like ours, we're going to change the model," Seidenberg told Dorman. "We're not going to discount every day. We're not going to give away our services. We're going to build a valuable network." Seidenberg realized that created a high hurdle to doing a deal for Dorman. "He was struggling with that. I also think he thought Ed would pay more."

Seidenberg also was surprised that Dorman was very interested in being a part of any new company and thought he would take the lead in public policy and related merger integration if the two companies merged. "We wanted to end the AT&T-style public policy framework and transform Verizon away from traditional regulation," Seidenberg said. But from a financial standpoint, buying AT&T was doable. Expensive, but doable.

Seidenberg convened a meeting of the senior leadership team to hash out the pros and cons. CFO Doreen Toben thought the likely price was too high but was still supportive of the idea. The wireless leadership didn't like the idea of devoting so many corporate resources to a legacy wireline business.

Verizon General Counsel Bill Barr raised a separate issue: Because there was so much geographic overlap in the eastern U.S. between Verizon's wireline business and AT&T's legacy long-distance network, especially in the Boston to Washington, D.C., corridor, the Justice Department might put up a serious fight on combining the two companies. "Ivan, this is one bridge that may be too far for you to go," Barr said. Seidenberg pressed him for a definitive answer, knowing that if Verizon looked elsewhere, everyone would want to know why they didn't go after long-distance market share leader AT&T. Barr said he wanted a day to think it over.

The next day, Barr was more emphatic: "Don't do this." The more he considered the issue and weighed recent government action, the more certain he was. Barr said, "This is a bridge too far." That was enough for Seidenberg. The Verizon team was done considering AT&T and did not follow up with Dorman. As the Verizon team suspected, AT&T would later pursue a union with SBC.

# MCI

That left MCI. Seidenberg had known MCI Director Larry Harris since their AT&T days, and through him arranged to meet quietly with MCI CEO Michael Capellas, the former CEO of Compaq Computer who had joined MCI in 2002 to lead it out of bankruptcy. Seidenberg and Harris got along well and agreed that MCI, which emerged from bankruptcy in 2004 (a move that Verizon initially fought), would be a good fit for Verizon. And unlike the asking price for AT&T—which in the spring of 2005 would be set at about $22 billion, when AT&T agreed to be merged into SBC—the estimated price tag of less than $7 billion for MCI would not be another bet-the-business investment for Verizon à la the Fios buildout.

On Valentine's Day 2005, the two companies announced a friendly offer from Verizon for MCI that valued the company at $6.75 billion, or $20.75 a share, in cash and stock, including a special dividend paid to MCI shareholders. MCI accepted the Verizon bid over a larger offer from much smaller and financially shaky Qwest Communications valued at $7.3 billion. Verizon said it wasn't worried that Qwest, already saddled with a junk bond rating on its debt, would come back with a higher bid. It said publicly that there wasn't much of a chance that Qwest would be able to effectively integrate MCI into its operations, so talk of cost-saving synergies was just that.

Qwest surprised Verizon and MCI with a higher bid for MCI on March 31. That set off a bidding war featuring a cast of characters including recalcitrant corporate leaders, angry hedge fund managers and image-conscious directors. The dramatic turning point was a clandestine visit by Seidenberg and strategist Diercksen to the armed compound of the wealthiest man in Mexico.

# "VERIZON TO MCI: DROP DEAD"

Corporate mergers, like politics, make for strange bedfellows. In 2003, less than two years before agreeing to buy MCI, Verizon was trying to kill it by forcing MCI into liquidation. The aggressive strategy was championed by Verizon General Counsel Bill Barr and approved by Seidenberg.

In arguments filed with the SEC as well as bankruptcy courts in four states, Barr alleged that MCI was a "criminal enterprise." He maintained that over three years, MCI's fraudulent accounting, which had already been revealed, inflated profits by more than $9 billion. That effectively made the phone company a "criminal enterprise." He took the position that "bankruptcy is not a mechanism for laundering stolen goods." That led *The Wall Street Journal* to write about the dispute on May 15, 2003, under the headline "Verizon to MCI: Drop Dead; Campaign Is on for Liquidation."

Verizon was concerned that if allowed to emerge from bankruptcy as planned, MCI would be relieved of much of its previous debt burden. That would enable it in theory to aggressively cut prices, putting more heavily indebted Verizon and AT&T at a disadvantage. Barr said, "For the life of me I could not figure out why the government was letting this happen." Verizon's aggressive stance toward the MCI bankruptcy plan had the effect of keeping the company in legal limbo for months on end. It finally emerged from bankruptcy in April 2004. "Then the irony of ironies," said Barr, "is we decided to buy it after bankruptcy."

# SLIM OFFER

Qwest CEO Dick Notebaert, former CEO of Ameritech, which earlier was sold to SBC, appeared not to take kindly to his company's financial strength and prospects being dismissed out of hand. He raised Seidenberg's counteroffer for MCI. The group of hedge funds that ended up holding one-third of MCI's shares after it emerged from bankruptcy also wanted as high a share price as possible and was cheering him on, if not actually prompting his bid. At Verizon, several board members cautioned Seidenberg that he shouldn't engage in a bidding war if he didn't have a plan to win the bid. What would it look like if they walked away and surrendered the field to puny Qwest (Verizon was over five times larger)? They were also concerned that investors would worry there would be a gaping hole in the strategy of the company, and how much more would it cost to address this?

When rumors spread that Qwest was going to jump the bidding for MCI, already in the mid-20s, to $30 a share, the Verizon team knew they had to take decisive action. Seidenberg and his team came up with a strategy that they predicted would tip the bidding war firmly in their favor.

Seidenberg and Diercksen flew to Mexico City on Friday, April 1, 2005. They were taken by private car to the heavily guarded urban compound of Mexico's wealthiest man, Carlos Slim. The telecommunications industry billionaire's 13 percent equity stake in MCI made him the largest holder of MCI shares. Seidenberg arranged the meeting through Slim's son-in-law Jaime Chico Pardo, a fellow Honeywell International board member for several years.

Verizon's strategy was to get Slim's support, which, with that of MCI management and their stock holdings, would give them nearly 30 percent of the stock, according to Seidenberg. That meant they had to get support of at least another 20 percent of the stockholders to have a majority. They then intended to put their offer up for a shareholder vote.

Once the Verizon executives passed the armed guards, Slim graciously gave them a tour of his collection of European old masters and other artwork collected over the years. Slim clearly was very engaged in building the art collection. They then settled in around a conference table, with

Seidenberg and Slim at one end and Diercksen and his chain-smoking Mexican counterpart, referred to simply as Arturo, at the other.

Slim opened the business portion of their visit by disclosing that Notebaert had just left earlier that afternoon. "Q West," as Slim called the Denver-based telecom, was prepared to pay him $30 a share for his MCI shares. Seidenberg pointed out that the Qwest bid included a heavy component of junk-rated debt, while the Verizon offer was all cash and perhaps some rock-solid Verizon stock.

The talks went back and forth, with Slim insisting that he couldn't appear to be leaving a higher-priced offer on the table. Seidenberg said that Verizon "might have a little more in the tank" and could increase its offer slightly from the then-current level of about $24 but that $30 in cash and Verizon stock was out of the question. Slim signaled that he wasn't interested in discussing the issue further.

The Verizon executives thanked him for taking the time to meet and got back in their hired car and started back to the airport. The car phone rang. It was Slim, who said that Arturo would be in their office in New York on Monday to continue discussions. "We didn't even know he knew which car service we had," Seidenberg said.

## "PATIENCE AND SAVVY WIN THE DAY"

Unbeknownst to the Verizon team, someone familiar with the talks with Slim had leaked that they were meeting in New York. That sent MCI's share price ratcheting still higher, from $24 to $24.50 to roughly $25 on Tuesday. Seidenberg said enough was enough. He called Slim Wednesday morning.

"Carlos, it's over," Seidenberg said. "Close the business today. Either we do the deal, or there's no deal." Slim said, "OK," though he insisted he be given options on Verizon stock as part of the deal. Verizon agreed, and they had a deal. Verizon bought 13 percent of the shares at $25.72. MCI CEO Capellas, whose management team controlled about 15 percent of MCI's shares and was backing Verizon, called up Seidenberg and asked, "How'd you do that?" Seidenberg said: "We paid $25.72. That's how we did it."

Seidenberg assured the handful of board members who were especially concerned about the MCI bidding process that if Verizon lost the vote because Qwest came in with a higher bid, they would pocket the $1- or $2-a-share profit and move on. "Ivan, do you know what you're doing?" a few asked him, Seidenberg recalled. His response was, "We could lose. It would be embarrassing, but we thought that once a shareholder vote was taken, investors would run to the safety of the Verizon bid, even though it was lower than the $30 offered by Qwest. I thought this was the right move for the company, but I also realized that it could cost me my job if we lost."

On April 21, Qwest made its last bid for MCI, which was valued at $30 as predicted. It offered $16 in cash and 3.373 Qwest shares for each share of MCI. Verizon's final bid was valued at $26. It included a cash dividend of $5.60, plus $20.40 for each MCI share, payable in cash, and 0.5743 Verizon shares. Verizon's argument that it had the stronger bid carried the day. A majority of MCI shareholders approved the $8.8 billion deal in an October shareholder vote.

Rather than take his badge, the Verizon board coalesced even more solidly behind Seidenberg and his team of dealmakers. Verizon's dealmaking prowess was also appreciated well beyond the confines of its board room. *Investment Dealers' Digest* crowned the purchase of MCI the 2005 "Deal of the Year" in the telecom/technology category. The headline to the write-up captured the financial world's appreciation for Verizon's accomplishment: "Unruffled Verizon Secures MCI Prize. Hedge funds tried browbeating via Qwest bid, but patience and savvy win the day."

## MCI'S COMPETITIVE EDGE

MCI was combined with several existing Verizon enterprise units serving large corporate clients in a new "wing of the mansion" called Verizon Business. Seidenberg and the leadership team valued MCI for its UUNET internet backbone network and global reach. Seidenberg also saw the purchase of MCI as giving Verizon, particularly its heritage landline business, a valuable infusion of competitive culture.

"MCI was a company that operated in competitive markets. It wasn't an incumbent," said Craig Silliman, an MCI attorney who joined the Verizon legal staff following the purchase. "The culture was very different. Culture at MCI was a very sales-driven culture. It was very scrappy. This was true with UUNET and everything else. These were companies that were built up to try to steal market share," he said.

Silliman said that Seidenberg shared his insights on buying MCI. "You're bringing an enterprise mindset and culture, which is very different. You're interjecting tens of thousands of employees who come from a different corporate culture, different market environment, and that's actually part of how we move the corporate culture at Verizon," Seidenberg said. "I thought it was a great insight," said Silliman. At the same time, Reed saw the purchase of MCI as an excellent opportunity to give rising leaders new experiences and exposure to MCI's technology and its highly competitive market. John Killian was named CEO of the newly created Verizon Business; Fran Shammo was named CFO, and Randy Milch general counsel.

# "WE WERE ALL ABOUT SCALE AND SCOPE"

Integrating MCI would take months. And it was not without its challenges. Yet even while it was being integrated, the successful purchase of MCI helped lay the foundation for a multibillion-dollar flurry of purchases and divestitures for the balance of the decade. "So, after the MCI deal got done, we were even more focused on building scale and scope," Seidenberg said.

The rapport established with Slim in the process of buying MCI served Verizon well going forward. For strategic reasons, and to raise cash, Verizon decided to sell off its international holdings and focus exclusively on the United States. In late 2006 and early 2007, Verizon sold its businesses in the Dominican Republic and Puerto Rico, respectively, to Slim, for a total of $3.9 billion, with very little haggling over price. "He liked doing business with us, and I think he would say because we didn't fool with him," Seidenberg said. Slim understood value and was a savvy and decisive decision maker.

Verizon also decided to sell its U.S print and internet Yellow Pages business for strategic reasons. In November 2006 Verizon spun off the directories business as a stand-alone enterprise called Idearc, based in Dallas. The company was spun off in the form of a tax-free distribution of shares, with shareholders receiving one share of Idearc for every 20 shares of Verizon they held. It was valued at roughly $13 billion. While some of Verizon's asset sales and spinoffs resulted in lawsuits against the company when these businesses foundered once detached from their former parent, Verizon was ultimately vindicated, sometimes after years of litigation.

"MCI was important, because we had to restructure the industry," Seidenberg said. "Once the industry now got restructured, and Southwestern bought AT&T, now you had the makings of, I think, a common-sense structure. Because you had us and AT&T, you had Comcast over here, so now you had the beginning of what was going to be the future of the industry."

Market forces were helping fashion the industry for the 21st century. But backward-looking regulations remained tight. "The thing that was troubling is the government was still regulating us like we were the old business," Seidenberg said. "And so, we still had work to do

## SELLING IN VENEZUELA

Verizon regretted passing on the opportunity to sell its stake in Venezuelan telecom CANTV to Slim in 2006 when he showed an interest. As a result, it got involved in a harrowing experience of selling its stake back to the Chavez government, which was nationalizing industries at an aggressive pace as the decade progressed.

Diercksen was leaving the Verizon offices one Friday evening and was passing the reception desk when the phone rang. He picked it up and found himself speaking with the vice president of Venezuela. He was calling for Seidenberg, whom he wanted to fly down to Venezuela the following day to meet with President Chavez. Diercksen said they would be in touch. After a flurry of calls, the Verizon team determined that Seidenberg wasn't going to Venezuela, period, in light of kidnappings and security concerns in the violence-prone capital of Caracas. It was agreed that, with proper security arrangements in place, Diercksen would fly down to represent the company the following week. "John was a great soldier and clearly took this assignment for the greater good," said Seidenberg.

Diercksen and others ended up making four trips to Caracas to negotiate the sale of Verizon's stake in CANTV, which had been a GTE holding at the time of Verizon's creation in 2000. On the final trip to close the deal in mid-February 2007, the Verizon team was shuttled between four hotels in Caracas by Chavez's Cuban security detail before meeting with the president in the evening. Diercksen even made a cameo appearance on Venezuelan television as part of the announcement of the sale of the stake back to the government for $572 million.

to modernize the template around which they were regulating." He emphasized: "It was never the regulators that were bad; it was their statutes that were bad. And if you're still stuck with the same statutes, you can't change the way you regulate."

"The regulators like to think they can interpret their statutes any way they want," he added. Verizon thought otherwise. "We sued them almost any time they did anything. Not because we thought they were not good people trying to do the right thing, but they were misinterpreting the power of their statutes," Seidenberg said.

---

# FIOS ADVANCES

---

Verizon's fiber buildout faced its own set of challenges. In 2006, Verizon's leadership and board took stock of Fios's progress and the challenges the new technology was encountering. There was no question Verizon had correctly gauged consumer demand for bundled phone, internet and TV service. And system maintenance reports plunged for Fios compared to the copper network.

Other issues raised serious concerns. The rollout, in some ways, was lagging expectations. The rollout of TV in particular was much slower than broadband in part because Verizon was required to go through an often laborious franchise-awarding process, similar to that required of cable companies, involving multiple meetings and drawn-out negotiations with municipal authorities in each community where it proposed offering the service. At the same time, installation and content costs were spiking. "After about two years, it became clear that it wasn't going to be the payback that we thought it was going to be," said Verizon board member Joseph Neubauer. "And that created a lot of discussion about, what do we do? Do we shut it down?"

It may have been a slower-than-projected start in some respects, but Fios was certainly trending in the right direction. Verizon's Fios internet subscriber base in 2006 jumped from 264,000 at the end of the first quarter to 687,000 by the end of the fourth quarter. After slightly more than two years in operation, the advanced fiber network passed 6.2 million homes and businesses. The TV service, including more than 25 high-definition channels and access to more than 8,000 on-demand movies and videos, passed 2.4 million homes.

Scale is key to the content business. Verizon was having to pay roughly the same amount for leading cable and broadcast TV programming whether it had 200,000 or 2 million homes subscribing to TV via the Fios network. Diercksen, who was named executive vice president of strategy, planning and development in 2003, said that Verizon at one point thought seriously about buying satellite-based DIRECTV as a source of TV programming and phasing out Fios. The company talked with cable giant John Malone, who had a majority ownership stake in DIRECTV at the time. Malone made a visit to New York City where Verizon demonstrated Fios. He was immediately struck by the latency of changing channels and how fast it was compared to DIRECTV, but didn't pursue a deal primarily because the satellite network was not compatible with the vision of a wireless and fiber-based network architecture.

The leadership team and board decided to stick with Fios and its promising long-term potential. The company told Wall Street analysts in the fall of 2006 that it was on track to have Fios pass 18 million premises by year-end 2010, or about 60 percent of the premises included in its landline network. It also projected that Fios would be cash-flow positive by 2008, a key indicator of network success, and contributing to operating income the following year.

Even as the board recommitted to Fios, it made it clear that it was concerned about long-term wireline costs. The board and management agreed that Verizon would trim its commitment to maintaining the copper landline network by beginning to sell off systems that were relatively remote from its core Boston to Washington, D.C., corridor and could not reasonably be converted to Fios technology. In the first of such moves, Verizon announced plans in 2006 to spin off access lines in Maine, Vermont and New Hampshire.

The board was very engaged during this period to make sure the leadership team was delivering on the financial promise of Fios, not just the technology promise. The board kept inquiring: How does the company scale Fios even further? Richard Carrion in particular would challenge the team about lacking a strategy to extend Fios beyond its core wireline market in the eastern U.S. Seidenberg said, "We never thought we would expand Fios beyond the Northeast and a few se- lect former GTE markets, but we were confident that over time a new approach to broadband deployment would develop. Later on, 5G sur- faced as the platform for this initiative."

## "WE CAN WIN AGAINST CABLE"

The company also decided to revamp the Fios leadership team in 2006 to provide additional leadership firepower and bring the busi- ness closer to customers. Virginia Ruesterholz, senior vice president of wholesale markets, was named president of the Fios service. Robert "Bobby" Mudge, senior vice president of the Northeast region for Verizon's Network Services Group, was named Fios chief operating officer.

The two realized that they needed "to market Fios in a much more granular and local, market-by-market-based approach against cable TV," said Mudge. "What we saw is that [with] the cable companies, there were no national companies. They were executing regionally.

We were set up nationally. We had to get much closer to the competitive intelligence, much closer to the marketplace," he said. "And to Ivan's and Larry's credit, they just kind of blew the place up and said, 'No, we're going to go in a different direction. We're going to have a regional approach here.' And Virginia and I were asked to lead that."

They were in uncharted territory. "The challenge is we had no playbook," said Mudge. "We were being asked to run a start-up company within a 100-year-old company. So, I think there were a few challenges."

Advances in fiber technology began to solve some of the installation challenges that were driving up the cost of deploying Fios. After working closely with key fiber-optic glass fiber supplier Corning, the Verizon team was able to begin to employ a new tool to speed installations and improve the performance of Fios by late 2007, especially in apartment buildings. One of the key limitations of the first generation of fiber-optic glass was that it could only bend slightly before starting to "bleed" light waves carrying information. That often required installers to run fiber from basements up to attics to cross a customer's living room, for instance, or to drill straight through multiple walls. With the new generation of glass from Corning, coated with nanostructures that act as microscopic guardrails, fiber-optic cable could snake around multiple corners in a room or apartment without losing any signal strength.

Ruesterholz said that as she and Mudge were stepping into the leadership roles at Fios, the workforce, union and non-union, were getting increasingly excited about the new service with its new technology. Suddenly the wireless workers weren't the only ones with the cool tools.

"I think the thing that was so exciting about that job for me was it was such a game changer for the techs—even the unions," Ruesterholz said. "They felt they could win. . . . You gave them fiber. You gave them the tools. You really changed the mindset. Now did everybody come along? Of course not," she said. "But there was a whole new group of employees that said, 'Wow. We can win against cable. And the enemy is cable. We're not now on our heels.' I think that was a very, very game-changing thing for the culture of the company."

Larry Cohen, president of the Communications Workers of America, was supportive of the Fios strategy because it demonstrated a huge commitment to invest in the legacy business and transform it to compete against cable. "Fios provided a huge, positive transition from our point of view for technical and customer service members into the 21st century," Cohen said. "Throughout the rollout, union heads applauded and encouraged communities to grant franchises for Fios, unequivocally," he added.

According to Ruesterholz, "It got very exciting—the competition among the different markets on how well they were beating cable. People rallied around that. They were fighting to be the next guy in how many video adds you had every month. It was a really fun, competitive growth opportunity."

The new Fios leadership injected a sales and marketing culture into the wireline business that too often in earlier years had received less emphasis than it had on the wireless side of the business. Ruesterholz and Mudge backed nine regional presidents, including Maura Breen in New York and Ellen Corcoran in New England, who drew upon sales and marketing backgrounds to drive success in their regions.

"Their excitement in building a team and bringing a sales and marketing and entrepreneurial spirit to an operations group of people was pretty infectious," Mudge said. "They were women with strong sales and marketing backgrounds who helped people that came through a regulated operation that really didn't think too much about how we competed and what sales and marketing work was needed. We were kind of buried in the factory for so many years just creating widgets, and that was it."

Yet the leadership, at least for a few years, still had to maintain a foothold in the old copper world and the new Fios landscape. It was a constant juggling act. According to Mudge:

> We were still in the mode of protecting the old network and the old business while growing the new one. At the time, because Fios was so new and small, the majority of the business was all still the core and copper folks. So yeah, there was some resistance to the new technology, but that was a rounding error. It was more— we had to say that everyone was still doing critical and important work, but that was a very tough balance because we didn't want to downplay Fios and fiber. But we couldn't overplay it for people to think they would be left behind. So, it actually had to play out. And then, over time, people saw so long as we were successful, there would be a future for our business and great jobs for the people involved.

## WIRELESS BACK ON TOP

Verizon Wireless accelerated by almost every measure as the decade progressed. Even though it would face a significant, if temporary, setback in terms of next-generation product offerings, it would surge to new heights year after year. In 2008, wireless business revenues grew by more than 12 percent, despite the fact that the world plunged into the global financial crisis beginning that September. With that performance, wireless revenues for the first time surpassed the wireline side of the business on a consolidated basis. And that was before the purchase of Alltel, the fifth-largest cellular service provider, in early 2009. With that acquisition, Verizon Wireless was once again back on top of the wireless industry—this time, to stay.

# "THIS IS GOING TO CHANGE THE WORLD"

Seidenberg was attending the annual media conference sponsored by the investment banking firm Allen & Co. in July 2006 when he saw Walt Disney Chief Executive Bob Iger. He was looking intently at what appeared to be an oddly shaped cellphone in his hand. Seidenberg asked him about it as Iger put away the device as discreetly as possible. "This is going to change the world," Iger said cryptically.

That was Verizon's first, albeit partial, view of the Apple iPhone that would indeed change the world of telecommunications. Seidenberg checked in with the Verizon Wireless leadership when he returned from the conference. "We've been hearing about this. We don't know," was the response. They knew that Apple CEO Steve Jobs was on Disney's board of directors. They assumed that meant Iger was looking at an Apple device. Tapping industry and Apple sources led them to the conclusion that Apple was readying a next-generation cellphone that clearly was intended to leapfrog the competition.

Two months later, Apple reached out to Verizon Wireless and requested a meeting. Jobs and several members of his iPhone team came to Basking Ridge and met with Seidenberg and the business and technical leadership of Verizon Wireless. Jobs and Seidenberg had gotten to know each other through appearing on telecommunications industry panels and were friendly, though there was no business relationship between the companies. "He came in and he started asking us all these questions about how we sort of did product development, and everything else," Seidenberg recalled. He clearly felt existing cellphone features were unduly limiting. "He just got off on us about voicemail," Seidenberg said. "I just remember the incident. And his issue was, 'You know, when you make a call, you can only answer your voicemails in the order in which the voicemails came into your phone.

You can't skip and go back to that one or this one.'" Seidenberg said. "He was sort of letting us know that he had designed something that was very different."

These were interesting points but sideshows compared to the main issue that was on everyone's mind. Was Jobs going to launch a version of his new product that would be compatible with Verizon Wireless' CDMA-based network? Apple clearly viewed itself as an international technology powerhouse. Its iTunes music products flew off the shelves from Beijing to Buenos Aires. And despite Verizon Wireless' tremendous success in the States with its CDMA standard, the international gold standard for cellular products remained Global System for Mobile communications, or GSM. The Verizon team was certain as a result that Apple would launch a GSM smartphone, as they would come to be called.

Would Jobs be willing to sell a version of the iPhone with a CDMA chipset as well? "Nah, I don't think so" is how Seidenberg recalled Jobs' response. Seidenberg said, "We kind of got the feeling when he left the room that we were not going to be selected to do that. And he was going to pick the GSM." That meant they were going to release the iPhone through Verizon rival AT&T—which they did, exclusively for AT&T customers, in June 2007. The decision was of a piece with Jobs' design mastery and therefore not really a surprise, even if it was a crushing disappointment, said Verizon Wireless CMO John Stratton. "Jobs had no intention of building multiple SKUs [shelf-keeping units, or iterations]. His great discipline was that he'll do more with less than anybody on the planet. And he had no desire to fracture or fragment his manufacturing, his design, his development, his delivery, the engineering. So, GSM was the worldwide standard. It was the obvious choice."

Strigl had anticipated as much as well. His ready response was "we'll school him," Seidenberg recalled. Verizon Wireless was not about to sit around waiting for Apple to change its mind. It was going to find other suppliers and take them on. Months of strategizing followed as the Verizon team considered product offerings and partners who could help them offset the impact of AT&T's exclusive rights to the iPhone.

The Verizon team realized that Disney's Iger was right. It was hard to overstate the impact of Apple's iPhone. Verizon realized it had to up its game, and fast. As Stratton said, "This device comes as if from another planet. Five minutes after I had an iPhone in my hand, it was very clear to me we couldn't do this. We didn't have the competency inside the business to produce the device that Apple had just put on the table. We recognized that the world was going to change."

# THE GOOGLE WALK

How to respond to the iPhone was at the top of Verizon's to-do list. Shortly after the iPhone launch, Seidenberg went on a previously scheduled visit to Google headquarters in Silicon Valley. Verizon and search giant Google at times found themselves on opposite sides of the issues concerning who was footing the bill for improvements to speed up the handling of mounting internet traffic. At the same time, Verizon considered itself primarily a network company, and Google was one of its largest customers.

Seidenberg arrived early for the meeting, and since it was a lovely, sunny afternoon, he wandered across the Google corporate campus toward the building where the meeting was to be held. He introduced himself to various groups of Google employees and chatted. By the time he got to the meeting room, Google CEO Eric Schmidt and founders Sergey Brin and Larry Page were waiting for him. "Well, how many trade secrets did they tell you?" Schmidt asked, only half-joking. Before the meeting started, Schmidt also thanked Seidenberg for the fact that Verizon introduced the wireless "dongle" he used on his laptop for internet access while traveling. "Your dongle changed my world," Schmidt said.

"You know what? Thank you, Eric," Seidenberg said. "But that's the reason I'm here. I'm here to remind you guys we're a network business. We start thinking we're a network business, and that's what we're trying to do. So, all this other stuff about we're both competing with each other. . . . There's going to be a level of overlap and competition, but we're primarily a network business."

Seidenberg freely admitted that the technical conversation among the three Google leaders was getting over his head. But that wasn't the dialogue he was looking for in the first place. "You know, we have to get together, and we have to do a couple of things," Seidenberg said. "We have to find a way to work a little bit closer together, introduce a few new devices that can compete with the iPhone, and we have to

## "THIS IS THE BEAUTY OF VERIZON"

Verizon Wireless CEO McAdam met regularly with Vodafone executive Vittorio Colao to discuss wireless developments and operational issues concerning their wireless joint venture. Colao, not surprisingly, was concerned about the impact of the iPhone and the ability of the planned Android phone to present a meaningful challenge to the new smartphone. The two were having breakfast in Shanghai one day during a swing through Asia to meet with regional customers, Colao said, when McAdam seized a handy prop to make his point. "If I tell my people that they have to sell this phone and that this phone is the best thing we have, I have to tell you they will do it even if this phone is not a phone, it is a banana, they will pretend that this banana is the best phone in the world," McAdam said.

"I have used this story endless times in Vodafone in saying this is the beauty of Verizon," Colao said. "They believe in themselves. They don't moan too much. They don't complain. And they have what they have and what they have becomes the best thing."

find a way to reduce the tension on the political side." He returned to the office and told Strigl, "OK, Denny, you and your team, you take care of that." The team realized that partnering with Google was key to effectively responding to Apple and its iPhone.

"One of the roles of leadership: Reduce the tension, get the process going. You don't have to negotiate every single detail. But you have to keep the lines open," Seidenberg said. "I think, overall, people view that as one of my responsibilities. I would always pass this advice along to our senior team. We did that with government. We did that with the industry. We did that with the competitors. We always tried to keep the line of communication going."

# DROID

Strigl, McAdam, Stratton and the wireless team followed up on Seidenberg's visit with Google. They were particularly interested in Google's Android operating system it had acquired in 2005. As McAdam recalled:

> We went to Google and said, "Look, we want to be open. We want to have devices on our network that we don't necessarily certify." Eric [Schmidt] looked at me across the table and he says, "Yeah, right." I mean, he was basically saying bullshit in a polite way. And I said, "No, listen, Eric, we understand now with the iPhone. And if you guys build a relationship with us, and we do so with Motorola, we could create something that would really rival the iPhone."
>
> And, at that point, Android wasn't doing anything. And Eric, today if you interview him, he would say that was the seminal moment for Android really becoming a rival to [the iPhone's] iOS. And we really turned that into something.

Working with teams from Google and handset maker Motorola, the Verizon team developed a smartphone alternative to the iPhone called the Droid. It was a crash development effort that collapsed a typical 18- to 20-month development cycle down to a year in order to get the new phone to market as soon as possible. So-called Tiger Teams worked in parallel on varying aspects of the hardware and software to speed production.

The Verizon version of the Droid phone launched in the fall of 2009, in time to meet traditional heavy holiday demand for cellphones. An aggressive $100 million ad campaign pointed out features it had that Verizon said outperformed those offered by the iPhone.

The Droid was an overnight success. It buoyed spirits and sales at Verizon Wireless. But at the same time, it had been a difficult two and a half year period to get through with rival AT&T having the undeniably hottest product on the market. The only issue that made the waiting for the Droid at Verizon tolerable was the dismal performance of the AT&T network as it struggled under the increased demand tied to iPhone use.

"Nothing kills a bad product like good advertising," said Stratton, who had moved over to be CMO of the parent company before the Droid was launched. "In this case, nothing drew attention to AT&T's substandard network quality than the needs of the iPhone user. Their network just wasn't ready for it. It really blew them up for a while." He added, "So we held our own. We were still growing pretty nicely during that period of time, but it was tough."

# 700 MHZ AUCTION

As Seidenberg had predicted, Verizon continued to find itself working alongside Google in one endeavor, in this case the development of the Droid phone software, and going head to head in other areas, such as auctions of cellular spectrum, or industry capacity. The FCC, to accommodate burgeoning consumer demand for cellular phones, planned an auction in 2008 of additional wireless spectrum that previously had been reserved for analog UHF television broadcasts, which had been rendered obsolete by the transition to digital television. Through a series of political moves, Google essentially lobbied the FCC to put restrictions on the biggest and most attractive nationwide C band of spectrum covering the contiguous 48 states. And those restrictions had to do primarily with ensuring access for all users.

The Verizon Wireless team, as a result, was focusing on bidding for A and B bands of spectrum. They were in smaller pieces located in patchwork fashion across the country, but they didn't carry the same restrictions as the C spectrum. True to the wireless business ethos, the wireless team didn't want to let regulatory fiat drive their business decisions. Nor did Seidenberg.

General Counsel Barr, and attorneys in the wireless business, took issue with that approach. Barr pointed out that if the industry figured out, as it was sure to do, that Verizon was only bidding on A and B bands of spectrum, not the C band, rivals were sure to run up the price of the A and B blocks Verizon was targeting. Barr understood the wireless point of view that they didn't want to encourage regulation of wireless spectrum. But he argued that to give the company as much leeway as possible in the future, they should position themselves as able to bid on C blocks if need be.

At the same time, a wireless business attorney realized that Google was planning on bidding just enough for the C-block spectrum to trigger the open access regulations. Verizon could come in with slightly higher bids and secure the nationwide block of spectrum. The attorney made the argument that while nobody wanted additional regulation of wireless, the C band was Verizon's for the taking if it could stomach a modicum of additional regulation.

# "SPECTRUM IS THE LIFEBLOOD OF OUR BUSINESS"

Verizon was already the industry leader in terms of the quality of its national wireless network at the time of the 700 MHz auction in 2008. The expected surge in wireless data usage in coming years, however, had the Verizon leadership team constantly on the lookout for ways to enhance their system's capacity. Wireless customers clearly expected to be transmitting more data, at a faster rate, in the future. And future systems would need to handle more devices per user as well as soaring demand from commercial users. Verizon was already planning for its next, or fourth, generation of wireless service, Long Term Evolution, to accommodate the enormous growth in data services. That 4G service would begin rolling out in 2010.

The 700 MHz auction offered what, in effect, was a one-stop shopping solution to Verizon's need for greater breadth and depth for the wireless network. The C block of radio spectrum offered a "once-in-a-lifetime opportunity to provide a long-term foundation for Verizon Wireless as a business," McAdam said shortly after the auction was completed. Seidenberg added that it was "nothing short of a transformative opportunity for our business."

Different portions of the radio spectrum have different characteristics and thus are suitable for different uses. Dick Lynch and his team at Verizon and other engineers identified the C band of 700 MHz spectrum as all but tailor-made to meet the needs of fourth-generation wireless systems coast to coast. "Spectrum is the lifeblood of the business," McAdam said, "so when something like 700 comes along, we look at it very, very closely. We saw a unique set of benefits here. It has been called beachfront property, but I think the benefits are of the best propagation, the best overall coverage results, the best penetration of buildings, the best throughput, which would lead to the best capital efficiencies, [and] were all in our minds as we entered this auction." And Verizon's commitment to an open development initiative for designers of devices to use the spectrum answered regulatory concerns about access.

McAdam bought in to the C-block approach. "I went back to Ivan and said, 'Look, it's going to cost you an arm and a leg to get the A and the B blocks.'" Google, meanwhile, had committed that it would bid the minimum on the C block but indicated that it wasn't interested in bidding higher. That left the field open for Verizon. McAdam called the C-block spectrum "by far the highest value-creating spectrum we've ever bought in the company because AT&T wouldn't touch it. Nobody else would touch it." He added, "We looked and said the market is going this way, anyway. We're not going to give away one thing, and we're going to steal this spectrum. And we did."

Verizon Wireless decided to go big. Verizon bid $9.36 billion for the C band of 700 MHz spectrum in 2008. It was a hefty price, but it helped future-proof the wireless business for its next phase of rapid growth. That would come two years later in the form of what would be called 4G, or fourth-generation wireless, also called Long Term Evolution, or LTE.

# ALLTEL

What the 700 MHz C band did for Verizon Wireless' need for additional spectrum, Alltel did for filling out its nationwide geographical footprint. Verizon bought the Midwestern company, the fifth-largest cellular service provider in the country, in January 2009 for $28 billion. Alltel, coming on the heels of the August 2008 purchase of Rural Cellular for $2.7 billion, put Verizon firmly back on top as the nation's largest cellular company. "Once Alltel was done, we had the biggest, most contiguous, most complete footprint," Seidenberg said.

He credited CFO Toben and her team for managing the short-term financing of the transactions, and the operations of Verizon as whole, as the world was being rocked by the global financial crisis that was triggered in September 2008 by the bankruptcy of Lehman Brothers. "The interesting thing about Alltel from my perspective is it was an all-cash deal," Seidenberg added. Sprint CEO Daniel Hesse called up Seidenberg when the Alltel deal was announced. "How could you do this, on top of everything else you've done?" Hesse wanted to know. Seidenberg's reply? Alltel wasn't even really a stretch in terms of Verizon's financial strength.

The ability to do the deal was a tribute to Verizon's rock-solid finances and the fact that it was a cash-generating machine. "The thing that's most powerful to me about Alltel," said Seidenberg, "is that we spent $28 billion, and we had it paid for in three years or so out of cash flow. It just tells you the amazing power of the business." When board members or others raised questions about the company's ability to withstand a potential severe slowdown triggered by the global financial crisis, Seidenberg pointed out that more than 90 percent of its wireless customers signed two-year contracts; they were not paying their bills month to month. The company could operate for about 120 days without any outside financing. Not many companies could say that as they watched global financial markets melt down in the final months of 2008 and early 2009.

# MIGRATIONS

With the successful acquisition of spectrum, Verizon Wireless was the unquestionable wireless industry leader. And it increasingly was the driver of Verizon's top- and bottom-line results as the company neared the end of its first decade in business.

To some the wireless tail appeared to be wagging the Verizon dog, said Stratton. "If you think about how wireless grew," Stratton said, "how it became the fuel for top-line and bottom-line expansion, how the culture of the company became shaped by this small sort of fairly nimble business that became very, very big but still had a well-defined, performance-based culture," he said, "that for us ultimately became very, very important."

The increasing importance of wireless didn't mean that the wireline side of the business was headed for obsolescence. The growth of Fios demonstrated the value of the new generation of fiber-based broadband service. The internet backbone provided by Verizon Business provided the crucial link carrying the skyrocketing volume of wireless voice and data communication from point to point.

Indeed, Marc Reed worked closely with Strigl, McAdam and others over time to revamp the wireless Credo so that it could accurately and effectively be applied to the entire company. Respect and diversity were key concepts that they highlighted for the company going forward. Verizon was preparing for the transition to the next generation of leadership.

# SCALING FOR MASS CUSTOMIZATION: C-SUITE INSIGHTS FROM RAM CHARAN

### __ DRIVE CONVERGENCE.

Integrate separate businesses and workforces as they mature to reap synergies as the whole becomes greater than the sum of the parts. Migrate cultures to replicate high-performance DNA across the enterprise.

### __ SCALE AND SCOPE.

Add capabilities to anticipate and meet customers' needs, from products and services to next-generation capacity.

### __ MASS CUSTOMIZATION.

Digitization drives tailoring offerings to individual clients' needs.

### __ SETBACKS SPUR INNOVATION.

Steve Jobs' launching of the iPhone on the AT&T network might have knocked Verizon out of the wireless race. Instead, the leadership created another path to success by spurring development of the Droid phone with Motorola.

# 09

# TRANSITIONS

—

## 2005-2011

Verizon's board of directors was accustomed to hearing more than a few startling pronouncements from the company's chairman and CEO over the years. Many on the board looked forward to Ivan Seidenberg's presentations—at the dinners before meetings or during official board meetings themselves—because they were so engaging and thought-provoking. Having served on several boards and watching some iconic CEOs run their boards, the directors often learned about engaging their own boards and making every board meeting an event. But at this particular meeting in March 2005, some of the directors were in a temporary state of shock.

Seidenberg, the master of the chessboard strategy who had positioned Verizon at the forefront of the telecommunications industry, was putting his own piece in play. Although just 58, Seidenberg told his directors, "You need to start thinking about my successor." After those words had a moment to register, some directors blurted out, "Are you leaving?"

"No, I'm not leaving," he reassured them. What he was doing, he said, was preparing the organization and its senior team for a multi-year transition to the next generation of Verizon leadership. He didn't want to risk all that he and the current leadership team had built being torn apart by a poorly thought-out and poorly executed transition.

# "WE'RE NOT HAVING ANY DISCONTINUITY"

Seidenberg, like many corporate executives and observers at the time, had been alarmed by the number of bumpy successions or outright succession crises at major American corporations in recent years. IBM and Hewlett Packard, for instance, had seen their businesses disrupted and their reputations tarnished, at least temporarily, by either poor succession planning or implementation. He and Verizon head of HR Marc Reed, who was at the board meeting that day, were determined that Verizon was going to put a process in place that would be a model for the company for years to come.

What's more, Seidenberg realized that successful transitions involved more than just picking a new CEO. "So, this is not just about a new CEO," Seidenberg said to the board. "This is about a full transition to make sure that when we pick a new CEO, and we populate some of the proxy positions, we will have continuity." He had watched in alarm at other companies where all the board did was pick a CEO. "Then all of a sudden, you change everybody, and you have discontinuity," Seidenberg said. "We're not having any discontinuity."

# 2-3-2 PLAN

Since Reed had moved from the head of HR in wireless to the head of HR for all of Verizon in early 2004, he and Seidenberg had been talking about making succession planning a much more robust process. "Talent development and succession planning should be a core system of this business, just like billing," Reed said. Seidenberg met with Reed one day, and he said, "You know, there's no magic to this, but I'm 58 years old. Well, before 65 I should be done. So, we've got seven years. How are we going to do this?" The two of them developed what they termed their 2-3-2 plan.

## "MAKE THE SYSTEM MORE OPEN AND MORE INCLUSIVE"

While CEO succession planning would capture much of management's and the board's attention for the next several years, less visible but just as important changes were evolving across the company in terms of hiring and promoting the next generation of Verizon leaders. When Reed took over HR for all of Verizon in 2004, he and Seidenberg expanded upon and formalized practices that Seidenberg had been encouraging for years as a corporate leader, as had Bruce Gordon, who retired in 2003. "It was always my mantra that I would make opportunity available to more people than anybody else. And I think over the years, what drove me is to try to find times and places to make the system more open and more inclusive, for outsiders with new talents and for diversity," Seidenberg said.

"Every year, I had a meeting with all of our top people," Seidenberg said. "And in addition to all of their objectives and everything else, the one question I would say to them is, 'How do you think your organization is doing on giving people more of an opportunity to do this?'" He recalled:

Almost all of our executives thought that being more inclusive was the right thing to do, but sometimes the pressure of the business resulted in people falling back on what they always did. Some executives would say we did not have the requisite talent base or that they felt long-standing employees should be rewarded. All of these points were valid, but in an organization that was experiencing the explosive growth that we were, we had to do better and demonstrate we were going to be a more open and inclusive company. We may have made some mistakes along the way, but the greater good was served by our diligence on this matter. And most important to me was that the succession candidates all stepped up to this challenge. The emphasis on minority hiring continues to this day.

As Reed explained, "We had a couple of years to create the jobs that we thought would be the future jobs. Then we had three years to get people positioned into those jobs because someone would have to retire" to create openings for younger candidates. "Once we had the field narrowed in terms of what would be the key jobs—then we had two years of working with the board and operationalizing it so people could be seen as the leader we wanted them to be seen as," he said. "And so, by the time you got to this magical moment, which we said should not be a magical moment, this should just work like anything else."

Seidenberg told the board, "There are seven to 10 candidates here that could be the CEO. And, oh, by the way, here's another dozen people that will populate the proxy positions" that would open up as candidates shuttled between new positions. Seidenberg also informed the board that he, Reed and the HR subcommittee of the board would track a list of external potential CEOs at the same time they were grooming internal candidates. Of course, since there were many seasoned veterans on the board, they immediately challenged whether there were really 10 CEO candidates and another 20 ready to fill proxy positions. "It was a fun discussion because some directors wanted me to rate them right away. Instead, we agreed to let the process work," Seidenberg said.

Implemented correctly, the succession plan would have a positive impact from those who were moving on to those who were advancing in their careers but not yet seasoned enough to be considered CEO material. "Not only did we have great leaders that have left a legacy move on and still be very supportive of the company," Reed said, "but as we were raising the handful of candidates that were eventually going to compete and succeed for Ivan's job, we then also built the new operating team. So as Lowell came up he had a team that was in place, ready to do their jobs."

# "I'M READY"

Director Bob Lane applauded the systematic approach Seidenberg and Reed were taking to succession. Like Seidenberg, Lane, the chairman and CEO of Deere & Co., had seen too many cases of rushed or poorly thought-out succession plans go awry. "For succession to work, the incumbent has to be ready. The candidate has to be ready, and the board has to be ready," Lane shared with the board. "If you try to move the process before one of the three is ready, there will be nervous energy in the system. And you'll get the wrong results." Seidenberg declared to the board that he was getting the process started. "I'm first. I'm ready."

Seidenberg told the board that he and Reed would discuss the succession process with the human resources committee of the board at every meeting but only with the full board twice a year, so the issue wouldn't become a distraction. Seidenberg also refused to tip his hand and suggest who the front-runners were, often to the frustration of certain board members. Aramark Chairman and CEO Joe Neubauer, chairman of the HR committee at Verizon, said that "it was a very long process again, very explicit deliberations, both by the human resource committee and the full board." Board members consistently prodded the CEO for more information.

"He was a very cagey player in this, and I admired him enormously," Neubauer said. "He never wanted to set a specific time frame, and he always said that if things worked out, it would be before" many board members expected a decision. "I will surprise you on the short side rather than the long side," Seidenberg told the board.

"Ivan was always close to the vest on his feelings about these guys," added Director Tom O'Brien. "He had a unique way about him. I admire him greatly, by the way, just for his business acumen and as an individual." O'Brien added, "He always felt that you could say 10 wonderful things about a person and one negative, and that's the only thing people remember."

The board would be able to evaluate the candidates, some of whom they had already met at board meetings, as they presented to the board more often during the selection process. Neubauer said, "We talked about letting them demonstrate their expertise, letting them demonstrate how they present to the board, how they handle questions from the board. I'm always amused when senior executives accuse me sometimes of giving them ongoing performance reviews. And I have to remind them that every time you present something to somebody else, there's a performance review going on. It's not explicit, it's not open, but that's what's going on. That's how you form opinions over a period of time."

Director John Snow, former chairman and CEO of CSX Corp. and former U.S. treasury secretary, was also a member of the human resources committee. "So, people were getting shuffled around, moved around, looked at, observed, tested and reported on to the human resources committee. Ivan would ask us, 'What do you think you see? Are they changing? Are they performing the way you would think they should?'"

## WANTED: COMMERCIAL LEADERS

What were Seidenberg and Reed, working with the board, looking for in the next CEO? "Commercial leaders," said Reed. "People who could look at our business, understand our technology and our operational processes, and then figure out how they could pinpoint external change and then transform our business models to monetize the assets and investments we had made in the company up to that time."

They also evaluated potential candidates according to their track record in four key areas: running large teams, P&L accountability, corporate staff assignments, and global experience.

To avoid the trap experienced by other companies, in which board members start to favor candidates based on their exposure to them at meetings or other events, Seidenberg and Reed intentionally had candidates sit by different board members from meeting to meeting and at dinners where executives mingled with the directors. At one event Verizon Wireless COO Lowell McAdam thought that his chances to reach the top might have faded. He had been seated next to Seidenberg's wife, Phyllis, not a high-powered board member. Then it occurred to him that his CEO's wife might have developed some fairly astute observations about what traits to look for in a future leader.

As much as Seidenberg and Reed were genuine in their willingness to consider external candidates, over time it became apparent that they were favoring a homegrown future CEO. For one, many of the initial external candidates they identified at mid-decade had demonstrated poor leadership in their careers or were snapped up by other Fortune 500 companies in search of fresh leadership as the Verizon search process neared its climax. More broadly, Seidenberg in particular felt that the next CEO should have deep vertical knowledge of the range of Verizon businesses and at the same time be immersed in the Verizon corporate culture. Seidenberg said simply, "I always thought we had a deep bench, and I always thought it was part of my job to give the board choices for succession, starting with qualified internal candidates."

Seidenberg recalled his discussion with Bill Ferguson when he was named CEO of NYNEX: "He said there were many outside candidates that had much more CEO experience than I might have had, but none of them knew our business. Sometimes it might be necessary to pick someone way outside the system, but after more than 10 major mergers and acquisitions and countless smaller deals, it was important to develop our own leaders to build on the foundation."

Neubauer quipped that he had his money on an internal candidate all along. "There was a very strong organ rejection system at Verizon," he said, meaning it was hard for the corporate culture at that time to accept outside leadership, just as it had been at many of the Bell operating companies.

## NAME IN AN ENVELOPE

The board was required to vote on and approve the next chairman and CEO of Verizon when the time came. Seidenberg left his recommendation for interim CEO in a sealed envelope with the corporate secretary if something should happen to him before the selection process ran its course. Many corporate CEOs have followed similar procedures.

The initial name in the envelope was Vice Chairman and COO Larry Babbio, who had known for years that he was not in the running to succeed Seidenberg as CEO. But Seidenberg did say, "If I'm not here, they may call you." Babbio thanked him for the recognition of his leadership skills and dedication to the company. Then Babbio asked, "What if I'm not here?" Seidenberg replied, "Then you're not on the list."

Their conversation set the frank tone Seidenberg maintained throughout the succession process. "Even though not everybody liked the conversation, everybody knew I was doing my job," Seidenberg said. "That's all I wanted them to know."

# CIRCUITOUS ROUTES

John Killian was still smarting years later from having not been considered in 2002 to replace Fred Salerno as Verizon CFO and executive vice president. Doreen Toben took that spot instead, and he reported to her briefly as corporate controller. As it turned out, what seemed like a setback at the time may have led—via a more circuitous route—to important career milestones that would in turn make him among the key candidates for Verizon's top job.

In 2003, Killian moved into the wireline business and served as CFO under Babbio. Two years later, as noted earlier, he was asked to lead the integration of newly acquired MCI. The combining of MCI into Verizon involved a lot of trade-offs. Killian adopted the MCI sales structure, for instance, while keeping the Verizon focus on pricing for what initially was a relatively low-margin business. Killian was named the first president of newly formed Verizon Business, with 31,000 employees and a global network covering six continents, in January 2006.

CFO Doreen Toben announced her retirement from Verizon in 2009. Seidenberg saluted her for her commitment to financial discipline and execution. Killian succeeded Toben as EVP and CFO. The experience he gained en route to the CFO's office made him a very well-rounded candidate as the Verizon succession sweepstakes progressed. Fran Shammo, CFO of Verizon Business, who had also held several financial and operating positions on the wireless side of the company, succeeded Killian as CEO of the Verizon unit.

# WIRELESS: FUEL FOR EXPANSION

Babbio, two years older than Seidenberg, had been discussing his retirement with Seidenberg on and off since they were in the midst of the Fios launch. But the actual event was always comfortably in the future. When it was time to announce his retirement in 2007, Babbio said, "It was probably a little earlier than I would have ordinarily gone, but not too much earlier. When I retired, I was 62. Would've been 63 in December of that year." He added, "Would I have stayed till 65? Probably. But you know, I understood the need for a planned management transition." Babbio's contributions to the success of Verizon were legion, but he was remembered, in particular, inside the company and out for his leadership role during the 9/11 crisis—especially the successful effort in 2001 to get the NYSE open for trading following the terrorist attacks.

Strigl moved from CEO of Verizon Wireless to serve as COO of the entire company in 2007. Lowell McAdam, COO of the wireless business, succeeded Strigl as CEO of Verizon Wireless. Dick Lynch moved from CTO of wireless to CTO of the parent company that year, and as noted, John Stratton moved from CMO of wireless to CMO of Verizon. Shaygan Kheradpir became the chief information officer for all of Verizon.

The board appreciated that this was much more than a flurry of corporate musical chairs. M. Frances Keeth, Verizon lead director and former Royal Dutch Shell executive vice president, said that Seidenberg led "the best process I've seen on succession planning." She added:

> He took the current management and positioned them so that we could bring [up] the new high potentials. Because the current management was basically the same age as Ivan. They had grown up together. Whether they had the capacity or not to be the CEO wasn't even a relevant question because they didn't have the runway.
>
> So, he managed those people to where he could position them where they were still contributors and then retiring at an appropri-

ate time and space between the different retirements and moved in the up-and-coming people and let the board see all the candidates and begin to make choices about, OK, this is clearly not going to work. These people clearly have an opportunity.

But I will tell you I still believe he knew where he was going, and he just let us get comfortable with it over maybe three years. I mean it was nice to have choices. Most of the time on boards, you don't have choices.

The shift of Strigl to Verizon COO was all about driving operating results across the company, Seidenberg told shareholders while reviewing the company's performance in 2007: "Under our chief operating officer, Denny Strigl, our leadership team is focused on the fundamentals of running a great business: growing revenue and taking market share, improving efficiency and productivity, delivering excellent service and strengthening our culture." With Babbio retired, Strigl's name replaced his in the envelope with the corporate secretary.

Opportunities in the legal department also opened up. General Counsel Bill Barr retired in 2008. He was replaced by Randy Milch, who had come up the legal ranks on the wireline side of the business. Craig Silliman, who had joined Verizon with the acquisition of MCI, replaced Milch as general counsel of the wireline unit.

One of the great challenges that Seidenberg and Reed often discussed was the fact that Verizon's next generation of leaders was replacing some renowned figures in the business. "Who replaces Larry or Denny or Fred or Doreen? We had to teach our people that change was constant and never defend or attack the past but constantly add new value to your position and the business," Seidenberg said. "This was one of the greatest lessons learned by serving on outside boards." Seidenberg learned from his experience and through serving on other boards that the CEO was in charge of all the bad news and also in charge of figuring out the future. "This made me sensitive to executives who could handle bad news by focusing on what to do next and those who had optimism and passion for the future," he said.

# "LIGHTNING BOLT" LEARNING

While Seidenberg spent a great deal of time mapping out career tracks for rising executives across the company during the succession process, he also continued in his role as mentor-in-chief. He counseled leaders during meetings and presentations and helped them to learn by doing, rather than dictating how they should approach or resolve challenges. CMO Stratton said that such lessons learned were often revelations that he and others valued, even if they didn't always appreciate how focused Seidenberg was on the learning process at the time:

I'll describe something that I'm embarrassed to say happened to me more than once. . . . Now Ivan's the chairman of the board. Ivan is flying at a much higher altitude than I. And once in a while, we'd come in, in a VLC [Verizon Leadership Council] meeting or whatever, we'd go down into the detail of a particular thing that was happening in the markets and would be describing the nuance of the initiative and where we were hoping to go, and here's the strategic aspect of it, and here's what we're going to do and how.

I'd be 15 to 18 minutes into the deal and Ivan would ask a question. And I would hear the question. I'd think to myself, "Uh-oh, he's not getting it. . . . Maybe I'm not explaining this the right way" or "I've got to cut him some slack; I'm doing this 24/7; you know, he's not really. . . ."

So, anyway, I'd try to answer the question politely and everything else and think to myself, "OK, I've got to figure out how to make sure that he's with me on this thing. But we're pretty good." And he would always say, "Look, it sounds like you've got it. Keep going. Do your deal."

So, I go back to work. I forget all about that exchange. And maybe 90 days, 100 days later, I'd be working on this thing, and as is always the case, it's fluid, the thing moves around, and all of a sudden I have this insight, maybe I should do this. And I'm telling you this happened way more than once. I stop in my tracks and go, "That's the question he asked me four months ago."

I have to say I can still feel what that felt like—you know, that moment? That lightning bolt that blasts a hole in your desk? It was, to me, an unbelievable thing that he could have such clarity and could be so many moves ahead of where I was, even though 1. I'm not a dope, and 2. I'm in this full time, driving it hard; I'm in the deep end of the pool. And that to me was an amazing gift.

Whatever the thing was that I was working on that was so essential, I think what was interesting about Ivan is he played the long game in everything he did. And I suspect that in many cases he thought that the development of me as a leader and as a businessperson was more important than the thing I was working on. So maybe he could help me cut four months off of my insight, but earning the insight was more valuable in the long run. And that's pretty extraordinary.

# PUTTING VODAFONE ON HOLD

For years Seidenberg and his leadership team, as well as the board, had been discussing various strategies they could pursue to buy out Vodafone's 45 percent stake in Verizon Wireless. Not owning 100 percent of the wireless business kept Verizon from garnering some important economies of scale and operating efficiencies. Verizon's business units were getting too big and interconnected for the joint-venture structure to remain viable indefinitely.

In preparation for the need to borrow to fund the purchase of the Vodafone stake, Verizon had been consistently reducing Verizon Wireless' debt load for years to well below industry averages. That had the added benefit of making Verizon even stronger financially than it might typically have been as the company entered the 2008 financial crisis. Vodafone, not surprisingly, had been advocating that highly profitable Verizon Wireless pay Vodafone an annual dividend with the cash it was generating, instead of consistently paying down debt. But as the operating partner with a 55 percent stake, Verizon did not yet have to compromise on dividends to please its minority partner.

"It used to drive them crazy because they would say, 'You've got to give us a dividend,'" Seidenberg recalled. "And I would say, 'No, the way you're going to get a dividend is you're going to sell your share'" back to Verizon. "It was a predictable conversation, done openly and in good cheer, but nevertheless a serious thorn in my side," he added.

Verizon's board was split on the issue of how Seidenberg should approach Vittorio Colao, Vodafone's CEO of Europe. The entrepreneurs among the group, including Richard Carrion, would say impatiently, "Just make him an offer; buy him." Others, including Sandy Moose, would balk at the figures being bandied about as the price for buying out Vodafone. Director Joe Neubauer grumbled that every time they looked at the issue again, the price had gone up another $5 billion based on the success of the business.

Seidenberg and Colao held a number of meetings at which they discussed the issue, including during long walks in Hyde Park in London and Battery Park in Lower Manhattan. Seidenberg even met with Vodafone's board of directors at Colao's invitation. They asked him what he would do in their shoes. "In a nice way, I said I'd sell" to Verizon and reinvest the proceeds in European markets, where Vodafone's market share had slipped due in part to under-investment, he said. Seidenberg left the meeting with the distinct impression that was not the message Vodafone wanted to hear.

By 2009, Seidenberg concluded that as much as he wanted to make a buyout of Vodafone the capstone of his career as Verizon CEO, it wasn't going to happen on his watch. The deal was a victim of his own success. He realized that Vodafone was very sensitive to not being perceived as "another notch on my belt, which was what one of the Vodafone directors jokingly said at their meeting," Seidenberg said. He met with McAdam and the board and told them that McAdam, first as COO and then CEO of Verizon Wireless, had developed a relationship with Colao at the operational level. He should be the point man going forward in advocating for a resolution of the partial ownership of Vodafone. Seidenberg also thought it was important to reassure Verizon shareholders that the company would not do an irresponsible deal and wildly overpay for Vodafone's share.

## NARROWING THE FIELD

Seidenberg broached the idea of Strigl's retirement with his COO in 2009. He pushed back initially, but a few weeks later, Strigl came into Seidenberg's office and announced that he had decided to retire because it was time to move on after 41 years of service. His retirement was announced that September, effective at year-end. Seidenberg described Strigl at the time as "truly one of the legendary figures of our industry. He built Verizon Wireless into one of the most amazing growth companies in this or any industry. His work ethic and high standards inspired generations of Verizon leaders and helped create a culture of performance that is his lasting legacy to our company."

After Strigl's retirement, there was no No. 2 at Verizon. Seidenberg and the board weren't tipping their hands on the succession race. Nor were they prepared to make a decision at that point.

To many the field appeared to have narrowed to a two-person race, however, based on the fact that Verizon SEC filings disclosed that the board had granted three-year retention bonuses to Lowell McAdam and John Killian in December 2009. Such bonuses are intended to provide financial inducements to stay with a company and not accept offers to take a senior position at another corporation. Neither Seidenberg nor the board made any commitments about the candidates' standing at the time, even though they had been granted the retention bonuses. As always, the board could pursue the option of an external candidate.

The two internal candidates, both in their mid-50s, were highly qualified, and each met the board's criteria for what they were looking for in a CEO. McAdam represented the company's wireless juggernaut that was Verizon's largest, fastest-growing and most profitable business. Killian had leadership experience in the company's traditional wireline business as well as the global internet backbone operations of Verizon Business. And his strength was as CFO, often a proving ground for Fortune 500 CEOs.

They each had spent a great deal of time with the board at this point and would, if anything, step up their exposure as 2010 progressed. But they were hardly cookie-cutter candidates. Killian was a natural presenter before the board. Smart, succinct, every hair in place and dressed as conservatively as a Brooks Brothers model, he looked and acted the part of a senior financial officer and corporate executive at the top of his game.

McAdam had been born in upstate New York and served in the Navy, but formative years spent in California gave him a taste for loafers, oddly colored shirts and loud ties. "Buy one blue suit," Seidenberg pleaded with him as they discussed his board interactions. "When they listen to you, all they can do is look at your tie." Trained as an engineer, McAdam's idea of a great day at work was breaking down processes and making them more efficient, not attending a board meeting.

When Strigl retired, institutional investors in particular, who had been following the company closely, saw both Killian and McAdam as the two most senior executives. "Everyone knew they were great exec-utives and both highly qualified. There was no drama," Seidenberg said, "because investors knew we had a plan and a deep bench, and John and Lowell were both committed to the other's success." He added, "I knew I was fast approaching the end of my run, and once the shareholders gave their implicit and explicit support for both John and Lowell, I was on the home stretch with the board."

## COACHING

McAdam said that Seidenberg worked closely with him and Killian during this period to expose them to issues a CEO faces. "He took me to meetings with John Chambers of Cisco, and I got to watch how Ivan handled John. And he'd occasionally throw me a question, and then if I didn't handle it right, Ivan would sort of come back in as he did without being confrontational or anything, but he'd come on, and he'd either ask you an obvious question or he'd make a statement. And you could see he was just sort of teaching you in the process," McAdam said.

In addition to taking McAdam along on meetings with key vendors, Seidenberg "did involve me as we got closer in a couple of the board recruitments," McAdam said, "when he was looking for somebody on the board. And then he started opening up about how you managed a particular board member a little bit more," McAdam said. "He was feeding me during the process."

"I got the sense that the only real two candidates, even though there were more on the list, were John Killian and me," McAdam said. "And he did similar things with John, I think."

In addition to working closely with the top two candidates, Seidenberg, who turned 63 in December 2009, also found himself needing to let his board know that the clock was ticking on the succession process. "At one meeting, they were having a hard time getting focused on it, and they thought, 'Eh, if we think John or Lowell need more time, we can talk him into staying another year or so,'" Seidenberg recalled. He had to make the process real for them and underscore that this was much more than an HR committee exercise.

Even though the board had yet to select his successor, Seidenberg told the board in reference to staying an extra year, "You're not going to talk me into doing that." He added, "Let me offer you a thought. In six months, I will no longer fly on company business. I'm done. No more overnight trips to California. No more overnight trips to Hong Kong. No more two-day trips to Asia. I'm not doing it. I remember one director, Fran Keeth, said, 'He's serious.' Then they got serious."

Seidenberg was increasingly comfortable with his two insider front-runners. "During 2009 and for a portion of 2010, I had the chance to discuss both Lowell's and John's views of the future of the business many times. They were both so far ahead of where I was at that point in my career. It just reinforced the idea about my own timing." He added, "It's a great lesson for boards and CEOs. There is a natural rhythm to industry evolution, company evolution and CEO tenures. Bob Lane was exactly right. All three have to be aligned for the process to produce a good outcome."

## JOHN KILLIAN BOWS OUT

In August 2010 Killian requested a private meeting with Seidenberg. "I went and saw Ivan and told him I was leaving," Killian said. His family had not moved to New York from Boston with him six or so years earlier. The weekend commuting was wearing on him. He made the decision that for personal reasons he would return to the Boston area and retire from Verizon.

"You realize this is taking you out of any consideration to be the top guy," Seidenberg said. Killian thanked his CEO for acknowledging that he was a contender for the top post but said, "We don't have to have that conversation."

During their talk, Seidenberg asked Killian if he thought he would have gotten the CEO job. Killian said that no, he thought McAdam was going to be the choice given the incredible success of the wireless business under his leadership and its contribution to Verizon as a whole. Seidenberg didn't respond. Killian emphasized that in any case he was taking himself out of contention for personal reasons, not because he thought he was trailing McAdam.

Seidenberg, who described Killian as "one of the best people I've ever worked with, a smart gentleman," said it was important in his role as CFO that Killian reach out to investor groups and Wall Street. He needed to make it clear that his departure was his choice. He was not leaving because he had been passed over for the top job. And whether they believed him or not, he needed to take the initiative.

When Killian's retirement was announced the following month, Seidenberg said, "In the decades that I've worked with John, I have been continually impressed with his ceaseless energy, his loyalty and his love of the business." Seidenberg added: "He has been a wonderful source of advice and counsel to me and to the rest of Verizon's senior team. A tremendous leader with intense focus on positioning Verizon to win, he has made a significant and positive difference to Verizon."

## COO LOWELL MCADAM

After Killian said he was going to retire, Seidenberg called McAdam into his office. He told him about Killian's decision and offered McAdam the COO job, with the expectation that it would lead to the CEO office when Seidenberg retired, if McAdam performed as expected. "Well, I don't know if I want to do this," McAdam told his stunned CEO. Seidenberg said, "Are you bargaining with me?" McAdam said that he was aware stepping up to COO, and eventually CEO, assuming that worked out, entailed an additional level of commitment on his part. He wanted to go home and talk it over with his wife.

His response may not have come as a complete surprise. McAdam had made it clear earlier to Seidenberg that he didn't see the CEO succession race as a do or die situation for him. "What are you going to do if you don't get the job?" Seidenberg had asked him when it was apparent to many that McAdam and Killian were the unofficial finalists. McAdam said, "Well, you know, you won't see me jump off the edge of the building here. Life's been pretty good. I've had a great run here, and if I do it, fine. If I don't do it, fine." McAdam recalled later, "I have to admit secretly I was thinking I wouldn't get it, and I'd just go do something else. It wasn't something that I felt I really needed. I think my philosophy is if you want this job too badly, you won't do it well."

While it wasn't widely known, McAdam had turned down a promotion several years earlier with the understanding that it might have permanently derailed his chance to become CEO of Verizon. Just as the Fios project was getting underway, Larry Babbio had pressed McAdam, then COO of wireless under Strigl, to move over and lead the Fios effort on the wireline side of the company. Strigl and Seidenberg both advised him to make the move for the benefit of his career. When he resisted, saying he was committed to his role in wireless, Babbio said that he was taking himself out of contention for the top job at Verizon. McAdam's stance was "so be it," and he assumed that the best he could hope for was to top out as the head of the wireless business. His performance in the intervening years leading wireless from strength to strength, however, ended up making him the Verizon CEO candidate to beat.

McAdam met with Seidenberg the day after speaking with his wife and said that he wanted the job. But he also said that he wanted further coaching from his CEO. Before the promotion was formally voted on by the board and announced publicly, McAdam also met with each Verizon director so they could get to know him better. "One of the things that I said was I wanted to make sure that none of you have any reservations, because if you think you've got a better option, you should go do it."

Director Sandy Moose said that by the time the decision was made, many on the board had been leaning toward McAdam. "We all agreed that the future of the business was really wireless. So, Ivan's successor was going to come out of the wireless business. We needed that experience/expertise," she said.

"By the time Lowell stepped into the role, the directors were very comfortable with him. They knew him. They had seen him in action and were well aware of his accomplishments," Moose said. "Lowell in many respects is like Ivan in being very straightforward, very honest," she added. "He's a man who knows what he doesn't know. I like to work with people who know what they don't know, and they're not trying to bluff you. They're willing to ask questions and discuss their misgivings.'"

Seidenberg told the Verizon board that he wanted to not only announce McAdam as COO but to go ahead and name him as Seidenberg's successor. Some board members objected. "What if he doesn't work out?" one asked. "Then fire him," Seidenberg said. "Most companies create a little drama about once you're COO you're not CEO, but my view was that we say it," Seidenberg said.

On September 20, 2010, Verizon announced that McAdam, 56, was the company's new president and COO, effective October 1. Seidenberg said, "The board's selection of Lowell to this key, central position underscores its commitment to reward success while working with me to prepare our company for an executive transition in the future. Lowell is undeniably the right executive at the right time, given his track record of growth while managing one of the most dynamic and successful businesses in America."

At the same time as the McAdam announcement, Verizon also announced that Fran Shammo, president of Verizon Telecom and Business, was promoted to Verizon CFO, replacing John Killian. Dan Mead, Verizon Wireless COO, succeeded McAdam as CEO of the wireless business and John Stratton, who had shifted from CMO of Verizon to CMO of Verizon Wireless in 2009, replaced Mead as COO of Verizon Wireless.

# LEADING VS. MANAGING

To no one's surprise, McAdam thrived in his new position as Verizon's chief operating officer. One of his immediate, lasting initiatives was to work closely with leaders on the wireline and wireless sides of the business to promote a greater focus on profitability in the face of the increasingly competitive arenas in which Verizon operated.

McAdam and Marc Reed worked with faculty from Duke University's business school to create a business program for company leaders. Out of that effort grew the Verizon Lean Six Sigma program focusing on return on capital, execution and customer service. The program has saved billions every year since it was implemented in terms of cost cutting and driving efficiencies across business lines.

McAdam also focused his attention on the rank and file across the company, including the unionized portion of the workforce. At his first employee meeting as the Verizon COO, he asked, "How many of you are technicians?' Nobody raised his or her hand. "How many of you are in call centers?" Again, no hands were raised. McAdam was astounded to learn that the local manager didn't invite union members to employee meetings. "How do you expect them to know what's going on in the business?" McAdam asked.

He took his share of haranguing from union stewards going forward, but McAdam insisted that employee meetings be opened up to all. "You just sort of stand in the line of fire and say, 'OK, well, here are the facts, and this is what we're trying to get done.'" He told managers, "If we don't include these employees, how do we get them to understand the Credo and the same sort of improve-every-day philosophy?"

# NEW CEO, NEW ERA

Verizon watchers were expecting a September 2011 announcement that McAdam would be named CEO in October, one year after his elevation to COO. Seidenberg told the board he wanted to move up the announcement to July and make the promotion effective August 1. That would give the new CEO more positive momentum for continuing to drive change at the company if his promotion was ahead of schedule.

Seidenberg had an ulterior motive as well. The early promotion would make McAdam the sole senior Verizon officer the unions would have to deal with when they renegotiated their contract, which was up in early August. "I had been through enough contracts," Seidenberg said. "Here was the issue: I wasn't going to be there, so why would I negotiate a contract that I wasn't going to be accountable for? So to me, I think that's playing team ball." Seidenberg remained Verizon chairman through year-end 2011, and then McAdam, as expected, assumed that title as well.

Seidenberg and Reed had worked for years to craft a succession process at Verizon that would be second to none in preparing the corporation for its next growth phase. As McAdam told *Fortune* magazine while still COO, "Ivan got all the tools and put them into the toolbox. Now it's up to us to take those tools and apply them to take the company to the next level." Seidenberg said, "At the end of the process, when the board selected Lowell, not only did they select a great executive but a passionate and dedicated person who cared deeply about the legacy and future of the company. As CEO, you could not have written a better script."

Verizon Director Richard Carrion joined the NYNEX board of directors just before Seidenberg took over as CEO in 1995. After Seidenberg's final board meeting in 2011, the directors held a dinner in his honor.

During the dinner, Carrion asked Seidenberg, what's been the key thing behind his and Verizon's success? "I never thought of the network as a commodity," Seidenberg told him. "I thought the network was going to be our competitive weapon, and we need to differentiate ourselves with a network."

"Looking back, what are the three things you're proudest of?" Carrion asked. "The company is a lot stronger now than it was," Seidenberg replied. "We're independent; we control our own destiny . . . and I'm very proud of how our people stepped up during 9/11. That will always be a source of pride to me."

Carrion echoed many Verizon insiders and those who have followed the company closely when he said recently, "People don't understand what was built here. If you go back and look at what the landscape looked like 25 years ago and what it is today, and how he maneuvered to create clearly a premier telecom company not only in the U.S., [but] in the world . . . and how he very deliberately put those pieces together, with one or two mistakes along the way without a doubt, but he put together a hell of a company, which is what we have today." He added, "With people knitting together the different organizations, you come up with a Verizon culture that is very clear today. . . . It's a great, great American company. It was put together in a short period of time by somebody who knew what the hell he was doing."

Seidenberg could look back on his term as Verizon chairman and CEO, and the leadership team he developed and assembled, with enormous satisfaction and pride. There was no question that the company and its leadership increasingly reflected the tremendous success of the wireless side of the business. Yet he was confident that McAdam and his senior team grasped the contribution to the company's success, and its prospects, provided by the Verizon Business global internet backbone and the Fios-driven spread of fiber-optic cable throughout the wireline core of the business.

There was no shortage of challenges facing the new Verizon leadership. They were determined to maintain the competitive advantage offered by their best-in-class network and develop more of a customer focus across their business lines. But with competition mounting across the board, they were keenly aware that wins in the past were not predictors of the future. At the same time, they would continue to push back on the regulatory front, especially concerning internet access. And McAdam was determined to finish the job Seidenberg started and buy out his wireless partner, Vodafone.

# TRANSITIONS: C-SUITE INSIGHTS FROM RAM CHARAN

---

## ___ NOTHING SUCCEEDS LIKE SUCCESSION.

Identifying and promoting high-potential leaders requires continual multi-year, multi-level succession planning across an organization. Not just at the CEO level. Value the capacity to learn new skills, not the mastery of yesterday's tool kit.

## ___ PROMOTE DIVERSITY.

Creating a broadly defined, diverse leadership team is key to a thriving succession process.

## ___ MAKE WAY.

Company icons need to be willing to move on so next-generation leaders can be groomed for more responsibility. Carefully orchestrated exit strategies are integral to the success of multi-dimensional succession planning.

# Handicapping HiPos

By Ram Charan

The most important job for the CEO and board of directors is to pick the CEO's successor. The trouble is, not everyone is what I call a high-potential leader, or HiPo, capable of being the near-term leader of a large and complex organization in tomorrow's world. In years past, CEOs-in-waiting sharpened their skills by extending brands, cutting costs and buying out weaker rivals. More and more radical changes are required of the next generation of CEOs. That includes transforming business models, quite possibly more than once during the CEO's tenure, reinventing the customer experience, and blowing up and rebuilding the supply chain and distribution networks.

The stakes could not be higher. In today's environment of accelerating digitization and discontinuity, companies can't afford to get succession wrong. That applies to companies operating in developed and developing economies alike. The well-chronicled succession shortfalls at Hewlett Packard, Infosys and Tata Group in recent years temporarily tripped up the organizations, or at least tarnished their reputations. Perhaps more than temporarily, in certain cases. Going forward, investors, customers and other stakeholders are likely to be much less forgiving of succession screwups. The marketplace won't stand still as the stumbling company rights itself. Rivals are more likely than ever to leverage another's failures, while customers' needs are met elsewhere. When it comes to handicapping HiPos, I have identified three essential characteristics that were not necessarily part of the skill sets of the previous generation of CEOs:

- They imagine on a large scale—they are fearless and prepared to scale up very quickly. If they don't have the information they need, they know the person or database to turn to;

- They seek what they need to make it happen—they ignore hierarchies and get the information or help they need, often from their seniors outside of their own organizations;

- They understand the concept of the ecosystem—HiPos have the ability to grasp the web of interrelationships around their company and how that might be transformed for the better.

Effective succession at the senior corporate level requires a multi-level, multi-year review of leadership team needs, inside and outside of the company. Succession is not a one-and-done affair. Internal candidates two and three levels down in senior leadership need to be assessed regularly in the context of succession. The peer group these HiPos are graded against should be potential CEOs. A key consideration: The accelerating pace of technological change across industries puts a premium on identifying tech all-stars who, by more traditional yardsticks such as breadth of management experience, might not make the cut.

One of the key issues in the succession process ought to be: What does past performance say about potential? Do HiPos have the capacity to learn, to change, to adapt and to embrace the future? To mold themselves into what the future requires?

The success of the senior leadership team at Verizon has been based consistently on moving the enterprise into the most competitive position possible relative to industry rivals, by expanding and engaging external influencers, starting with customers and suppliers and including regulators and government entities at multiple levels. Dealing with externals is a clear requirement for HiPos and, crucially, leaders at secondary and tertiary levels for an organization to thrive going forward.

Measuring C-suite capacity is not a cut-and-dried exercise that can be determined by asking a few pointed questions. It requires digging into the kind of messy world of real-time, simultaneous decision-making that the Verizon story has been describing. And it ought to be a continuous, multi-year process. If you are an HR person, if you are a CEO, monitor these context-driven, behavioral decisions of the HiPos in your organization. When you see how they perform over a period of time, in multiple positions of authority, you will be able to pull it together. Gauging the potential of external candidates adds another layer of complexity to the succession process but is essential in order to ensure that you are considering the best possible group of high-performance potential CEOs.

High-performance organizations typically have a bias for learning built into their DNA. Bill Ferguson knew that the next CEO of NYNEX had to be a change agent prepared to lead the company into uncharted territory that he couldn't define with any accuracy. In my consulting work with Ferguson, I had highlighted Ivan Seidenberg's leadership potential and clear ability to pursue non-linear solutions. He obviously had caught Ferguson's attention, as well. We both agreed that he was far from a textbook choice for CEO. After all, he did not have much operating experience, nor had he risen through the financial ranks of the company, which were the two most direct career paths to the CEO office at the time. Ferguson concluded (correctly, as it turned out) that Seidenberg's clear curiosity and potential to learn outweighed the negatives, including the fact that not all of the NYNEX board had supported his choice.

I continued to consult with Seidenberg for another 15 years. We were constantly adapting the idea of what the CEO of the future would need to focus on. As the industry evolved—with greater regulatory impact and consequences, dramatic technological changes and the broad trend toward mass customization—it became obvious to both of us that the next CEO was facing a range of challenges that in key ways exceeded those faced by Seidenberg when he took the top job.

These conversations helped drive the multi-year succession process at Verizon that ultimately led to the choice of Lowell McAdam as the current chairman and CEO. His dominant skill and his capacity to learn in the broadest meaning of the term, coupled with his natural curiosity and his willingness to adapt to the demands of the future—on top of outstanding career performance—made him the unanimous choice of the Verizon board. It is importance to re-emphasize that this type of succession sorting doesn't just happen at the top. It has to be applied to the second layer of management and the third layer of management, so everybody is trying to figure it out across the top tiers of leadership.

While no one can predict the future, the accelerating trends of technological change and ongoing mass customization serve as clear indicators as to where the potential of HiPos ought to be focused.

---

Portions of the above material derived from *The High Potential Leader: How to Grow Fast, Take on New Responsibilities and Make an Impact*, by Ram Charan with Geri Willigan, John Wiley & Sons Inc., 2017.

# A NEW ERA BEGINS

2010-2015

Verizon's succession process wasn't happening in a vacuum. Even before McAdam was named CEO, he was building on Verizon's earlier successes to spur future growth. The biggest challenges—and opportunities—facing Verizon in the first years of the current decade were in its rapidly growing wireless business, where McAdam made his reputation as a dynamic leader.

His new leadership focused on meeting the broadband communications needs of tomorrow's consumers, initially in the wireless arena. Driving performance across the entire company continued to be a top priority as well. In the process, McAdam and his team positioned Verizon as the decade progressed to reinvent itself once again as an integrated broadband juggernaut. And McAdam would complete the journey begun by Seidenberg and finally make Verizon the sole master of its destiny by buying out its longtime wireless partner.

McAdam realized that even though he could draw on years of experience in the business, he had to up his game as CEO. "When I first took over, I thought a CEO is just a COO on steroids," he said. Not so. "You've really got to be a lot more into strategy," McAdam said. "Ivan said this to me at one point: 'You're the chief future revenue officer . . . you've got to be thinking what will build the revenue of this business three, four, five years from now.' That was a big change for me."

# APPLE TALKS

It had been a tough few years for the wireless business following the launch of the iPhone exclusively on AT&T's network in 2007. By late 2009, early 2010, however, Verizon was on the rebound. As noted, the Droid smartphone created in partnership with Google and Motorola launched on Verizon's network in the fourth quarter of 2009 and was an instant best-seller. Its success further underscored the limitations many iPhone users faced being tethered exclusively to the AT&T network. Behind the scenes at Verizon, even bigger changes were underway. Apple was talking quietly with Verizon about rolling out its own version of the iPhone as soon as the exclusive clause in the AT&T distribution agreement expired. The deal had been renegotiated to 2011 from 2012.

McAdam and Seidenberg each had made multiple trips to Apple's corporate campus in Cupertino, California, to meet with Chairman and CEO Steve Jobs and COO Tim Cook. Dan Mead, who was named COO of Verizon Wireless in 2009 and succeeded McAdam as CEO in 2010, also joined in forging closer ties with the technology trailblazers.

Early on, Jobs consistently told the Verizon executives that he was a loyal team player when it came to AT&T. But as the end of the exclusivity agreement loomed, he did indicate that he appreciated Verizon's commitment to quality and that at least some customers continued to chafe at the service they received from AT&T. "You know, there's an element of the way you guys think that we think," Jobs told Seidenberg. "Your singular focus on your network is the way we singularly focus on our product development." Seidenberg made sure he had Jobs' OK to share that story with his team, since it validated the commitment they had long made to the quality of the Verizon network.

Jobs added, "I've got to tell you a story. I was in my dentist office yesterday. As he's working my cavity, he was complaining to me about his AT&T iPhone. And it was dropping calls, and everything." Jobs changed the subject, but Seidenberg sensed an opening for a closer relationship between the two companies.

"So how are we going to get to the point where you take us more seriously than you have in the last couple of years?" Seidenberg asked. "I'm a good partner," Jobs reiterated. "The contract goes for another 14 months." Seidenberg nodded in agreement and then offered, "So what if we had some of our technical people begin the conversation?" Jobs, who was struggling with cancer, agreed. "Yeah, have them call Tim Cook."

That was the opening Verizon was waiting for. McAdam took part in talks with Cook as well as Jobs. The technical discussion seemed to be getting hung up on the pages of specifications around important but time-consuming details. Verizon needed to change the terms of the negotiations.

McAdam and his team had an insight. To demonstrate the superiority of the Verizon network and how much better an iPhone would function with Verizon rather than AT&T, they offered to build a Verizon cell tower on Apple's Cupertino campus free of charge. Apple could test its network's abilities however they wanted. "You don't have to tell us what you're doing," McAdam said. "We guarantee you'll get a better experience than you're getting today."

Unlike the biblical Tower of Babel, the Verizon tower on the Apple campus quickly had the two companies speaking the same language. Seidenberg marveled at the change in attitude. "Three months later, they were so hot to figure out how to add us to the mix, all these issues—they couldn't redesign the chip set, they couldn't fit in the radio license—they all went away." He added, "It was the tower that turned it around." He credited Jobs' dentist with an assist.

# VERIZON IPHONE

The two companies worked in secrecy as much as possible throughout 2010 as plans for the new phone advanced rapidly. Speculation about the phone spiked in the fall of that year when Verizon started selling an Apple iPad with a "MiFi" card that enabled it to run on the Verizon network. A *Fortune* cover story dated October 29, 2010, began, "The most talked-about cellphone in America is one that doesn't officially exist: the Verizon iPhone."

Roger Gurnani, who was president of the Verizon Wireless Western Area from 2005 to 2008, witnessed the pent-up demand for the iPhone firsthand. He said that some die-hard iPhone customers in his area actually added a Verizon phone to get their work done and then accessed the iPhone's smartphone features on off hours. "I used to see [iPhone] customers where they would literally be dropped four times, five times on the same call. I would see customers who had our service when they needed to make calls and do their work, but they had an iPhone, which was not available in our network but was available on AT&T's network" when they wanted to access the smartphone features.

While the Verizon iPhone was in development, Verizon and AT&T regularly traded barbs about the ability of their networks to handle the strain created by data-intensive smartphone use. AT&T maintained that its network was "battle-tested" and that Verizon wasn't prepared for the deluge of data demand that would accompany the iPhone launch. McAdam pointed out that, even though there were fewer Droid phones in circulation than iPhones, the average Droid user had a greater appetite for data than the typical iPhone owner. Bring it on.

Verizon was confident that the demand for a Verizon iPhone was likely to be huge, given AT&T's impressive iPhone sales. The company's

# CELEBRATING "VZ DAY:" VERIZON IPHONE LAUNCH

The problems with and complaints about the poor quality of AT&T reception using the iPhone had become a part of popular culture by the time the iPhone 4 was ready to launch on the Verizon network. On the day of the Verizon iPhone announcement, comedian Jon Stewart caught the spirit of the moment, which he christened "VZ Day," on his *Daily Show* cable TV program:

> For the past three or four years, those of us in the iPhone community have sacrificed one thing for the ability to carry around every photograph we've ever taken or song we've ever listened to or home video or compass: We have sacrificed the ability to make phone calls. For years, for years, for years . . . struggling with the world's most popular "almost phone." Well, our long national nightmare may soon be over.

research was buttressed by a Credit Suisse survey that found that 18 percent of AT&T iPhone users would consider switching to Verizon for an iPhone. Hollywood mogul David Geffen even told *Fortune*, "I can't wait to get the iPhone with Verizon."

The first version of the Verizon iPhone was formally unveiled in January 2011. Verizon Wireless CEO Dan Mead shared the stage with Apple COO Tim Cook. Jobs was too ill to attend. "This is just the beginning of a great relationship between Verizon and Apple," said Cook.

David Geffen wasn't alone in being anxious to get his hands on the new phone. Lines formed around the block outside Verizon stores across the country when the new smartphone was offered for sale in February 2011. It was the iPhone 4, which launched on Verizon's CDMA-based 3G network. It was essentially the same phone available to AT&T customers with a few extras, including the ability to use the phone as a mobile hot spot.

The Verizon iPhone was a sales sensation. On the eve of the product launch at year-end 2010, smartphones accounted for 28.1 percent of Verizon's retail phone base. At the end of the first year the iPhone was sold through Verizon, smartphones accounted for 43.5 percent of retail phones. By the end of 2012, smartphones as a percentage of Verizon's retail phone base had more than doubled since the iPhone launch to 58.1 percent. Of course, Droid smartphones continued to sell well for Verizon, but the iPhone clearly was driving the rapid sales gains.

"When we put the iconic device on the world's best network," Mead said, "it just lit things up." Mead pointed out that by the time Verizon launched the iPhone, nearly everyone in America who was going to buy a cellphone already owned one. That meant that new customers were going to come from those already being served by rival carriers or those trading up from earlier phones.

What better way to win the cellphone shootout than offer the best smartphone on the best network? After experiencing a few years of slow growth after the launch of the iPhone on AT&T, "we got on this massive growth curve again" with the Verizon iPhone, Mead said.

# WIRELESS DREAM TEAM

Not even a product as hot as the iPhone sells itself. Mead credited his wireless leadership dream team with driving the business to new heights. "I had this philosophy: Surround yourself with people better than you, and things are going to work out. And I've always tried to do that."

Marni Walden was one of Verizon Wireless' most senior executives. After serving as president of the 15-state Midwest Area for Verizon Wireless, Walden was asked by McAdam to relocate to Basking Ridge and serve as wireless chief marketing officer in 2009. She was named a Verizon executive vice president and chief operating officer of Verizon Wireless in late 2011, making her No. 2 in wireless and Verizon's highest-ranking woman.

Walden helped accelerate the trend underway to focus the marketing of products and services on partnerships with suppliers in the United States and increasingly around the world. In a first for the industry, Walden's team also led the development of a data-sharing plan for families with multiple wireless devices on the same Verizon account. "That was revolutionary at the time," she said, and the sharing plan gave wireless sales an additional boost.

In addition, Walden led a revamping of Verizon Wireless' network of stores as showcases for the products and services Verizon offered. Verizon's first Destination Store opened in the Mall of America in Bloomington, Minnesota, in 2013. It showcased lifestyle zones that highlighted the myriad ways customers use wireless products daily.

Walden was a tenacious saleswoman with off-the-charts people skills, but like the rest of his senior team, she was more than that, Mead said. "One of my management convictions is you're a great businessperson first, and you're a functional specialist second," Mead said. To use Marc Reed's term as he applied it to the succession process at Verizon, Walden was an outstanding "commercial leader" whose career was being closely tracked by Verizon's senior leadership and board.

Walden wasn't alone in her business acumen, Mead said. "My head of HR, Alan Gardner; my general counsel, Bill Petersen; my lead in finance, Holly Hess; my chief operating officer, Marni Walden; Shankar Arumugavelu and Ajay Waghray, our two IT guys; Tony Malone and Nicky Palmer and David Small, our CTOs—any of them could go out and do store visits or conduct an operations review of the overall businesses, effectively probably better than I could."

"We were all together as one team in driving the results," Mead said. "We'd go into our board meetings, and I'd always have the whole team there and . . . I'd be so proud—I'd want the board to see my team and what they were doing and the results we were getting and how we were drawing blood from the other guys."

# LTE — 4G WIRELESS

As Verizon was secretly working on its version of the iPhone, the company was rapidly developing its fourth-generation LTE wireless network. There was no question that the first Verizon iPhone would operate on the existing 3G network. McAdam, Mead, Walden and others, however, were pushing for Apple to develop an iPhone capable of operating on Verizon's 4G LTE network, which began rolling out in late 2010, as quickly as possible.

The LTE payoff for device makers, network providers and especially consumers was huge: Migrating from 3G to 4G LTE wireless service was going to produce at least a threefold to eightfold increase in download speeds to 15 megabits. That speed increase was expected to not only keep up with consumer demand but spur another wireless industry growth spurt driven by a flurry of new applications, including in social media. Other versions of 4G wireless service were promoted by rivals, including AT&T, but they weren't considered true 4G service by Verizon and others because they lacked the speed and versatility of LTE.

McAdam pitched an LTE iPhone to Jobs early in the process of developing a closer relationship between Verizon and Apple. But just like when Jobs was considering Verizon's CDMA standard the first time around, the Apple executive was concerned that the LTE standard was not going to be widely adopted by the industry. "Lowell, this is like GSM all over again. You guys are going to be out there with LTE; nobody else wants to do it," Jobs complained.

McAdam cut to the core of the issue and the reason Verizon was confident LTE was going to prevail in the wireless marketplace. "We think we can do 15 megs of download," McAdam said. "Think what you could do with an iPhone that could do 15 megs of download." Jobs was still for nearly 30 seconds. "OK," he said. "I've got it. You had me at 10. And when you went to 15, I was all in." The iPhone 5, the first to support LTE, was released in September 2012.

# 4G PIONEERS

Jobs' concern about Verizon being too far out in front of the industry with LTE was founded in part on Verizon's pioneering role in promoting LTE as a global standard for fourth-generation wireless networks. Verizon CTO Dick Lynch concluded as early as 2007 that the next generation of CDMA and GSM wireless standards were in effect converging in many ways. "It was amazing how the GSM sequence of technologies had evolved to adopt all of the CDMA capabilities within it and used the same technologies," Lynch said. "The only differences were seemingly minor. And at that point, I saw the wisdom of conforming the world to a single highly beneficial future technology path so that no matter where you went you would have the ability to use your device." All he had to do was convince the rest of the world.

As an indicator of how closely the rival wireless standards had evolved, Lynch, Verizon's champion of all things CDMA, attended the Mobile World Congress, the European meeting of GSM providers, in 2007 in Barcelona. A few suppliers were aware of his interest in LTE, but not the industry at large. In concert with Seidenberg, Strigl and McAdam, he had decided that the meeting would be the right time and place to announce Verizon Wireless' intent to develop LTE as the 4G standard of choice. He also thought it made sense given that Verizon's 45 percent partner in wireless was European-based Vodafone.

Lynch stood in front of more than 2,500 people at the conference and announced that Verizon was going forward with LTE, "and we were going to do it soon." A few small network providers, including one in

## "NO ONE WILL EVER WANT TO HAVE LTE ON A SMARTPHONE!"

Marni Walden was one of the Verizon Wireless executives in the vanguard of promoting LTE, first as CMO and then as COO. For months at a time, she seemed to be in constant motion, meeting with external partners from the United States, South Korea or another locale as she drummed up support for new LTE devices and applications. Data use was exploding on smartphones. Everyone expected that growth to accelerate further as more LTE devices and applications drove greater consumer usage, which prompted the creation of more devices and applications in a classic "virtuous circle" of growth.

So, imagine her surprise when some of the strongest turbulence she encountered in promoting LTE was close to home. "I was presenting to the Verizon Wireless board at that time. We were still in the Vodafone joint venture." Vittorio Colao, Vodafone's senior representative on the Verizon Wireless board, said to her: "No one will ever want to have LTE on a smartphone! Why would they need that?"

Walden thought the answer was obvious. "To watch videos and stuff and have their music stream and get [rid of] the buffering thing. I remember being pretty nervous because I'm running around the world trying to develop this ecosystem, and hopefully people are going to want to buy it," but Verizon's own business partner was questioning the wisdom of the LTE project. Colao, and Vodafone, were won over in due time. Walden, and Verizon, were more than vindicated. "Lo and behold," Walden said, "here we are now, where people just can't get enough data consumption."

Sweden, had committed to LTE, but Verizon was the first major global provider to do so. He realized many of the attendees were taken by surprise when a group of reporters in the front of the meeting took his picture and then ran out of the hall to call in the news to their organizations. Other attendees huddled in groups talking among themselves.

"We got a tremendous amount of support from the suppliers because they were anxious to get LTE out there" and profit from equipment sales, Lynch said. "I got a tremendous amount of, shall we say, cold shoulders of discomfort from a lot of carriers around the world, because they had yet to finish deploying 3G and/or they wanted to have 3G last a lot longer before they began an investment cycle in 4G." Nevertheless, Lynch and his team kept their focus squarely on providing the best network experience for the customer as Verizon's key competitive advantage. "I believed that in order to stay ahead of the competition in the U.S.—in order to maintain the best quality of service possible for the customer, which is how you compete and succeed—early LTE was the right thing to do," he said.

# INNOVATION CENTERS

Verizon CTO Lynch wanted to kick-start the collaboration among Verizon and its suppliers and developers that was necessary to make the transition to 4G a success. Gurnani moved from president of the Western Area to head of wireless new products in 2008 and joined Lynch to help develop and launch LTE. As an initial step, he created a 4G venture forum that brought together equipment manufacturers and "chipset ecosystem application services." More was needed, said Lynch:

At this point in time, all we have is Verizon announcing they're going to deploy LTE, and Lucent and Ericsson and Nokia and [the industry association] GSMA announcing that they're going to support it. We don't really have yet the ecosystem that supports the applications and the revenue opportunity on the LTE network. So how do you get one?

What I thought we could do was take one of the technology hubs of the country and develop a facility where potential application developers and potential technology companies and large customers could go and see the benefits of LTE and get some help with developing their applications for use on LTE. And so, I thought that we needed a place where you could innovate as necessary.

We knew that the customers would appreciate LTE if they knew what could be done with it. We knew that there would need to be an ecosystem of developers around LTE in order to assist the customers or position the customers to utilize the benefit of LTE.

---

## "WOW FACTOR"

---

Lynch and his team decided to locate the new Innovation Center on the site of an old GTE lab in Waltham, Massachusetts, along the famed Route 128 technology corridor outside Boston, the Silicon Valley of the East Coast. There was also a Fios research facility nearby. And they wanted the facility to make an impression. "Let's create a marketing-focused innovation center and build that innovation center in such a way that when people drive up to it they know that it's Verizon, the forward-thinking company," he said.

"When you walk in, you say, 'Wow, this is Verizon?' And then in each of the rooms, you see a demo or a development underway where the customer or the developer can say, 'Wow, LTE can do that?'" He added, "So at different levels, what I tried to do was to create a wow factor that had credibility to it."

Verizon broke ground on the Waltham center in April 2010, and it was open for LTE customers in July 2011. To spur development during construction, Verizon in October 2009 created a replica of the 4G LTE network in company lab space onsite in Waltham. That enabled clients to develop and test more than 30 products before the commercial network launched. Verizon built a second Innovation Center in downtown San Francisco focusing on application development for the 4G LTE network.

# LAPPING THE COMPETITION

The early development of LTE, and the launch of the 4G service in December 2010, was a tremendous coup for Verizon Wireless. Not only did some industry players want to slow the transition to the next-generation service in order to enjoy the fruits of their 3G networks as long as possible, but industry standards groups and regulators were hardly supportive of Verizon getting too far out in front of the industry. The company politely but firmly forged ahead, saying it could set standards that others could follow as it strove to provide its customers with the best and most rewarding wireless experience available. As a result, Verizon had its 4G LTE service, and a growing number of devices and applications, available a full two years ahead of the competition.

A year after deployment, the reviews were in: LTE was a smashing success. *PC World* magazine ranked 4G LTE at the top of its "100 Best Products of 2011." For the year, Verizon Wireless received the No. 1 consumer satisfaction ranking from a major consumer magazine. By the end of 2011, Verizon's LTE network reached 200 million people in 195 markets across the United States. It helped spark a 21 percent jump in wireless data revenue for the year. At year-end 2013, the 4G network reached 500 markets and 97 percent of the U.S. population.

# NET NEUTRALITY

Apple wasn't the only Silicon Valley technology leader to receive a Verizon cell tower free of charge. Verizon also installed a few towers on Google's corporate campus. The use of the towers was tied in to the continued development of the Droid smartphone, of course. But they also served another important purpose in Verizon's positioning relative to the ongoing debate over net neutrality. Analyzing data from the towers, Google executives witnessed how network performance declined, for instance, with the impact of movie downloading.

The two companies began finding common ground on the previously divisive issue of net neutrality during 2010. In August, they issued their joint "framework" on net neutrality to the FCC. They supported net neutrality as it applied to internet traffic but agreed the wireless networks and some new wireline ventures should be excluded from the regulatory mandate.

# ENTERPRISE LEARNING CURVE

In January 2012, McAdam asked Verizon CMO Stratton, who had spent most of his career in the wireless business, to move over and run Verizon Enterprise. This was clearly an opportunity to broaden his skill set. It was also an opportunity for McAdam and Reed to see how Stratton functioned in this new environment. It proved to be a trial by fire, but Stratton more than survived.

To help learn the business, Stratton asked his team to diagram out all the steps in a typical Enterprise engagement, from the negotiating of a contract to full implementation. "Find a room somewhere in Basking Ridge, and map it out on a wall," he told them. Two weeks went by, and he hadn't heard anything. His team told him they hadn't been held up by other projects; they simply needed more time. They wanted another two weeks. Stratton had trouble understanding what was taking so long, but he agreed.

The day arrived for his meeting, and he was escorted down a dimly lit hall he'd never seen. On the way, his team member prepped him by saying he was going to be shown the process map for a single trans-action for a customer buying a managed service, a network. Stratton wondered what took so long. The team member explained that Post-it notes had been used to illustrate the process: Tan ones represented "manual"; blue ones represented "automated."

With that introduction, he was ushered into a long, narrow conference room. Three of the four walls were plastered with Post-it notes. String connected the paper squares to illustrate workflow.

"I don't even know what to say. I look at this thing, and it's unbeliev-able," Stratton recalled. "And the first thing that comes to my mind is, where's the blue? There was, I think, of the 7,000 Post-it notes on these three walls, four of them were blue, meaning automated pro-cesses. Everything is manual."

Basking Ridge, we have a problem. "In that moment," Stratton said, "I went, OK, I know what I'm going to be doing for the next three years." The business had grown via acquisition, first at MCI and then as part of Verizon. Not enough time and effort had been directed at rationalizing fundamental engineering and business processes.

The Enterprise legacy businesses were in secular decline, with revenues "dropping by a very high single- to low double-digit levels. And it's a very, very big business that's coming down. That's where all the profit is, too," Stratton said. "So, you're running to replace those revenues with new businesses like cloud, like cyber security, like IP communications and all the rest."

Stratton had his team get to work. Their first goal was to get their arms around the processes and start to streamline:

> If I don't streamline process, I also can't fix my labor model. I can't take costs out of the business. It is really, really a challenge. For the next couple of years as the leader of that business, it was the least sexy thing that I can say without hesitation that I've done in my entire life, but it was important. For me, personally, I've learned more in those two years that I maybe did in any other phase of my career on 10 levels.

The complexity of the product sets and the solutions were beyond anything he had experienced in the wireless side of the company, Stratton said. He also had a great opportunity to interact with multinational company leaders around the world and understand their business problems. There were some "dark moments" in the process of learning about running a business that's in decline, and how to regenerate it and build a leadership team. But they managed to turn the business around.

"All I had known in my entire career in Verizon and Verizon Wireless was top-level growth and success. And so just from the personal side, that was tough; those were tough periods. As the saying goes, 'If it doesn't kill you, it makes you stronger.'"

# HANDLE-WITH-CARE
# ACQUISITIONS

Stratton, as well as McAdam, focused intently on driving the standardization of business processes and practices in the Enterprise business. Each drew upon his experience in building the wireless business. In the process, they learned an important lesson that shaped their approach to acquisitions and managing workforces going forward: One size does not fit all. They learned that just as they had walled off wireless from too much interference from the wireline companies, key acquisitions often benefit from a hands-off policy as well.

To boost its presence in the rapidly growing data center/cloud computing business and further its goal of providing integrated solutions for Enterprise customers, Verizon in 2011 acquired two companies, Terremark Worldwide and CloudSwitch. They "complement our existing expertise in managed security services and accelerate our global IT services strategy," McAdam said. The following year Verizon added Hughes Telematics Inc., a leading provider of internet connectivity in the machine-to-machine, fleet and connected car services.

Verizon paid $1.4 billion for Terremark in January 2011. It was Verizon's first major Enterprise acquisition since its $6.8 billion purchase of MCI in 2005. The Verizon team acted as if there was little difference between the established internet backbone provider and the cloud computing upstart. In retrospect, McAdam said, that was a mistake.

Terremark became the shiny new penny, and we brutally ruined that company, to be honest. We changed all their compensation procedures, changed all their systems. All their capital had to go into the big melting pot of Verizon's capital budget. And it got lost, and so we underinvested in it, and we didn't respect the culture that they had in that company, a cloud company versus the big bureaucracy. And literally I think it was 24 out of 25 of their top people left within 12 months.

It was a lesson McAdam wouldn't forget.

# BUYING OUT VODAFONE

With Seidenberg stepping down as chairman of Verizon at year-end 2011, McAdam started 2012 as Verizon's sole leader. The company was firmly launched on a new era. Yet at the top of McAdam's to-do list for 2012 was unfinished business: what to do about Vodafone's 45 percent interest in Verizon Wireless. Coincidentally, that was also the most important issue that Vodafone CEO Vittorio Colao needed to resolve.

The two telecommunications executives had known each other for more than 15 years. They had grown up together in the business and were of the same generation. With McAdam, Colao no longer felt like, or was perceived as, the junior partner in talks with his Verizon counterpart as he had with Seidenberg. Each executive, successful in his own right, reasoned that it was time to move beyond their joint venture that, while highly successful, was keeping both corporate parents from investing most effectively for the future.

They had some basic questions to answer. Should they consider merging the two companies? Did Verizon want to buy Vodafone, or conversely, sell to Vodafone, assuming the price was right?

The status quo was increasingly leaving McAdam and his team hamstrung. "If you started to look at things like mobile video and the

Internet of Things," McAdam said, "Vodafone blocked everything we wanted to do that was across business units . . . I knew we had to get Vodafone out of the picture. Or we were just going to be so bureaucratic and so slow we'd never be able to get there." He added:

> If you look at mobile video, all of our content relationships were with Fios. . . . But we knew the future was going to be more mobile-centric, where we had a lot more customers—100 million customers versus 5 million customers. So, we were not getting the scale advantages. Every time we tried to do something with video on mobile, we would find out that the contract that we had didn't give us the rights to do that. . . . So you either had to try to figure out a way to measure everything and reward everything cross-boundary, or you just got rid of the boundary. And I decided to take the easy way and get rid of the cross-boundary.

Among the options under consideration, McAdam and his board found it difficult to imagine selling out to Vodafone. Verizon was the controlling, operating partner of their joint venture. At the same time, Verizon was aware of how Vodafone operated its global business. Frankly, McAdam said, it didn't look like a good fit. "They don't do the things that we do. They don't invest in networks the way we do. They outsource more things than we do—they outsource a lot of their customer service. We don't do that," he said. "There were just some cultural, some fundamental differences in how you run the business."

The issues went beyond investing and outsourcing. "I think if we had sold to them, I think most of the senior team would've left" at Verizon, he added. "I think it would've been a very different business. And Ivan had sort of instilled in all of us, you're always a buyer; you're never a seller of anything in core like that. And I think the board had that same philosophy."

Many operating and cultural issues weighed against Verizon buying Vodafone. As did the fact that relative to the United States, Europe did not have nearly as bright economic prospects as Verizon's home market. As much as Verizon pushed back against federal regulation in the States, when it thought it was being treated unfairly, European regulators had a tradition of being even more likely to wade into business issues.

At the same time, uncertainty in Europe made the Vodafone board less anxious to part with its U.S. investment. "They were schizophrenic about it," McAdam said. "Every time they'd have a bad quarter in the rest of Europe, their board would say, 'How can you get out of the U.S.?'"

# MARATHON TALKS

For more than a year, from the spring of 2012 through the summer of 2013, most of the negotiations between Verizon and Vodafone were carried out in the form of personal meetings between McAdam and Colao. Everywhere from Italy's Lake District to a sporting event in New York City, the two executives discussed various options before they finally reached a deal.

At some point, the press learned of their interest in changing the terms of the relationship between the two telecommunication giants. They were tracking when Colao was coming to the States and when McAdam was visiting Europe. At one point, Colao was in New York, and the two decided that rather than arrange furtive meetings they would get together in public. McAdam and Colao went to a hockey game and watched the New York Rangers in Madison Square Garden and the rabid fans, and the press, took no notice.

# SEPARATION AGREEMENT

McAdam next visited Colao at his home in London. "We had a dinner at my house . . . a very nice dinner. It was really very personal, and at the end of the day, he said, 'Listen, relationships go the way they go, and that's it." McAdam, not physically expressive by nature, gave his counterpart a hug. "You have a wonderful family," he told Colao. "It sounded like this was the end of one phase; a new phase has to start," Colao recalled. That's when the two companies started negotiations in earnest over what price it would take to get Vodafone to agree to sell its interest in the wireless joint venture back to Verizon.

Their final meeting of the negotiation phase was on side-by-side stationary bikes in the exercise room of a San Francisco hotel. Colao had arrived from New Zealand, having just completed the Pacific Ocean

## "YOU REALLY WANT ME IN THE TRUNK"

While the two companies were wrestling with the issues surrounding their joint venture and the best path forward for both parties, Colao invited McAdam to address the Vodafone board a few times so they could hear his point of view firsthand.

"I went to his full board a couple of times and talked about where we were going. The analogy that Vittorio used is that he was sitting in the front seat of the car but was not allowed to touch anything. And he wanted to have more control," McAdam recalled.

"Vittorio, in order to do what I need to do in the market going forward, I need you in the backseat," McAdam had stated. Colao had responded, "No, I think you really want me in the trunk."

"Well, the trunk wouldn't be bad, either," McAdam said.

leg of an around-the-world trip visiting suppliers and customers. McAdam said, "We were both early risers, and we were both in the gym riding our bikes in the morning. Then we went and had breakfast, and that was sort of the final breakthrough meeting when we just said, 'Yeah, OK.' At that point it was down mostly to price."

"They're very good negotiators; they just kept pushing and pushing and pushing it. But we had decided as a board that we were in the range" at roughly $130 billion, said McAdam. Colao and his board, meanwhile, wanted to use proceeds from the sale of its 45 percent interest in Verizon Wireless to fund further investments in Europe.

The Verizon board was anxious to conclude the deal before some of its veteran members, who had discussed the issue for years first with Seidenberg and then McAdam, were likely to step down from the board. Sandy Moose described the Vodafone buyout as "one of the more difficult decisions that the Verizon board has had over the years. It was a decision virtually 10 years in the making to buy out the rest of Vodafone, so it had been discussed any number of times with the board," she said. "It was good to have a board that was pretty well informed." They wanted to get the deal done before her scheduled retirement, as well as that of longtime board members Joe Neubauer and Hugh Price.

"We felt we needed to make this decision while the company still had the people with the history and the experience on the board," Moose said. "Asking relatively new directors to make such a significant decision without having all that context . . . would have been more difficult. So, fortunately, the stars were aligned and we were able to do that before the three of us retired," Moose added.

The Verizon board also prepared for the impact of the increased debt load by creating a finance committee to monitor the financial performance of the company in the context of its additional payment obligations and other factors.

## "I WISH I COULD 'CONTAMINATE' MORE OF VODAFONE WITH THE VERIZON CULTURE"

Looking back, Vodafone CEO Colao said selling the minority stake to Verizon when he did was clearly the right thing to do. But he did miss the impact Verizon had on Vodafone, even if it was in the form of an arms-length joint venture. "In hindsight, I wish I could contaminate more of Vodafone with the Verizon culture, which is as I said a culture of ruthless implementation, avoiding wastage . . . when it's not necessary. And good results."

"If I had one regret, it's simply I wish I could use more of their way of working to influence and shape Vodafone's way of working," Colao said. "But in terms of the decisions, in terms of everything else, it was a pretty good decision not to split early on when Ivan was with my predecessor pushing for that. And it was a great decision to hang on until the last moment because we got the great value out of it. And Verizon [Wireless] actually got their own adulthood and independence in the right moment for them as well."

There were a lot of details involved. McAdam and Verizon General Counsel Milch made multiple trips to Europe to iron out how best to separate Verizon's and Vodafone's interests. "We were doing some systems development together; we had roaming agreements; we were buying handsets together . . . we had sort of integrated some of the supply chain. So, figuring out how we were going to undo all of that . . . it wasn't just a price discussion. It was an operational untangling, almost," McAdam said. Tax and regulatory issues also consumed weeks of negotiating time.

# "A UNIQUE ASSET"

On September 3, 2013, Verizon announced that it had agreed to buy Vodafone's 45 percent stake in Verizon Wireless for a staggering $130 billion, payable in cash and Verizon stock. That valued all of Verizon Wireless at roughly $290 billion. At the time that was more than the market capitalization of Google Inc. As part of the transaction, Verizon agreed to sell back to Vodafone its 23 percent stake in Vodafone's Italian unit for $3.5 billion. The $130 billion price tag trailed the $181 billion Vodafone itself paid for Mannesmann AG in 2000 at the peak of the dot-com boom but otherwise put Verizon uncomfortably near the top of a list of the world's big spenders, which was not company Verizon was used to keeping.

It was a lot of money, McAdam allowed, but worth it. "Where could you go out and buy a business that has no integration risk that has a great path in front of it for additional growth, which has 50 percent margins?" he said at the time of the announcement. "This is really a unique asset."

To help fund the cash portion of the mega-deal, Verizon engineered a $49 billion mega-bond offering, the largest ever. The Verizon deal was more than twice the size of the next largest bond offering, a $17 billion debt offering from Apple Inc. in April 2013, and was roughly equal to the total outstanding debt of the Slovak Republic.

McAdam and Shammo were concerned that they would need to sell multiple rounds of debt in the United States and abroad to raise the $49 billion they were targeting. "We thought we were going to have to do it in many different tranches, and we thought we were going to have to go to many different markets around the world," Shammo said. As a first step, they estimated they would be able to raise about $20 billion to $25 billion in the States.

They had clearly underestimated investors' appetite for debt from such a highly regarded borrower as Verizon. "We had a business plan that said on a consolidated basis, I want to get the $49 billion at an aggregate average rate of 5 percent," Shammo said. The demand was so strong that Verizon was able to raise $49 billion at an average borrowing rate of 4.5 percent, and just in America. Their investment bankers' "book" for the deal that reflected investor interest soared to $120 billion, indicating that they could have raised a multiple of what they actually did.

# DECADE OF TRANSFORMATION

The 2013 purchase of the Vodafone interest in Verizon Wireless capped a decade of transformation at Verizon, noted John Diercksen, who retired from Verizon as EVP of strategy, planning and development in September of that year. Since 2003, the company had executed key acquisitions totaling $178 billion. That included the Vodafone stake, as well as Alltel, MCI, SpectrumCo, Rural Cellular and others.

*(see chart on opposite page)*

During the same period, Verizon divested businesses worth a total of $36 billion. The funds generated by these sales were instrumental in strengthening the company's balance sheet, funding further acquisitions and being available to return to shareholders in the form of dividends. The sale of Frontier and FairPoint systems, and overlapping systems relating to the purchase of Alltel, accounted for more than $13 billion of that amount. Directory businesses brought in about $15 billion.

Also impressive was the evolving mix of businesses over the decade and the company's significant increase in valuation. In 2003, 71 percent of Verizon's $27 billion in earnings before interest, taxes, depreciation and amortization—the company's core earnings engine—was generated by the wireline and other businesses. A decade later, EBITDA had increased by 56 percent to $42 billion, with 81 percent coming from the wireless business. Revenues and earnings were also on a stronger growth path than in the first few years of the millennium, a fact investors noticed and rewarded with a higher stock price multiple. The company was in a strong position to address the competitive challenges and opportunities that lay ahead.

**Verizon has successfully transformed itself over the past several years and positioned itself as one of the fastest-growing large-cap telecom operators in the world.**

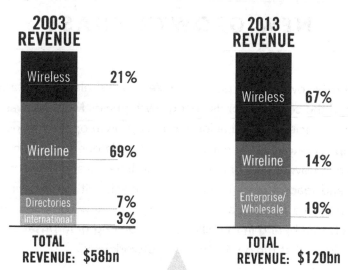

### 2003 REVENUE

- Wireless 21%
- Wireline 69%
- Directories 7%
- International 3%

**TOTAL REVENUE: $58bn**

### 2013 REVENUE

- Wireless 67%
- Wireline 14%
- Enterprise/Wholesale 19%

**TOTAL REVENUE: $120bn**

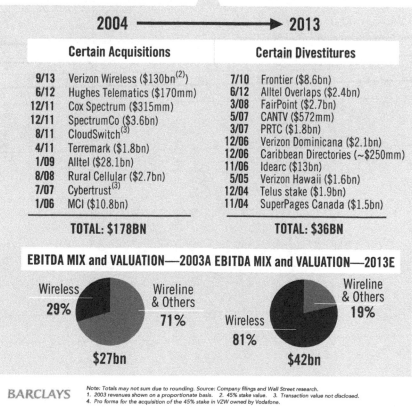

**2004 ⟶ 2013**

| Certain Acquisitions | | Certain Divestitures | |
|---|---|---|---|
| 9/13 | Verizon Wireless ($130bn[2]) | 7/10 | Frontier ($8.6bn) |
| 6/12 | Hughes Telematics ($170mm) | 6/12 | Alltel Overlaps ($2.4bn) |
| 12/11 | Cox Spectrum ($315mm) | 3/08 | FairPoint ($2.7bn) |
| 12/11 | SpectrumCo ($3.6bn) | 5/07 | CANTV ($572mm) |
| 8/11 | CloudSwitch[3] | 3/07 | PRTC ($1.8bn) |
| 4/11 | Terremark ($1.8bn) | 12/06 | Verizon Dominicana ($2.1bn) |
| 1/09 | Alltel ($28.1bn) | 12/06 | Caribbean Directories (~$250mm) |
| 8/08 | Rural Cellular ($2.7bn) | 11/06 | Idearc ($13bn) |
| 7/07 | Cybertrust[3] | 5/05 | Verizon Hawaii ($1.6bn) |
| 1/06 | MCI ($10.8bn) | 12/04 | Telus stake ($1.9bn) |
| | | 11/04 | SuperPages Canada ($1.5bn) |

**TOTAL: $178BN**    **TOTAL: $36BN**

### EBITDA MIX and VALUATION—2003A    EBITDA MIX and VALUATION—2013E

- Wireless 29%
- Wireline & Others 71%

**$27bn**

- Wireline & Others 19%
- Wireless 81%

**$42bn**

BARCLAYS

Note: Totals may not sum due to rounding. Source: Company filings and Wall Street research.
1. 2003 revenues shown on a proportionate basis.   2. 45% stake value.   3. Transaction value not disclosed.
4. Pro forma for the acquisition of the 45% stake in VZW owned by Vodafone.

# NEW GROWTH PHASE

Once Verizon owned 100 percent of Verizon Wireless, the leadership positioned the company for its next growth phase. McAdam was intent on gaining efficiencies and unlocking new growth opportunities across the company once the barrier created by Vodafone's ownership stake had been removed. That opened up possibilities to align Verizon's businesses, and leadership structure, more closely with customer needs. And it created a global platform for tapping a new customer universe potentially numbering in the billions by acquiring enterprises and content providers that run on the Verizon network itself.

# A NEW ERA BEGINS: C-SUITE INSIGHTS FROM RAM CHARAN

**—— FOCUS ON QUALITY CREATES LONG-TERM VALUE.**
Partners and customers reward a focus on quality over time and across product and market cycles.

**—— NEW TECHNOLOGIES POWER NEW REGULATIONS.**
For companies and customers to fully reap the rewards of innovation, regulators have to be engaged as well as challenged.

**—— REMAIN IN CHARGE OF YOUR OWN DESTINY.**
Leaders need independence to realize their goals.

# "WE'RE GOING TO HAVE TO DISRUPT OURSELVES"

2014–

**W**ith Vodafone in his rearview mirror, CEO Lowell McAdam, the car buff, couldn't wait to shift Verizon into an even higher gear. He and his leadership team saw Verizon at a strategic inflection point. Their world, and the world of their current and future customers, was changing rapidly. They needed to change with it.

McAdam's challenge was how to take the inherent strengths of Verizon—operational excellence, a robust culture and network superiority—and position them for a world in which Verizon would not only operate the best telecommunications network but also compete for billions of new consumers of content running on Verizon's and others' global networks.

In some ways, McAdam and his team were going back to the future. Like Ivan Seidenberg and his team a generation earlier, McAdam's senior team was moving the company toward the shifting center of the competitive chessboard. Their goal was to maximize their value-creating potential and dodge the threat of commoditization. They realized they needed to reposition Verizon for a digital future driven increasingly by mobile-first, digital media and video-centric technologies. This was where millennial and even younger customers worldwide lived. Verizon also needed to be open to embracing new and evolving business models to stay in step with changing consumer habits.

In some ways, the leadership team was operating from a position of strength compared to the first generation of Verizon leaders. Whereas their predecessors faced a declining market share in their core business and geographic constraints, McAdam's team was building upon best-in-class businesses. That gave them great flexibility in considering future moves. The only thing they couldn't afford to do was stand still.

But McAdam and his team understood that assembling and building businesses to meet customer needs was only part of the process. They also had a cultural challenge. "It's one thing to have the building blocks," McAdam noted. "It's also important to demonstrate flexibility and creativity in how you run your company to meet the changing needs of the market." While maintaining a culture of operational excellence, "you've got to be curious and hungry and willing to do things differently," McAdam said. "We're going to have to disrupt ourselves."

Given Verizon's dominance in its core businesses, generating change from within would be no easy task. Most of its employees had grown used to being the market leader, so McAdam would have to shake the organization out of its complacency. "When you're performing well, it takes somebody with a vision and a willingness to take a few body shots along the way" to lead an organization to the next level of performance, McAdam said. But the pace of the competitive marketplace was making the challenge increasingly urgent.

"The flywheel of change is rotating at least a hundred times faster than it was when Ivan took over," McAdam said. "We compete against more people; we have to be better on more levels as the organization gets more complicated."

To illustrate, McAdam said, think in terms of a classic X- and Y-axis diagram. In Seidenberg's era, the company needed to fill in the white spaces on its coverage map by expanding its wireless business nationwide, building its Fios business and adding MCI for global reach—in other words, growing horizontally along the X axis on the diagram. Seidenberg and McAdam had often talked about the need to capture some of the profits generated by businesses riding on the network, along the vertical Y axis.

With Vodafone out of the way, it was up to McAdam and his team to tackle that challenge. Verizon immediately began to move up the Y axis by moving into the broadband media and content marketplace and taking an early lead in the development of the next generation of wireless capability: 5G.

# HUNDREDS OF MILLIONS TO BILLIONS

With more than 110 million customers—about one-third of the U.S. population—Verizon couldn't expect the kind of wireless sales growth in the years ahead that it had experienced in decades past. McAdam threw down the growth gauntlet for his team. "If you had somebody that really knew the internet and knew how to get a large number of customers to view the information that you get off your network, you could use that along with location and a few other things to really do targeted advertising," he said. "You can create a multibillion-dollar business in the next three to five years. And those were the kinds of businesses we needed to move the needle" in a company with more than $126 billion in revenues.

For years, dating back to Seidenberg's term as CEO, Verizon had eyed the billions of customers, and billions of dollars in revenues they generated, belonging to social media and other internet companies using its networks. Yet these companies hadn't invested a dime directly in building a public network. Verizon led the industry with the introduction of

4G LTE technology. But while Verizon continued to invest in its network superiority, it was the social media and content giants—the Amazons, Googles and Facebooks of the world—that were profiting from the services those networks made possible. McAdam and his team were determined to find opportunities to monetize the company's millions of customer relationships and investments in world-class technology.

"I use the term that you stand on the shoulders of the people that came before you all the time," McAdam said. "We knew we wanted to do more software that rode on the network. Ivan always said, and I think he was right, that just being the connectivity company and letting everybody else do the software that rides on that—they get all of the profitability from the software. We basically get cost of capital for the big investments that we put in." Now, on his watch, McAdam said, "we're finally at the point where we're putting the software on the network to get the better value."

## AOL'S AD TECH ALLURE

The Verizon team believed that the most logical way to tap into the revenues generated by today's mobile-first younger generation of social media consumers was via what is known as advertising technology, or ad tech for short. While ad tech comes in a variety of flavors, in general it refers to technology that enables advertisers to identify and target customers as they search the internet for airfares to Mexico, for example, or shop online for a car. "We've got all these assets, and all of these assets drive a lot of great information," Roy Chestnutt said, "but we don't have the . . . advertising technology infrastructure."

In their search for an entry point to the ad tech space, McAdam's team kept coming back to AOL. "They've got the ad tech infrastructure;

they know how to use the internet. We think their systems with our systems would create—we talked about one plus one had to equal at least six" to make the investment pay off, McAdam said.

McAdam met AOL Chairman and CEO Tim Armstrong at the Allen & Company media industry conference in 2014. "I sat down with Tim for the first time, and we had a half-hour meeting scheduled that went for 90 minutes. And we kind of kept going, because I kept hearing the vision from Tim about what he could do if he had more access to mobile data and some of the content relationships that we had. So we started in negotiating a commercial agreement."

The more they talked about some form of commercial deal, the more they thought it might be better to combine the two enterprises. "If Tim was inside the house, you'd be able to give him access to more things," McAdam said. "That's when it moved more and fairly rapidly into a purchase versus a commercial deal."

## "A MAJOR ENGINE FOR US"

In the years following the dot-com collapse in the early 2000s, AOL's surviving business had been reorganized and revived as a much slimmer, more focused operation by its management. In 2009, Tim Armstrong joined AOL from Google, where he had served as head of its Americas operations. He started directing AOL even more intently toward mobile ad tech tied to digital and video platforms. Though a fraction of Google's size, and with a fraction of its ad tech market share, AOL was recognized as an ad tech contender that aspired to punch above its weight class. AOL also acquired well-known online content providers, including The Huffington Post, Engadget and TechCrunch. But ad tech was the prize that brought Verizon to the negotiating table.

Verizon announced on May 12, 2015, that it had agreed to buy AOL for $4.4 billion, and that Armstrong would remain at the helm. In announcing the deal, McAdam said, "AOL has once again become a digital trailblazer, and we are excited at the prospect of charting a new course together in the digitally connected world."

## "WE NEEDED TO SCALE THE AUDIENCE"

McAdam believed that, just as the wireless business was built up over several years through organic growth and a series of acquisitions, Verizon's media business could be built out from its AOL core and become, in his words, "a major engine for us as we go forward."

As a step toward greatly expanding its potential content audience, Verizon closed on the purchase of Yahoo in mid-June 2017 and merged that business with AOL. The newly combined assets were rechristened Oath and put under Armstrong's leadership. The name underscored Verizon's long-term commitment to the media business, Armstrong said.

Oath at birth had around 1 billion users monthly in 40 countries and generated $7 billion in revenue, close to three times that of Twitter.

"Our goal is to open up relationships with consumers in a differentiated way," Armstrong told a group of advertisers shortly after Oath was formed. Oath's brands are "trusted places to do marketing," he said. "We are probably the single largest, cleanest source of consumer traffic and data."

McAdam and his team are acutely aware that, with AOL and the group of content businesses, they are back where the Verizon Wireless team was when the company was formed. They pulled together a patchwork of growth-oriented businesses that require long-term investment and integration to realize their potential and contribute to the bottom line. With the success of wireless as their template, Verizon's leadership team and board committed themselves to the long-term challenge of funding Oath's future. Verizon's goal is to double its user base to 2 billion or more by 2020, which would put it in the same league as Facebook in terms of users, and increase revenue to $10 billion to $20 billion.

## GROWTH ENGINES

Telematics, building on the acquisition of Hughes Telematics, and the Internet of Things, or IoT, comprise added growth engines for Verizon. In late 2015, Verizon formed ThingSpace, a web-based IoT development platform. To expand its ability to offer its own IoT solutions, Verizon in September 2016 acquired Sensity, which makes "smart city"-connected LED light systems and had more than 40 smart city light installations around the world.

Telematics growth accelerated over two years and was augmented in July 2016, when Verizon acquired Telogis to leverage its fleet telematics connected solutions on a global scale. In November 2016, Verizon bought Dublin-based Fleetmatics Group PLC for $2.4 billion, making Verizon the global leader in fleet and mobile resource management.

# "WHAT'S THE RELATIONSHIP BACK TO THE CORE?"

While McAdam was leading the drive to create new businesses, he also knew he couldn't neglect Verizon's core businesses, particularly the network superiority at the heart of the Verizon brand. The strategic repositioning of the company would require a continuous emphasis on integrating new businesses with old, and retooling the latter in the process.

The new era would require a more holistic view of network architecture, as the logic of digital technology erases boundaries and renders definitions about wireless and wireline, old business and new, obsolete. The new network vision was of a multi-use fiber architecture supporting both wireless and wireline access in the last mile. As John Stratton said, "The critical point for us will be not that we go and build the media and ad-serving business. The question is, what's our point? Why would we do that? What's the relationship back to the core? For us, the Holy Grail is that we make the core asset matter in terms of how we develop, build and succeed in the ad-serving and media side of our business."

# 5G

Even as Verizon continued to enhance and strengthen its 4G wireless network, it was already looking ahead to the next generation of wireless infrastructure that could open new market opportunities and support the hyper-connected world that was rapidly emerging. Its technology team was leading the industry on the path to fifth-generation, or 5G, technology—whether the industry was ready or not. In fact,

Verizon had begun to lay a pathway for developing 5G while Seidenberg was still CEO. "We didn't even know what it was going to look like at first," Seidenberg recalled.

In McAdam's view, 5G wireless differs from preceding generations of technology in three fundamental ways, which combine to make it a breakthrough technology with enormous growth potential. The first is sheer speed, which will be exponentially faster than current technologies. Instead of 10 megabits of throughput, he said, "you'll be somewhere between 1 and 2 gigabits of throughput," which opens the door to mobile transmission of 3D images, virtual reality, holograms and other immersive experiences. Second is what engineers call "latency," or the response time on the network. By the time you blink your eye, says McAdam, the network will be able to transmit a signal and get a response from across the country or around the world. "That opens up . . . gaming, that opens up control of anything that's mechanical, even if it's going down the road at 60 miles an hour," he said. The third advantage is battery life, which on a 5G network could be as much as 10 years for some devices. The advantages for the Internet of Things will be enormous, McAdam predicts. "You'll be able to put chips in the paint striping in a parking garage so that the cloud will tell you where to go to park," he said. "Basically, anything that has a chip in it will be able to be controlled by the network, which today you can't do."

All of this enables the ability to make many connections almost simultaneously. The research firm Gartner estimates that 8.4 billion internet-connected things were in use worldwide in 2017 and will reach 20.4 billion by 2020. Mobile data traffic is expected to balloon at an even faster pace as the IoT links everything from handheld devices to devices in smart homes, smart cities, connected utility grids, health care systems and smart cars.

That tremendous innovative potential is what makes 5G figure so importantly in Verizon's plans for its future. In Marni Walden's words,

---

# FUTURE-PROOFING THE VERIZON CULTURE

When McAdam became CEO, he thought that technology, customer service and other operational issues "would be No. 1 on my hit parade." Instead, he found that his job boiled down to one word: culture. "It's how hungry are you, how innovative are you, how do you take care of people, how are you viewed as a great place to work? To me, all that comes down to culture. You can go buy technology. But if you don't have the culture to turn it into a competitive advantage, that's the missing link. So, culture is the biggest thing for me."

Culture isn't something that a CEO presents via PowerPoint to the staff. "Culture is how you get things done, so operations is your culture," McAdam said. Verizon starts from a culture of operational excellence that McAdam and his team brought forward from the early decades of the wireless business. The Credo evolved from that era as well, and is as relevant as ever to the new businesses Verizon has been adding to leverage the profits available to businesses riding on its network.

As much as McAdam admires the creative culture of the media companies brought into Verizon and would like to see some of that creativity travel over to the operations side, the reverse has to happen as well. "I don't care about impressions; I care about impressions that make money," McAdam said. In his view, the Credo and the values are crucial to Verizon's future success. "You abandon culture," he said, "you abandon the business."

---

Verizon doesn't intend to take a backseat to anyone when it comes to introducing products that run on the 5G network. "When we go out with 5G, you don't let Apple have the greatest innovation on top of that. Don't let Facebook have the greatest innovation. Verizon will because we have the sandbox first." (Walden announced in October 2017 that she would be leaving Verizon in February 2018 to pursue other opportunities.)

Verizon began to plan for 5G in earnest in 2015. The company was already increasing the density of its wireless network by deploying small cells, a critical enabler for 5G. In addition, they convened a technology forum to develop standards and began working with technology partners to jump-start the ecosystem of equipment and devices that will be key to deploying 5G at scale. In 2016, the company announced 5G test sites in 11 cities across the country, where it would stress-test the 5G across a variety of geographies, topographies and building types, and continued its progress in 2017 with pre-commercial testing of such services as fixed-wireless broadband to the home.

In addition to a dense network of small cells, two other crucial building blocks would be necessary for a 5G infrastructure: fiber capacity to connect those cells and carry the oceans of data generated by the 5G network, and spectrum in the millimeter wave frequencies required to carry a large amount of data over short distances. Verizon quickly acted to fill both needs. In November 2016 the FCC approved Verizon's $1.8 billion purchase of XO Communications' national fiber-optic network, which closed in early 2017. The 26,000-mile XO network gives Verizon fiber "rings" providing high-speed access in 45 of the country's top 50 metropolitan markets, from Seattle to Chicago and Miami, and from New York to Los Angeles. The company also gives Verizon a portfolio of spectrum in the 28 GHz and 39 GHz bands. In May 2017, Verizon announced plans to further strengthen its fiber assets by buying Straight Path Communications Inc. for $3.1 billion in stock.

The additional fiber capacity and strong millimeter wave spectrum position not only enhance 4G LTE and lay the foundation for 5G, they also will enable Verizon to take its broadband services outside its Fios footprint, making Verizon, in McAdam's words, "a nationwide broadband provider." Fixed broadband over 5G could be available in certain markets as early as late 2018, with mobile applications and other innovations to follow.

With Verizon's fiber and spectrum assets, dense high-speed wireless network, and track record of engineering excellence, McAdam and his team believe they are positioned to lead the next era of wireless growth. At the same time, McAdam acknowledges that not everybody in the industry shares Verizon's aggressively optimistic view of 5G as a platform for the future. "It's funny," he said, "if I look over my career, I remember people saying, why would anybody need a cellphone in their car? Then, why would you need something you can carry around in your pocket? Then, why would you need any data service over your phone? [Now it's] why would you need 10 megabits of throughput? I wouldn't be surprised if 10 years from now, they're going to say, well, we need 10 gigs, not 1 gig."

## "THE BUSINESS OF TOMORROW"

While McAdam and team are confident about the bets they've made for the future, they know that, in an industry that reinvents itself by the day, success is anything but guaranteed. In contemplating this complicated chessboard, McAdam often invokes the precedent of his predecessor and the choices Ivan Seidenberg and his leaders made in Verizon's early days.

As he often tells his lieutenants, it's tempting to look back at the path Verizon has traced and assume that its success was obvious, almost pre-ordained —but nothing could be further from the truth. Verizon was built by a team of bold leaders making sometimes risky decisions that were often deeply controversial in the industry and on Wall Street. Investing in wireless and seeing the network as more than a commodity, pushing ahead with the rollout of Fios, and buying MCI all were company-altering decisions that were denounced at the time. Today, they form the foundation of Verizon.

Now, he says, the company must take equally bold steps to build the Verizon of the future. Some steps will be unqualified successes, some will fail, and others, just as in years past, will attract naysayers focusing excessively on short-term results and easy wins. But as McAdam says, "We're going to build the next business of tomorrow"—making the risks of inaction greater than the possibility of failure.

The key—then as now—is a culture focused on what's most important to success for customers, employees and communities, framed in the company's mission statement as "delivering the promise of the digital world." As McAdam explained to employees:

> The emerging requirements needed to enable customers to manage their digital lives are very different today than they were a decade ago. Ubiquitous, high-bandwidth, instantly responsive digital services are a necessity, not only in managing customers' personal lives, but are also paramount in driving a global digital economy. The move to smartphones and all the changes associated with that transformation over the last 15 years are just the tip of the iceberg for what lies ahead.

These are just the sort of challenges that have energized Verizon's leaders at every major turning point in the industry's history—reaching all the way back to AT&T CEO Charlie Brown's historic announcement in January 1982 that Ma Bell was going to divest itself of its local operating companies. The future of communications wasn't any clearer in 1982 than it is now. The risks today are just as great. Yet there is a palpable sense of excitement within Verizon as the company pivots toward a digital future it's already helping to shape.

# "WE'RE GOING TO HAVE TO DISRUPT OURSELVES": C-SUITE INSIGHTS FROM RAM CHARAN

___ **HIT THE GAS.**
Accelerating technological change requires ever faster decision-making and leadership agility.

___ **LINK YOUR FUTURE TO YOUR PAST.**
Our successor leadership team moves to the center of the competitive chessboard—where the customer is king—to align growth alternatives with the core enterprise.

___ **CULTURE RULES.**
A strong culture for the times ahead will help you win. Monitor culture on your leadership dashboard, and make sure the values are practiced daily.

# Epilogue

T he story of Verizon in many ways is the story of the transformation of the global communications industry. The transformation continues, and so does the Verizon story. When we assembled our leadership team two decades ago, we were focused, ambitious and hungry. We were underdogs, and we liked it that way. We assembled the pieces of a coast-to-coast communications powerhouse and gave it a new name, Verizon, that was all about future possibilities. We took risks and remade ourselves to meet the evolving digital needs of the American—and later global—consumer. We achieved scale by way of creating the best national wireless network, bar none. That was the company decision that required all-in support from the board. So was going all-in on a $20 billion-plus Fios initiative and our commitment to high-speed internet communication.

We could not have pulled off this technology revolution without driving a revolution in corporate leadership as well, which is a cornerstone of the Verizon story. This was a team effort. We committed early on to contingency planning as central to our strategy, short-term and long-term, not as a Plan B left in a drawer. Flexibility was a key component of our approach to competition, and that made us as agile as any rival. We also committed to deep engagement with our board, whose knowledge and commitment furthered our ability to deeply analyze our options.

In *Verizon Untethered*, we have tried to explain our purpose, our convictions and how we went about doing our work. Embedded in the narrative are several big lessons about strategy, board engagement, risk, managing both the short and long term, the need for constant change, and succession. Ram Charan serves as the reader's guide in elucidating many of these key takeaways. There also are many everyday lessons about culture, the meaning of serving your customers, being a part of something bigger and more important than yourself, and having the humility to address one's shortcomings and challenges head on.

Life in any corporation is always changing. The last two chapters capture the dynamic approach Lowell McAdam and his team are taking as they reshape Verizon yet again and create a better future for its customers and stakeholders. This, indeed, is the most gratifying part of my personal 46-year journey, to see that the company is stronger than ever today and confident it can capture the promise of tomorrow.

Ivan G. Seidenberg

# Acknowledgments

R am Charan played a pivotal role in my decision to write this book, and his contributions to the text and his encouragement greatly enhance the Verizon story. The History Factory team, led by founder and CEO Bruce Weindruch, was also very instrumental in helping to shape the structure of the book and the process of conducting the research and interviews that form the basis for this narrative, written by The History Factory's Scott McMurray. Other members of The History Factory team include Caelin Niehoff, Michelle Witt, Hannah Stogsdill, Zack Hopkins, Reyna Boyer, Jason Dressel, Michael Leland and Verena Calas. Joellen Brown, part of the Verizon executive communications team for more than 30 years, helped to provide historical context and research materials. She also reviewed the text for accuracy multiple times. And, of course, my wife, Phyllis, was able to help structure my contributions to the story and remind me of so many of the important details and everyday events that make the narrative really work.

The body of the text relies heavily on extended research-oriented interviews with more than 45 current and former executives and directors of Verizon and its predecessor companies, including myself, regulators, securities analysts and others who had an important role in the history of the company and the telecommunications industry. In some cases, The History Factory conducted multiple interviews with a single subject. In addition, I have personally spoken with at least 30 to 40 former executives and colleagues over the past three years to get their thoughts on certain aspects of the narrative.

When the text mentions specific dates or events, such facts were cross-checked with Verizon and third-party records, including books, magazines and newspaper articles from the period being discussed. Opinions offered by interviewees represent their personal points of view and not those of me or Verizon.

Those with whom The History Factory conducted formal interviews are listed below, in alphabetical order:

| | |
|---|---|
| Larry Babbio | Randy Milch |
| Mary Beth Bardin | Sandra Moose |
| William Barr | Robert Mudge |
| Joellen Brown | Joseph Neubauer |
| Richard Carrion | Don Nicolaisen |
| Ram Charan | Tom O'Brien |
| Larry Cohen | Clarence Otis |
| Vittorio Colao | Marc Reed |
| Jim Cullen | Virginia Ruesterholz |
| John Diercksen | Fred Salerno |
| Simon Flannery | Alan Schwartz |
| Jim Gerace | Ivan Seidenberg |
| Bruce Gordon | Fran Shammo |
| Roger Gurnani | Craig Silliman |
| M. Frances Keeth | Ray Smith |
| John Killian | John Snow |
| Rose Kirk | John Stratton |
| Paul Lacouture | Denny Strigl |
| Robert Lane | Paul Taubman |
| Charles Lee | Tom Tauke |
| Dick Lynch | Peter Thonis |
| Lowell McAdam | Doreen Toben |
| Dan Mead | Marni Walden |
| Stephanie Mehta | Greg Wasson |

# Biographies

**IVAN SEIDENBERG** is the former chairman and CEO of Verizon Communications. His career began in 1966 when he started out as a cable splicer for New York Telephone. He was a key part of the leadership team that transformed Verizon into a premier global network by building the nation's best wireless network, deploying high-speed fiber broadband directly to homes, and expanding Verizon's global internet backbone network. Seidenberg retired from Verizon in 2011; the following year, he joined Perella Weinberg Partners as an advisory partner. He serves as a director for a number of organizations, including BlackRock Inc. and New York-Presbyterian Hospital. Seidenberg earned a bachelor's degree from Lehman College, part of the City University of New York, and a master's degree from Pace University.

**RAM CHARAN** is an advisor to CEOs and boards around the globe and the author or co-author of 26 books that have sold more than 2 million copies worldwide. He is widely sought for his ability to cut through the clutter and provide practical insights into today's most pressing business problems. Charan earned an engineering degree in India, where he was born and raised, and earned MBA and doctorate degrees from Harvard Business School, where he later taught. He has also taught at Northwestern, Wharton, Duke and GE's famous training center at Crotonville, NY. He serves on several boards, and is a Distinguished Fellow of the National Academy of Human Resources.

**SCOTT MCMURRAY** is vice president—editorial at The History Factory. He has conducted hundreds of oral histories with CEOs and other corporate, nonprofit and government leaders. He is an award-winning author of corporate history publications and has written books for clients including Time Warner Cable, Accenture and Saudi Aramco. A Phi Beta Kappa graduate of Grinnell College, Scott has written for *The Wall Street Journal*, *U.S. News & World Report* and *Institutional Investor*.

# Bibliography

American Telephone & Telegraph. Annual Report to Shareholders. 1983. http://www.beatriceco.com/bti/porticus/bell/att/1983/att_1983.htm.

Andrews, Edmund, "AT&T Completes Deal to Buy McCaw Cellular," *The New York Times*, September 20, 1994.

Ante, Spencer E. and Crockett, Roger O., "Rewired and Ready for Combat," *BusinessWeek*, November 7, 2005: 112.

Arenson, Karen, "At NYNEX, X is the Unknown," October 27, 1983, *The New York Times*: D1.

Associated Press, "Verizon to Move Operations Center to Former AT&T Headquarters in Basking Ridge, N.J.," March 29, 2005.

Auletta, Ken. *The Highwaymen: Warriors of the Information Superhighway*. New York: Random House, 1997.

Brooks, John. *Telephone: The First Hundred Years*. New York: Harper & Row,1975.

Bell Atlantic Corp. 1984 Annual Report to Shareholders.

Bell Atlantic Corp. 1987 Annual Report to Shareholders: 9.

Bell Atlantic Corp. 1989 Annual Report to Shareholders: 15-16.

Bell Atlantic Corp. 1992 Annual Report to Shareholders: 39.

Bell Atlantic Corp. 1994 Annual Report to Shareholders: 42.

Bell Atlantic Corp. 1990 Annual Report to Shareholders: 10

Bell Atlantic Corp. 1996 Annual Report to Shareholders: 20.

Bell Atlantic Corp. 1997 Annual Report to Shareholders: 3.

*Business Wire*, "PCS PrimeCo Wins Big at Auction in 11 Cities," March 13, 1995: 1.

Cauley, Leslie, "Bell Atlantic and NYNEX Discuss Merger to Form Second-Biggest Phone Firm," *The Wall Street Journal*, December 18, 1995: A1.

Cingular Wireless, Securities and Exchange Commission Form 10-K for the Fiscal Year Ended December 31, 2003.

CNNMoney, "Vodafone Wins AirTouch," January 15, 1999.

CNNMoney, "SBC, BellSouth Venture Named Cingular Wireless," October 5, 2000.

CNNMoney, "Verizon Buying MCI," February 14, 2005.

Coll, Steve. *The Deal of the Century*. New York: Atheneum, 1986.

Creswell, Julie, "Is the Most Powerful Man in Telecom Pulling a Megabluff?" May 31, 2004, *Fortune*: 20.

Demsey, Seth, "AOL's Demand Side Platform (DSP) Named a Leader by Independent Research Firm,"AOL Blog, June 3, 2015.

Ellison, Sarah, "Lowell McAdam: Seidenberg's 'Air' Apparent," *Fortune*, October 29, 2010.

Fleming, Heather and Wolf, Alan, "Bell Atlantic, NYNEX Merger OKed," August 15, 1997, Bloomberg News.

Gannes, Stuart, "The Judge Who's Reshaping the Phone Business," April 1, 1985, *Fortune*.

Glassman, Paul, "AT&T Building," in *Encyclopedia of Twentieth Century Architecture*, ed. R. Sennott, Stephen, New York: Fitzroy Dearborn, 2004: 84-86.

GTE Corp. 1991 Annual Report to Shareholders: 3.

GTE Corp. 1992 Annual Report to Shareholders: 2.

Gallegos, Raul, "Venezuela to Pay $572 Million for Verizon's CANTV Stake," February 13, 2007, *The Wall Street Journal*.

Hernandez, Raymond, "President Is Leaving N.A.A.C.P.," *The New York Times,* March 4, 2007, http://www.nytimes.com/2007/03/05/us/05naacp.html?_r=.0.

History of Verizon Communications Inc., http://www.verizon.com/about/sites/default/files/Verizon_Corporate_History.pdf

*Investment Dealers' Digest*, "Unruffled Verizon Secures MCI Prize," January 16, 2006: 65.

Isidore, Chris, "AT&T, Kodak, IP Out of Dow," April 1, 2004, CNNMoney.

Kane, Margaret, "Merger Mania: Bell Atlantic, GTE to Combine in $53B Deal,"zdii.com.

Kanter, Rosabeth Moss; Raymond, Douglas; Raffaelli, Ryan L., "The Making of Verizon," February 6, 2004, Harvard Business School Case 303-131: 14.

Kanter, Rosabeth Moss and Bird, Matthew. *Transforming Verizon: A Platform for Change.* Harvard Business School, 2012.

Keller, John J. "GTE Agrees to Buy BBN, Sets Plans to Boost Spending,"May 7, 1997, *The Wall Street Journal.*

Keller, John J., and Lipin, Steven, "Jumping off Sidelines, GTE Makes a Cash Bid for MCI," October 16, 1997, *The Wall Street Journal.*

Koten, John A. *Building Trust: Leading CEOS Speak Out: How They Create It, Strengthen It, Sustain It.* New York: Arthur W. Page Society, 2004.

Kupfer, Andrew, "Mike Armstrong's AT&T: Will the Pieces Come Together?" *Fortune*, April 26, 1999.

Latour, Alma, and Blumenstein, Rebecca, "Verizon to MCI: Drop Dead; Campaign Is on for Liquidation," *The Wall Street Journal*, May 15, 2003.

Lee, Charles, "When Disaster Strikes: Putting Corporate Values to the Test," October 31, 2001, speech to the 2001 CEO2CEO Conference, New York, NY.

Levine, Daniel, "My First Job," *Reader's Digest*, January 1997: 90.

Lieberman, David, "Verizon Faithful Finally Get iPhone," *USA Today*, January 12, 2011: B1.

Mehta, Stephanie N., "Bend It Like Corning," August 6, 2007, *Fortune*: 69.

Moose, Sandra. V*erizon: Decision to Deploy Fiber Optic Broadband.* MIT Sloan Management case study: 1.

Moritz, Scott and Thomson, Amy, "Verizon Agrees to $130 Billion Vodafone Deal," Bloomberg, L.P., September 3, 2013.

NBC News, "Cingular Agrees to Buy AT&T Wireless," February 17, 2004.

NYNEX Corp. 1993 Annual Report to Shareholders.

NYNEX Corp. 1994 Annual Report to Shareholders: 6.

Pastor, Andy and Guyon, Janet, "Regional Phone Firms May Sell Services Outside of Areas Without Prior Approval," August 18, 1989, *The Wall Street Journal*: 5.

Poletti, Therese, "Verizon's Dueling Comments on Yahoo Deal May Confuse Investors," MarketWatch, January 6, 2017.

PR Newswire, "Verizon Names Diego Scotti Chief Marketing Officer," October 2, 2014.

PR Newswire, "Verizon Relocates Corporate Headquarters to Lower Manhattan," December 8, 2005.

PRNewswire, "Verizon and Yahoo Amend Terms of Definitive Agreement," February 21, 2017.

PR Newswire, "Verizon Launches Nationwide Advertising Campaign to Introduce New Company Name," July 31, 2000.

Ramirez, Anthony, "Bell Atlantic to Buy Metro Mobile," September 25, 1991, *The New York Times*: D1.

Robichaux, Mark. *Cable Cowboy: John Malone and the Rise of the Modern Cable Business*. Hoboken, NJ: John Wiley & Sons, 2002.

Romero, Simon and Atlas, Riva, "WorldCom's Collapse: The Overview; WorldCom Files for Bankruptcy; Largest U.S. Case," *The New York Times*, July 22, 2002: 1.

Schiesel, Seth, and Holson, Laura M., "Reshaping the Phone Business: The Deal; Two Phone Giants Reported Merging in $52 Billion Deal," dnet.com, July 28, 1998.

Seidenberg, Ivan, speech at National Press Club, December 3, 2001.

Seidenberg, Ivan, remarks prepared for delivery to the Consumer Electronics Show, Verizon Communications Inc., January 8, 2004: 4.

Shields, Mike and Gryta, Thomas, "Verizon Agrees to Buy AOL for $4.4 Billion," *The Wall Street Journal*, May 12, 2015.

Smith, Hilary, "Verizon is New #1," *RCR* Vol. 19, issue 15, April 10, 2000: 1.

Smith, Raymond, "Creating Partnerships: What Works and What Doesn't," *Beta Gamma Sigma News*, Summer 1995: 1.

Smith, Raymond, "The Measurement Trap," November 3, 1989, speech to the University of California at Berkeley CEO Forum: 9.

Smith, Raymond, "The Googolbit Network: Innovating, Standardizing, Democratizing and Fantasizing," July 15, 1991, speech delivered at the Symposium on Gigabit Networks, Washington, D.C., in *Vital Speeches of the Day*, Vol. 57, No. 24, Oct. 1, 1991: 746-749.

Spangler, Todd, "Tim Armstrong Unveils Oath: AOL-Yahoo Combo Is as Big as Netflix and Looking to Expand," *Variety*, June 19, 2017.

Strigl, Denny F. and Swiatek, Frank. *Managers, Can You Hear Me Now?* New York: McGraw Hill, 2011.

Tell, Lawrence J., "Footloose and Fancy Free: The Bell Operating Companies Are Doing Splendidly," November 12, 1984, *Barron's*: 43.

Thomson Financial, "Verizon Conference Call to Discuss FCC Spectrum Auction Results," April 4, 2008: 5.

Tichy, Noel M. *Succession: Mastering the Make or Break Process of Leadership Transition*, New York: Penguin, 2014.

Tucker, Elizabeth, "Bell Atlantic Told to Divest Cellular Unit," February 25, 1986, *Washington Post*: F1.

U.S. Congress. Office of Technology Assessment. *Wireless Technologies and the National Information Infrastructure*. Sept. 1995: 85.

Verizon Communications Inc. 2000 Annual Report to Shareholders: 6, 26.

Verizon Communications Inc. 2002 Annual Report to Shareholders: 8.

Verizon Communications Inc. 2005 Annual Report to Shareholders: 1, 3.

Verizon Communications Inc. 2003 Annual Report to Shareholders: 5.

Verizon Communications Inc. 2004 Annual Report to Shareholders: 9, 34.

Verizon Communications Inc. 2006 Annual Report to Shareholders: 16.

Verizon Communications Inc. 2007 Annual Report to Shareholders: 2.

Verizon Communications Inc. 2008 Annual Report to Shareholders: 16.

Verizon Communications Inc. 2009 Annual Report to Shareholders: 5.

Verizon Communications Inc. 2011 Annual Report to Shareholders: 3

Verizon Communications Inc. 2012 Annual Report to Shareholders: 30.

Verizon Communications Inc. 2013 Annual Report to Shareholders: 1, 2.

Verizon Communications Inc., Verizon Launch Day Communications Guide: 13.

Verizon Communications Inc., *One Year. One Day. One Verizon.* 2001: 3.

Verizon Communications Inc. SEC Form 10-K Filed for the Period Ending 12/31/03, 2003.

Verizon Communications Inc., "Verizon Wireless Says Spectrum Additions From FCC's Auction 73 Will Further Company's Broadband Strategy," April 4, 2008

Verizon Communications Inc., "John Killian Named Verizon Chief Financial Officer," February 12, 2009.

Verizon Communications Inc., "Verizon Clarifies Succession Plans; Names Lowell McAdam as COO," September 20, 2010.

Verizon Communications Inc., Hurricane Irene case study, 2015.

Verizon Communications Inc., "Verizon to Acquire Straight Path Spectrum to Accelerate 5G Deployment." May 11, 2017

Verizon Wireless Inc., SEC *Form S-1 Registration Statement*, August 24, 2000: 1.

Verizon Wireless Inc. news release, January 7, 2004, "Verizon Wireless Announces Roll Out of National 3G Network."

White, James A., "In Antitrust Accord AT&T Bets on Future by Writing Off Past," *The Wall Street Journal*, January 11, 1982.

Young, Shawn, and Grant, Peter, "Bell Tolls: How Phone Firms Lost to Cable in Consumer Broadband Battle," March 13, 2003, *The Wall Street Journal*: A1.

# Image Credits

Seidenberg in *New York Post*: From *New York Post*, May 26, 1996 ©1996 *New York Post*. All rights reserved. Used by permission and protected by the Copyright Laws of the United States. The printing, copying, redistribution, or retransmission of this Content without express written permission is prohibited.

Seidenberg, Gent and Lee: Henny Ray Abrams/AFP/Getty Images

Gordon: Kevin Winter/Getty Images Entertainment/Getty Images

Neubauer: Sean Zanni/Patrick McMullan/Getty Images

Damage to 140 West Street (bottom left): U.S. Navy photo by Chief Photographer's Mate Eric J. Tilford

Capellas: Ken Cedeno/Bloomberg/Getty Images

Barr: Photo courtesy of the United States Department of Justice

FiOS takes to the streets: Getty Images Publicity/Getty Images

Meade and Cook: Ramin Talaie/Bloomberg/Getty Images; Colao: Jason Alden/Bloomberg/Getty Images

McAdam: David Paul Morris/Bloomberg/Getty Images

Armstrong and Walden: Steve Jennings/Getty Images Entertainment/Getty Images for TechCrunch

Oath announcement: Nicholas Kamm/AFP/Getty Images

Stratton: Denise Truscello/WireImage/Getty Images

All other images courtesy Ivan Seidenberg and Verizon Inc.

# Index